ICONOCLASM

ICONOCLASM

The Breaking and Making of Images

EDITED BY

Rachel F. Stapleton
and Antonio Viselli

McGill-Queen's University Press
Montreal & Kingston | London | Chicago

ICONOCLASM

The Breaking and Making of Images

EDITED BY

Rachel F. Stapleton
and Antonio Viselli

McGill-Queen's University Press
Montreal & Kingston | London | Chicago

ISBN 978-0-7735-5736-9 (cloth)
ISBN 978-0-7735-5737-6 (paper)
ISBN 978-0-7735-5838-0 (ePDF)
ISBN 978-0-7735-5839-7 (ePUB)

Legal deposit third quarter 2019
Bibliothèque nationale du Québec

Printed in Canada on acid-free paper that is 100% ancient forest free (100% post-consumer recycled), processed chlorine free

Funded by the Government of Canada | Financé par le gouvernement du Canada | Canada
Canada Council for the Arts | Conseil des arts du Canada

We acknowledge the support of the Canada Council for the Arts.
Nous remercions le Conseil des arts du Canada de son soutien.

Library and Archives Canada Cataloguing in Publication

Title: Iconoclasm : the breaking and making of images / edited by Rachel F. Stapleton and Antonio Viselli.
Other titles: Iconoclasm (2019)
Names: Stapleton, Rachel F., 1981– editor. | Viselli, Antonio, 1985– editor.
Description: Includes bibliographical references and index.
Identifiers: Canadiana (print) 20190104074 | Canadiana (ebook) 20190104104 | ISBN 9780773557376 (paper) | ISBN 9780773557369 (cloth) | ISBN 9780773558380 (ePDF) | ISBN 9780773558397 (ePUB)
Subjects: LCSH: Aesthetics—Case studies. | LCSH: Image (Philosophy)—Case studies. | LCSH: Iconoclasm—Case studies. | LCSH: Icons—Case studies. | LCGFT: Case studies.
Classification: LCC BH301.I52 I36 2019 | DDC 701/.03—dc23

Set in 10.5/14 Adobe Caslon Pro with Univers Next Pro
Book design & typesetting by Garet Markvoort, zijn digital

to our families

— R.F.S. & A.V.

CONTENTS

FIGURES

ACKNOWLEDGMENTS

This volume arises from papers presented at the conference "Iconoclasm: The Breaking and Making of Images," which took place at the Centre for Comparative Literature at the University of Toronto, 17–19 March 2011. The conference committee of then graduate students worked tirelessly for almost a year to put together an international conference with plenary lectures by Carol Mavor (University of Manchester), Michael Taussig (Columbia University), and Eric Cazdyn (University of Toronto), and featuring more than forty papers by scholars from around the globe.

The 22nd Annual Conference of the Centre for Comparative Literature was organized by Olga Bazilevica, Natalie Pendergast, Jeannine M. Pitas, Rachel F. Stapleton, Kristina Syvarth, and Antonio Viselli, with assistance from Jonathan A. Allan, and with the unwavering support of the Centre: Neil ten Kortenaar, who was our sounding board from writing the CFP to preparing this volume; Linda Hutcheon, who sponsored and supported our successful Social Sciences and Humanities Research Council of Canada grant; Ann Komaromi, who supported the latter phases of this publication; Aphrodite Gardner, whose administrative wizardry kept us on track and on budget; and Bao Nguyen, whose design acumen made for a visually impressive conference.

Of course, any conference, and subsequent volume, is only as good as its participants, and so we gratefully acknowledge all the participants who attended the University of Toronto on that March weekend, and particularly Christopher van Ginhoven Rey, Beth Saunders, Emily Hoffman, Brendon Wocke, T. Nikki Cesare Schotzko, Adam Swann, Angela Toscano, and Helen Hester, who have worked with us over the intervening years – with exemplary patience – as we brought this volume to fruition. We also offer our thanks to the two reviewers whose generous comments helped shape this volume. And finally, we'd like to thank Jonathan Crago and the staff at MQUP for their work in making this book possible.

– Rachel F. Stapleton and Antonio Viselli

ICONOCLASM

RACHEL F. STAPLETON & ANTONIO VISELLI

INTRODUCTION

If It's Broke, Don't Fix It: The Back-to-Front Logic of Iconoclasm

Make or Break

All icons have their limits, their breaking points. In *Iconoclasm: The Breaking and Making of Images*, we explore this threshold by examining the *how* and the *what* of symbolic and material images, and the many ways these venerated and despised images often exceed or transgress themselves, especially when they are broken, altered, or recontextualized.

A recurring concept that unites the chapters in this work is what Michael Taussig identifies in chapter 1 ("Iconoclasm Dictionary") as a "back-to-front logic," a Foucauldian conception in which icons "seem to come alive only with their defacement": "You smash them and – lo and behold! – they have become icons."[1] The transgressive act against the image or belief system pushes that same object or concept beyond its boundaries, in a distorted sublime that re-envisions the threshold of the icon, and in which "iconoclasm is written into the icon."[2] The destructive act now metonymically stands in place of the once sacred object: transgression is now the idol.

Before unpacking the various definitions of iconoclasm and how they relate to what this volume recognizes as *conceptual iconoclasm*, let us illustrate a fairly recent example of this "back-to-front logic" at play, one which demonstrates how current and pervasive instances of iconoclasm are, instances that merit critical attention now more than ever.

On 7 January 2015, two gunmen entered the offices of *Charlie Hebdo*, a satirical newspaper in Paris, and opened fire, killing twelve people and injuring several others. The attackers were two brothers, Saïd and Chérif Kouachi, who identified with Al-Qaeda, and who killed the cartoonists and staff as revenge for the satirical portrayal in a cartoon of the prophet Muhammad. This case demonstrates the Taussigian principle in action, since iconoclasts on each side – both satirists and terrorists – have bestowed iconic status on what they meant to desecrate. As a publication, *Charlie Hebdo* is now both iconic and iconoclastic: its front cover is immediately recognizable and carries with it an aura of provocation, subversion, and shock value from the masthead down. Such provocation, following the attacks, was quickly converted into sales: the first issue published after the shooting saw a record number of sales domestically and internationally, as the issue was also translated into several other languages. Yet, it is the content of the magazine that underlines its iconoclastic tendencies, content that tends toward the sacrilegious and the blasphemous, in particular its offensive portrayals of the prophet Muhammad; it dismantles, via ridicule, individuals and ideologies, from the politically relevant to anything (everything) considered sacred.

Not unlike the Danish *Jyllands-Posten* cartoon controversy in 2005, *Charlie Hebdo*'s continuous representations of the prophet Muhammad – a representational act considered sacrilegious within many aniconist Islamic traditions – were an instigating element that led to the massacre of the cartoonists and their staff. This violent, iconoclastic act is at once direct, metaphoric, and metonymic. To destroy, tear up, or burn an issue of *Charlie Hebdo* is one matter, but to spill more blood than ink by massacring the hands behind the satirical drawings pushes the purification and punishment of the iconoclastic act from the image beyond its pages. In interrogating iconoclasms, iconoclashes, and iconocrises, Bruno Latour demands that we do not ignore the hand at work in creating icons; the *Charlie Hebdo* massacre simultaneously creates icons of the creators' hands, hands that, in creating an icon, had had to be hidden: to claim an icon as

Figure 0.1 | Je suis Charlie.

"'man-made' you nullify the transcendence of the divinities, you empty the claims of a salvation from above."[3] Thus, in moving past the physical object of *Charlie Hebdo*, its images-as-objects, the assailants effectively removed or rejected the possibility of the iconicity of the reproduced images: in linking the images to the hands that created them, the images can no longer be iconic, but the hands now are. In this sense, the cartoons perform what Fabio Rambelli and Eric Reinders name *hieroclasm*: "the elimination of sacred value from formerly religious artifacts once they are re-signified as cultural relics or art," similar to the "dead" Buddhas placed in museums discussed below.[4] Yet due to the impossibility of wiping out the cultural memory of *Charlie Hebdo*'s heritage – *damnatio memoriae* – punishment is transposed onto the cartoonists and their editors, they who turned the prophet into "art." However, the socio-political repercussions also participate in a curious dynamism of iconicity and iconoclasm: the creation of a polarized "Je Suis Charlie" community, of "us-versus-them" rhetoric, because "the idol is always the idol of the *other*."[5]

The slogan "Je Suis Charlie," an initially simple claim of solidarity with the artists who were killed, and a defence of free speech, quickly gained traction by going viral, becoming itself arguably iconic: thousands of Facebook users, for example, adopted virtual icons of the slogan as profile pictures, signalling their outrage over the atrocities, repeating and perpetuating it. Going viral, in this case, is symptomatic of iconicity. However, this solidarity rapidly found its contrapuntal echo in the "Je Ne Suis Pas Charlie" image-slogan that appeared soon afterward, followed by the spread of "Je Suis Ahmed," which commemorated the Muslim police officer killed during the attacks. The possibilities are endless. And merchandise almost always follows.

This brief evolution of the slogan demonstrates several things: first of all, that an utterance can become an image, which in turn, becomes an icon. Second, it seems natural to have a visceral reaction against the murder of cartoonists, yet an initially uncritical rallying of support for the weekly cartoon can add fire to an already implicit religious rhetoric of "us" versus "them," one that does not take into consideration the racism and hatred underpinning the satire. In fact, one could argue that a subliminal Islamophobic message exists within the slogan; after all, in the scheme of alphabets, there are relatively few letters that separate "Je Suis Charlie" from "Jesus Christ." Therefore, to "be" Charlie could mean to abide by the reactionary, provocative establishment that is *Charlie Hebdo*. Yet it is simultaneously reductive to think that only Muslims would be offended by the satirical representations of Muhammad that instigated these atrocities, or that Christians are the only ones appalled by the murderous act.

Although this volume focuses almost entirely on iconoclasm from a Western perspective, the Charlie Hebdo example allows us to compare at a glance traditions of tolerance and acceptance of icons, as the frame shifts from the prohibition of iconographic representations of the prophet Muhammad to the pervasive plastering of "Je Suis Charlie" – a "permitted" image according to Noyes (in contrast to the aniconism of Muhammad), which performs "in exactly the same way as iconoclasm."[6] Here, there is seemingly no place for a critique of the satirical drawings, where we witness – and witnessing is a loaded term within the study of iconoclasm – and participate in an "iconoclash," a war of, on, and by, images as Latour defines it, a very material and yet very symbolic war.

Speaking in the aftermath of the massacre of the necessity for the magazine to live up to the public's expectations, Patrick Pelloux, one of the survivors, explained that *Charlie Hebdo* had now become a symbol, and "being a symbol … becomes an obligation."[7] Yet a critical reader might ask: is there a new, hidden digital-age *cogito* behind the recognizability of icons, their symbolic value, and the way we distribute and interact with them? What verb, action – and therefore responsibility – has replaced the Cartesian epithet here: *Je ______, donc je (ne) suis (pas) Charlie*? Is it witnessing, copy-pasting, tweeting, liking, or ignoring "in the age of digital reproduction,"[8] a new, perverted *cogito* that makes one complicit, in which "I" (*Je*) naturally becomes "we" and, often, "us" versus "them"?

From Icon to Iconoclasm

In order to scrutinize the transition from image to icon to iconoclasm that we see played out in one instance in the evolution of the "Je Suis Charlie" image-slogan-meme, we must attempt to define, albeit incompletely, the notions of icon and iconoclasm. The definitions that follow are incomplete because it is impossible to foreground empirical meaning when dealing with icons, iconicity, and the processes of iconoclasm, as they are context- and culture-dependent. Rambelli and Reinders, in *Buddhism and Iconoclasm: A History*, go so far as to question this nomenclature entirely, claiming that they "employ the term [iconoclasm] also in consideration that, so far, there is no better term."[9] The fundamental reason for this ambiguity is precisely that iconicity and iconoclasm, beyond their historical evolution, are reciprocal processes and cannot exist in a vacuum: they rely heavily on context, and their signs exist only in relation to other signs, to suggest something akin to Derrida's notion of *différance*, whereby meaning – constantly deferred and refracted – lacks a centre. Meaning's foundation therefore depends, at least partly, on contiguity, with signs brushing up against other signs, resisting our slippery attempts at signification. Despite this impossibility, we propose the following recurring characteristics related to iconoclasm, elements that underpin our understanding of *conceptual iconoclasm*.

Martin Kemp, in *Christ to Coke: How Image Becomes Icon*, explains that "an iconic image is one that has achieved wholly exceptional levels of widespread recognizability and has come to carry a rich series of varied associations for very large numbers of people across time and cultures, such that it has to a greater or lesser degree transgressed the parameters of its initial making, function, context, and meaning."[10] An iconic image is inseparable from its recognition as such. After all, icon means likeness. An unseen icon would therefore be an oxymoron, at least in a Western context.[11] Thus, if the destruction of such images and belief systems constitutes iconoclasm per se, this term also refers to precise historical periods in which the sacred notion of the icon becomes subverted. For example, many critics accept that the Byzantine Empire's war on images was the initial occurrence of a formal policy of iconoclasm in the Western Tradition; the "First Iconoclasm" was instigated by Emperor Leo III between 726 and 787 CE and later continued by his successors between 814 and 842 (the "Second Iconoclasm"). With the physical destruction of objects of idolatry, the extreme veneration of (in this case religious) icons was a contributing factor to a schism that was beginning to develop between eastern and western Christianity. The Protestant Reformation, which began in 1517, is often viewed as the "third" major religious iconoclasm, whereby, in an attempt to reform the Catholic (Western) Church, viewed by many as corrupt, reformers took literally the Ten Commandments' admonition against idolatry, destroying religious idols and icons. Yet, as Kristine Kolrud and Marina Prusac explain in *Iconoclasm from Antiquity to Modernity*, it could instead be argued that the beginnings of religious iconoclasm truly lie in the Old Testament, where, in 2 Kings 23, King Josiah bans the worship of idols on discovering the Deuteronomic texts.[12] Nevertheless, idolatry and veneration, icons and idols, no longer limit themselves – if they ever did – to uniquely religious policies or practices.

Along with Kolrud and Prusac, as well as Bruno Latour, Stacy Boldrick, Leslie Brubaker, Anne McClanan, Jeffrey Johnson, Richard Clay, and James Noyes, we do not limit iconoclasm in this volume to a religious context, but believe in appropriating the term to facilitate discussions of the destruction of cultural objects beyond vandalism, which does not necessarily maintain a political, religious, historical, or aesthetic agenda. Such a critical understanding of the term allows us to interrogate and engage with "attacks on traditional cultural authority," a usage, according to McClanan, that dates back to the 1860s,[13] and which the *Oxford English Dictionary* places in 1842, when Elizabeth Barrett Browning wrote of some Greek poets, "an iconoclast of their idol rhyme."[14] Iconoclasm or *iconomachy* – understood as "image struggles," to borrow Leslie Brubaker's term[15] – offers a flexible framework to study not only the more radical conception of iconoclasm defined above, but also the critique and destruction of institutions, philosophies, and dogmas, as examined in Adam Swann's discussion, in this volume, of English identity from Milton to Nietzsche.[16]

A definition that exhaustively acknowledges the numerous complexities of iconoclasm throughout history is impractical, and, we would argue, entirely undesirable, to echo Dario Gamboni's metaphor of iconoclasm's grammar; he claims that "the recurrence of several traits in phenomena separated by time and place does not mean that there exists a timeless grammar of iconoclasm."[17] An absolute or all-encompassing definition of iconoclasm is unreasonable and impossibly dependent upon the socio-historical, political, and religious contexts wherein one studies the icon's symbolic value and its destruction. Nonetheless, there are indeed recurring elements specific to iconoclasm in its varied iterations: its many pronouns, subjects, direct objects, declensions, and even dangling modifiers, that our volume addresses. Whether religious, political, or artistic, iconoclasm is, as McClanan writes, "a principled attack on specific objects aimed primarily at the objects' referents or at their connection to the power they represent."[18] Iconoclastic acts therefore engage with the materiality of the object, but also, and most importantly, with the power and value hidden within and beyond the object, which are almost always tantalizingly out of reach.

An icon stands in for a greater referent or power, at times metaphorically, at others metonymically. For example, the digital reproduction of a saint, in most cases, does not carry the beatific qualities of that saint; however, it may be used for ceremonial and sacramental purposes, in which case ambiguity ensues, raising the question as to whether one is praying to a statue or to the symbolized and mediated divinity, as discussed by Beth Saunders in this volume. Yet, while destroying or even removing any statue or depiction of a saint is an iconoclastic act, the reasons behind such destruction can vary – for example, a *damnatio memoriae*, in which the destruction of the icon is synonymous with the obliteration of cultural memory, an attempt to overthrow the previous institution, empire, or religion, something that has become ever more difficult in a digital age of replicated copies and aura-less images. To eradicate the icon, however, can extinguish both its iconicity and indexicality – in other words, what it mimics and represents, as well as that toward which it points or directs the viewer.

The cases discussed in *Iconoclasm: The Breaking and Making of Images* are primarily Western. It is essential to note that, although the semiotics of iconoclasm can function in a similar manner in Eastern and Western contexts, there are some noteworthy differences that merit further attention. Similarities include the manner in which the attacks on icons can either destroy or alter their signification, transforming their semiotic status via "demolition, redefinition, humiliation" or "acts of piety, sacrifice, communication, provocation, or renovation" – all potential forms of obliteration, but also of "destruction as a mode of cultural production."[19] A point of divergence between East and West, however, is found in Buddhism, where images of the Buddha incarnate, literally bring into flesh, the Buddha's beatific qualities. Rambelli and Reinders explain: "Buddha images were created and maintained as living presences, produced through consecration rituals, obeisance, and various discursive means. Icons were imagined and treated as organic beings, and the effective life of the icon was always intimately related to regular offerings and obeisance."[20] These icons are considered animated, to the point that when they needed to be moved – for reasons of renovation or simply to be placed elsewhere – an eye-closing ritual took place, in which paper covered their dotted eyes, thus removing their soul. "Images on display at exhibitions," Rambelli and Reinders add, "are, therefore, quite literally 'dead' – empty receptacles devoid of their sacred essence," objects that are often given funerals before being subjected to the potential violence against their meaning (being placed in a museum, for example).[21] Buddhism also raises the question of karma – "ultimately, what you do determines what is done to you" – and making sense of destruction: Rambelli and Reinders give the example of an angry monk who is reborn as several rats, a punishment for having destroyed a sacred icon.[22] The monk's act of iconoclasm or icon destruction results in his being split into multiple bodies. Beyond these preliminary differences that arise between Eastern and Western forms of iconoclasm, further enquiries – enquiries beyond the scope of this book – might examine to what extent the Taussigian principle of "back-to-front" logic holds true in Eastern examples.

In *Negating the Image: Case Studies in Iconoclasm*, Anne McClanan and Jeffrey Johnson discuss yet another impetus for the destruction of icons beyond *damnatio memoriae*, and the redefinition, recontextualization, and humiliation discussed by Rambelli and Reinders – that of iconoclasm as "punishment to the human or supernatural figure represented by the icon."[23] In this volume, we argue that iconicity and iconoclasm merit scholarly attention now more than ever; we take as merely one example among many the 2015 *Charlie Hebdo* massacre, to demonstrate that it is possible and vital to study the process and speed at which images become icons, how contagious their iconicity can be – particularly in a digital world – and, finally, how (quickly) an icon can be subverted or become iconoclastic.

Given the interdisciplinary and historic transformation of our understanding of iconoclasm, we ask, with Kolrud and Prusac, whether "a continuous widening of the definition is useful or counterproductive."[24] *Iconoclasm: The Breaking and Making of Images* offers, at least in part, an answer to this question by analyzing the sacrality of objects and belief systems, from religious to secular iconoclasms, within a framework based on what we recognize as *conceptual iconoclasm*. This notion takes into account both the destruction and productivity of icons: their representation, their language, and, most importantly, the manner in which they signify once shattered, as well as the reactions to such events. *Conceptual iconoclasm* is therefore a dive into the back-to-front logic that exposes within the image the very seeds of its own destruction, as well as those of new creation. We are attentive here to the reciprocal and often contradictory processes of creation and destruction, as well as the socio-political, cultural, and historical ramifications to such practices.

In the introduction to Boldrick and Clay's *Iconoclasm: Contested Objects, Contested Terms* (2007), Boldrick notes the *unwieldiness* of iconoclasm – both the subject and the term – and maintains that any project which tackles the subject must necessarily be focused.[25] And yet our volume does the opposite, taking the position that the combining of seemingly disparate approaches to and engagements with iconoclasm is the way forward – to precisely poke at its *dis-ease* as the etymology of "unwieldy" suggests.[26] While iconoclasm has elements of the de(con)structive and the trans/formative, as Boldrick notes, in our conceptualization, iconoclasm is also very much productive: it is not only the *breaking* of images or semioclasm – "the destruction of meaning" – but also the *making* of new images and new signs out of the ruins.[27] Nevertheless, we agree with Boldrick that the "diversity of iconoclastic intentions and methods means that there can be no useful meta-history of iconoclasm."[28] This volume's very aetiologies demand that we accept this impossibility before we even begin.

The ABCs of an Icon(oclasm)

The volume that you are holding in your hands had its genesis in the University of Toronto Centre for Comparative Literature's 2011 conference "Iconoclasm: The Breaking and Making of Images," and its form contains some remnants of Michael Taussig's keynote address, "Iconoclasm Dictionary."

Although this volume, *Iconoclasm: The Breaking and Making of Images*, does not follow a linear narrative, as an organizational strategy each chapter in our volume unites and engages with aspects of Taussig's opening article, an initial dictionary that lays out various thematic perspectives related to iconoclasm. These most prominently and most generally include the creation, transgression – perhaps the main thread throughout Taussig's headwords – and de(con)struction of icons, and the meaning we, as readers and cultural observers, make of the plurality of these processes of (de/re)signification that are iconoclasm.

Taussig's keynote lecture, which has since been adapted to a textual format, was delivered on a fine March day in 2011, in the Victoria College Chapel at Victoria University in the University of Toronto. The Chapel of "Old Vic" is used mostly for classes, events, weddings, and lectures, rather than regular religious services. The erstwhile Old Vic "Chapel" is a relatively plain space, with a stage at the front of the room beneath the windows (the altar is set up for events that require it). There is a podium rather than a pulpit, organ pipes at the back, some subdued stained glass featuring iconoclastic "icons" of the Reformation (including John Milton, discussed later in this volume by Adam Swann), and the padded, theatre-style seats with folding tablet arms suitable for taking notes common in many university halls. The chapel lacks much of the more explicit iconography of religious worship – permanent altar, crucifixes, etc. – that its name suggests. In taking the stage to deliver his address, Professor Taussig sat to one side while he was being introduced, carefully taking off and folding his blazer, and removing his shoes, lining them up beneath his chair and speaking in socked feet, a subtle iconoclasm of the expectations of academe. In delivering his lecture, there is an almost childlike cadence in the introduction of each headword: "'A' is for Antiquated," "'B' is for Body," and so on. We recall learning our ABCs to a similar rhythm – although the listener or reader is quickly reminded that, even here, our icons must be broken, as Taussig meanders through the alphabet out of order, repeating or skipping letters at will.

Taussig's dictionary, somewhat like this book, is fluid. It breaks the tyranny of alphabetically ordered headwords, of historical chronologies and etymologies, instead focusing on a flowing progression and evolution of themes from diverse theoretical, philosophical, and mediatic perspectives. Evolution, then – with its mongrel cousins, mutation and transgression – might be considered one of the organizing principles of this volume, a principle that favours, despite its kinship to etymology, the eclectic over the formal, further emphasizing the inconstancy of iconicity and iconoclasm. We have structured *Iconoclasm: The Breaking and Making of Images* in four sections that gravitate around keywords. These link our chapters hypertextually and unite them thematically, while echoing Taussig's broken dictionary with our own pseudo-headwords. These are somewhat arbitrary, however thematically appropriate, and their "definitions" are often as interrogative as explanatory, and as playful as formal, with the dismantling of clichéd or iconic language and the intrusion of other literary and iconographic forms.

Our chosen headwords – *religion*, *pop art*, *nation*, and *sexy* – are words of, if not iconic, then of ideological force. They are all thematically relevant to the chapters that follow them, sections we introduce below, deliberately out of order, so as to emphasize the multiple threads that connect them and the fluidity of a topic that lends itself to multiple ways of reading: whether from front to back cover, or back to front, or everything in between. These headwords are, of course, merely four of the many possible words we could have chosen to index this volume. The four we settled on, however, are all recurring sites or tools of iconoclasm, terms that also follow the four stages of iconoclasm explicated below. While *religion* is the term perhaps that most immediately comes to mind in regard to both icon and iconoclasm, we would argue that in our current post-modern (or even "post-truth") world, the notions of art, nation, and sex are equally sites of provocative iconoclastic – or, to build on Latour, icono*clashtic* – labour.

The Four Stages of Iconoclasm

The authors in *Iconoclasm: The Breaking and Making of Images* each address at least one of the four stages of iconoclasm set out by Taussig: 1) the "stage of invisibility or taken-for-grantedness of the icon"; 2) the "destruction or humiliation" of the icon; 3) the "resurrection" of the icon, which is now visible thanks to its destruction (this stage is crucial and particularly problematic, as it forms a palimpsest of the damaged icon out of the memory of "its noble, pristine, pre-traumatized, form"); and 4) this new object, "bred of violence and death," is "now mixed with sacred or magical emanation."[29] Iconoclasm thus inevitably results in the icon's transgression of itself.

This dynamic engagement is present in varied and diverse perspectives, from its theoretical approaches to its genres and media, in an attempt to create a comparative understanding of the creation, destruction, and glorification of icons, and the political, aesthetic, and poetic ramifications of this binary, which suggests the existence of an intermediary space between icon and iconoclasm – a "delay," as Christopher van Ginhoven Rey terms it in chapter 2 ("An Aesthetics of Splendour"). Such a study is in no way exhaustive; it aims instead to contribute to the constantly shifting notions of iconicity and iconoclasm by addressing, in various forms, the process of signification at work in iconoclasm, particularly its logic of transgression, its politics, and, most importantly, its ambiguity, in many languages and cultures and over several centuries, in the Western world.

In the opening piece of our collection, Michael Taussig begins his dictionary with entries whose lexical fields relate to iconoclasm by positing the presence of the body as central to iconicity and iconoclasm, an "intimacy of destruction" that further underlines the aesthetics and politics of witnessing, as discussed by T. Nikki Cesare Schotzko in chapter 6 ("What The Disaster Writes: Contemplations of the Fall"). Cesare Schotzko's contribution is not alone in discussing the process of iconoclasm; in fact, every chapter answers the question of not only what icons and iconoclasm signify, but *how* they signify, alongside the problematic understanding of "likeness" in the representational act that defines iconicity and iconoclasm. Furthermore, this volume considers the performative and intersubjective aspects of the icon and its agency *beyond* viewing and witnessing, as well as the image's various semiotic transformations from historical photograph to object of art and adaptation.

This transgression can be manipulated, serving a capitalist, artistic, or even humanitarian need; such is the case in chapter 4 ("The Bluest Eye: Paul Newman, Iconoclasm, and the Shameless Exploitation of Beauty"), wherein Emily Hoffman discusses the cyclical vigour behind Paul Newman's conscious effort to manipulate the public's desire for his iconicity – an economy of iconoclasm per se. Inextricably tied to the notion of transgression are questions of desire, sexuality, and therefore the body. Taussig writes of icons in Benjaminian terms: "their aura owes much to the curious ambivalence of taboo as the prohibition of desire: that which endows an icon with its respect and prestige also demands its defacement."[30] He adds that "breaking the taboo results in yet another taboo and the effort multiplies, feeding on itself."[31] This Ouroboros-like dynamism embodies precisely the back-to-front logic explored in this volume – present from the very title – and, although *breaking* precedes *making*, these two concepts become fundamentally interdependent and oftentimes interchangeable. In a similar vein, Hoffman's study of Paul Newman engages with the actor's use of his own iconic body, or the synecdoche of his blue eyes, as they are consumed first via his celebrity and later as a brand of consumable goods.

This autophagic dynamism at the heart of iconoclasm appears most loudly in chapter 9, Helen Hester's "Vampire, Cannibal, Iconoclast: Displacing Genitality and Desecrating Genre," in which she analyzes the "self-devouring" (autophagic) genre that is pornography, as it adopts and reappropriates conventions from other forms and genres – from reality TV and game shows to war propaganda – thereby transgressing beyond itself into a new genre that is quite unsexy: the *pornedy* displaces sex and arousal, which itself engenders novel forms through the "misuse" of other genres. This logic arguably also functions in reverse, whereby the designation "porn" is adopted in contexts far removed from sexual acts and genres: such as "food porn" images posted on Instagram or Facebook.

In chapter 8 ("The Idolatry of the Real: Form, Formula, and Happy Endings in Romance Literature"), Angela Toscano discusses a similarly autophagic, back-to-front logic in the area of genre studies. From a meta-narratological perspective, the formulaic "happily ever after" in popular romance literature works against the romance narrative, but is also a response to, and distinction from, an imposed, seemingly uncritical desire to conflate popular romance and literary realism. By theorizing iconoclasm alongside genre studies, Toscano blurs the boundaries between the notion of the real, what is representational, and what constitutes a copy.

In chapter 5, vandalism, usually a destructive act without a necessary ideological agenda, combines here with iconoclasm in Brendon Wocke's essay "Q Is for Queer: Banksy, Iconoclasm, and the Queering of British Traditional Authority." Wocke's title echoes the ABCs of Taussig's dictionary and childhood primers, yet in his choice of headword Wocke immediately transgresses, queering the dictionary for his readers, even as he helps us to understand how street art queers our icons. In his dictionary, Taussig mentions the iconicity of Queen Elizabeth's behind, which roared when the Australian prime minister touched it – another instance of the back-to-front logic at work in the iconicity of a cultural object to which no one had yet pointed any attention! Wocke takes the royal body one step further, not only by focusing on the semiotics of British authority in Banksy from the point of view of two policemen kissing, but, more importantly, by demonstrating the imbued power dormant in Queen Victoria's metonymic bottom, as, scantily clad, she sits on another woman's face in a same-sex sex act, potentially also enacting the very notion of a drag *queen*. Icon and logos meet, as the polysemy of linguistic registers in the utterance "queen" creates a clashing acoustic image. These representations are also self-devouring, in that through the replication of these portraits in counterculture on canvasses and t-shirts, the recycled iconoclastic image itself becomes iconic, consumed, and proliferated.

Also critical of British identity as iconic, Adam Swann's analyses of John Milton and Friedrich Nietzsche question the misconceptions encountered in idealizing a nation's past. In chapter 7 ("Twilight of the Idle, or How to Historicize with a Hammer: Milton, Nietzsche, and the Iconoclasm of English Identity"), Swann explores Milton's unfinished *History of Britain* (1670) as a neglected iconoclastic text, bypassing *Eikonoklastes* (1649), which, even more than Banksy's subversion of the queen(s) of England, justifies the beheading of King Charles I in response to the *Eikon Basilike* (icon of the king). In *History of Britain*, Milton's refusal to accept the narrative of a Saxon Golden Age as iconic relates anachronistically to Nietzschean thought in that both men prioritize a cyclical notion of history in lieu of a linear conception of humanity and temporality.

Christopher van Ginhoven Rey, in chapter 2 ("An Aesthetics of Splendour"), questions the paradigmatic role iconoclasm plays in the creation of aesthetics, from Albert the Great and Thomas Aquinas to Hegel, through the lens of Catholic mysticism. In a close reading of Teresa of Ávila's *The Interior Castle* (1577), van Ginhoven Rey examines not only the notion of "an iconoclastic climax" that occurs in prayer, one paralleled by Christ's ascension, but also the aesthetic and philosophical implications of iconoclasm's role in regard to love and beauty.

Examining more modern iterations of mysticism and aesthetics, chapter 3 ("Visionary Camera: The Polaroid SX-70 and Marian Apparition Photography"), by Beth Saunders, considers Polaroid pictures used by pilgrims at sites reputed to have been venues of apparitions of the Virgin Mary. Saunders's study demonstrates the immediacy and performative nature of this camera in terms of contemporary photographic culture, thinking particularly of the specular position of photography in the digital age: once these pictures are placed online, they reflect one's "faith in photography's ability to reflect back to us our own beliefs."

From a historical understanding of aesthetics in relation to iconoclasm, to the iconicity of Polaroids and their performativity coupled with apparition sites – and without forgetting the use of iconoclasm in relation to genre studies – we come to T. Nikki Cesare Schotzko's essay in chapter 6 ("What the Disaster Writes: Contemplations of the Fall"). Cesare Schotzko examines the iconoclastic break of 11 September 2001 and the politics of photography and witnessing, as well as the political and aesthetic evolution of Richard Drew's visually stunning image, "The Falling Man." As photograph, documentary, and novel, "The Falling Man" acts as a kind of primitive theatre. Cesare Schotzko examines the intersubjective relations between readers and observers of the photograph, and the multiple aesthetic, political, and psychological implications that ensue, such as the reproduction of the image in the opening credits of HBO's *Mad Men* TV series, the complex complicity of the viewer, and the image's paradoxical autonomy.

As readers explore the contents of this collection, they will engage with the interdisciplinarity of icons – their sacredness and authority, as well as the aesthetic, moral, political, philosophical, and religious repercussions of iconoclasm. The concerns of time and history, creation and destruction, art, signs and representation, and the spaces between all these themes result in tensions at once troubling and productive. We emphasize, through the examples in this volume, that the privileging of particular images – iconophilia – and their prohibition or destruction – iconoclasm – share the same space, and are often two sides of the same coin. The spaces between the chapters – the connections and resistances that push and pull iconoclasm from creative to destructive and back again – are manifest in the very conceptions of this project. We encourage readers of *Iconoclasm: The Breaking and Making of Images* to approach this collection in diverse ways, according to their needs or wishes: as a manual, a commonplace book of case studies, or an iconoclastic dictionary.

NOTES

1 Taussig, "Iconoclasm Dictionary," pages 21–32 in this volume. Previously published in *TDR: The Drama Review* 56, no. 1 (2012), and another version in Michael Taussig, *The Corn Wolf* (University of Chicago Press, 2015). A video recording of Prof. Taussig's talk is archived and publicly available through the website of the Centre for Comparative Literature at the University of Toronto (complit.utoronto.ca).

2 Ibid., pages 21–32 in this volume.

3 Latour, "What is Iconoclash?," 16.

4 Rambelli and Reinders, *Buddhism and Iconoclasm*, ix.

5 Kolrud and Prusac, *Iconoclasm from Antiquity to Modernity*, 5.

6 Noyes, *The Politics of Iconoclasm*, xiv.

7 Devichand, "How the world was changed."

8 Noyes, *The Politics of Iconoclasm*, xiv.

9 Rambelli and Reinders, *Buddhism and Iconoclasm*, ix.

10 Kemp, *Christ to Coke*, 3.

11 The example of the *hibutsu*, the "secret, hidden Buddha," is an exception to this statement: they are so precious that they remain hidden, invisible, further complicating their status as icons. "How can they convey meaning if they are hidden?" ask Rambelli and Reinders (*Buddhism and Iconoclasm*, 152). They add, "Buddha images underline an inaccessible, mysterious, and fundamentally other dimension of the real, while at the same time constituting (being) the symbolic,

bodily, and material aspects of deities" (152). Their invisibility therefore stands in for the inaccessible, they who are both icon and symbol, a complete sign.

12 Kolrud and Prusac, *Iconoclasm*, 5.

13 McClanan and Johnson, *Negating the Image*, 1.

14 *Oxford English Dictionary Online*, s.v. "iconoclast, n. 2," http://www.oed.com/ (accessed 4 October 2016).

15 Brubaker, "Making and Breaking Images," 18.

16 Kolrud and Prusac, *Iconoclasm*, 2.

17 Gamboni, "Image to Destroy," 89.

18 McClanan and Johnson, *Negating the Image*, 3.

19 Rambelli and Reinders, *Buddhism and Iconoclasm*, 172.

20 Ibid., 148.

21 Ibid., 148.

22 Ibid., 187, 179.

23 McClanan and Johnson, *Negating the Image*, 4.

24 Kolrud and Prusac, *Iconoclasm*, 7.

25 Boldrick and Clay, *Iconoclasm*, 1.

26 Indeed, it is in the spaces between our chapters, our nominal "headwords," which demand that our readers answer for themselves the questions that Bruno Latour asks in "Why Has Critique Run Out of Steam?": "Should we be at war, too, we, the scholars, the intellectuals? Is it really our duty to add fresh ruins to fields of ruins? Is it to recall the task of the humanities to add deconstruction to destruction? More iconoclasm to iconoclasm?" Bruno Latour, "Why Has Critique Run Out of Steam? From Matters of Fact to Matters of Concern," *Critical Inquiry* 30, no. 2 (2004): 225–48.

27 Rambelli and Reinders, *Buddhism and Iconoclasm*, 172.

28 Boldrick, "Introduction," in Boldrick and Clay, *Iconoclasm*, 5.

29 Taussig, "Iconoclasm Dictionary," pages 21–32 in this volume.

30 Ibid., pages 21–32 in this volume.

31 Ibid., pages 21–32 in this volume.

BIBLIOGRAPHY

Boldrick, Stacy, and Richard Clay, eds. *Iconoclasm: Contested Objects, Contested Terms* Aldershot, UK: Ashgate, 2007.

Brubaker, Leslie. "Making and Breaking Images and Meaning in Byzantium and Early Islam." In *Striking Images, Iconoclasms Past and Present*, ed. Stacy Boldrick, Leslie Brubaker, and Richard Clay. Farnham, UK: Ashgate, 2013.

Devichand, Mukul. "How the World Was Changed by the Slogan 'Je Suis Charlie.'" BBC News. 3 January 2016. http://www.bbc.com/news/blogs-trending-35108339 (accessed September 2016).

Gamboni, Dario. "Image to Destroy, Indestructible Image." In Latour and Weibel, *Iconoclash*, 88–135.

Kemp, Martin. *Christ to Coke: How Image Becomes Icon.* Oxford: Oxford University Press, 2012.

Kolrud, Kristine, and Marina Prusac. *Iconoclasm from Antiquity to Modernity.* Routledge, 2016.

Latour, Bruno. "What Is Iconoclash?" In Latour and Weibel, *Iconoclash*, 14–37.

Latour, Bruno, and Peter Weibel, eds. *Iconoclash: Beyond the Image Wars in Science, Religion, and Art.* Cambridge, MA: MIT Press in association with ZKM (Centre for Art and Media), Karlsruhe, 2003.

McClanan, Anne, and Jeffrey Johnson, eds. *Negating the Image: Case Studies in Iconoclasm.* Aldershot, UK: Ashgate, 2017.

Noyes, James. *The Politics of Iconoclasm: Religion, Violence and the Culture of Image-Breaking in Christianity and Islam.* London: Tauris, 2013.

Rambelli, Fabio, and Eric Reinders. *Buddhism and Iconoclasm: A History.* London: Bloomsbury, 2012.

Taussig, Michael. "Iconoclasm Dictionary." This volume, pages 21–32.

Michael Taussig

1

Iconoclasm Dictionary

Antiquated

Why does iconoclasm seem so dated? Are there no more icons to smash? After all, who builds statues these days or, like Hugo Chavez and Saddam Hussein, has portraits of themselves hugging skyscrapers? Only Third World dictators, and they quickly put a stop to the slightest sign of iconoclasm. Of course the Stars and Stripes fly proudly over every second-hand car lot, gas station, and fast-food outlet, but nowadays people seem wary of taking it on – not like the good old days when people would wear the flag on their jeans bottoms or burn it to make the Great Communicator mad. But then you have to consider the proposition that nothing could be more iconoclastic than using the flag to sell cars, gasoline, and fast food, such that this particular icon now exists in a special limbo preserved for retired icons or icons that have seen better days and now deserve some well-earned rest. Today it seems the world has been divided between places begging for a little bit of iconoclasm and those where it has lost its bite. Truly, protests have gotten harder to launch in the Western democracies. Along with kettling by police of mass demonstrations and the erection of chain mail fences closing off targets, as occurred at the G20 protests in Toronto, so-called free speech and free markets allow everyman to be an iconoclast and yet search in vain for a protest site to get close to. That in itself, of course, is a belated sign of success – that the forces of law and order have to expend such spectacular military force to stop iconoclasts; and yet it must make the bankers and politicians feel grand as well. Of course what's important here is that even in this digital age, iconoclasm must be largely a physical affair with the human body in close proximity to the icon. It seems that no amount of ferocious blogging or vile, anonymous online commentary can get even close to the impact of human bodies marching down streets or tearing down a statue. How strange, you say, that even today the human body could assume such presence! Could it be that the power of icons, like the power of iconoclasm, depends on this presence made intimate? And what could be more intimate than destruction?

This would explain why icons suddenly burst into consciousness and seem to come alive only with their defacement. You smash them and – lo and behold! – they have become icons. This back-to-front logic is of a piece with the rhythm of taboo and transgression, attraction and repulsion that runs through all societies and all of social life. Even in good old days – especially in the good old days – icons begged for a little bit of iconoclasm because their aura owes much to the curious ambivalence of taboo as the prohibition of desire: that which endows an icon with its respect and prestige also demands its defacement. When the prime minister of Australia, a politician not especially fond of Australia's allegiance to Britain, touched the queen's butt many years ago … what an uproar! He said it was an accident. Well, so what! But that butt had been crying out for a touch and, what's more, in being touched, accidentally or not, its iconicity soared. Iconoclasm is written into the icon. Taboos are meant to be broken. Well, that's how it used to be anyway. In the good old days.

Sacred

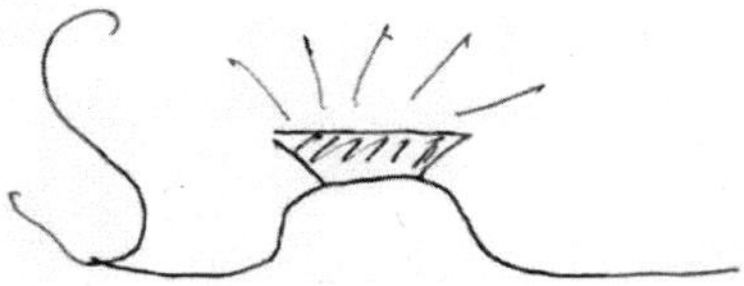

Now, however, it seems that something strange and wonderful has taken place. Before, there was a discernible distinction between sacred and profane, between the taboo and its transgression. But now it seems as if transgression itself has become the new sacred. Is that possible? It was complicated enough before. But now? Oh my God!

Icons

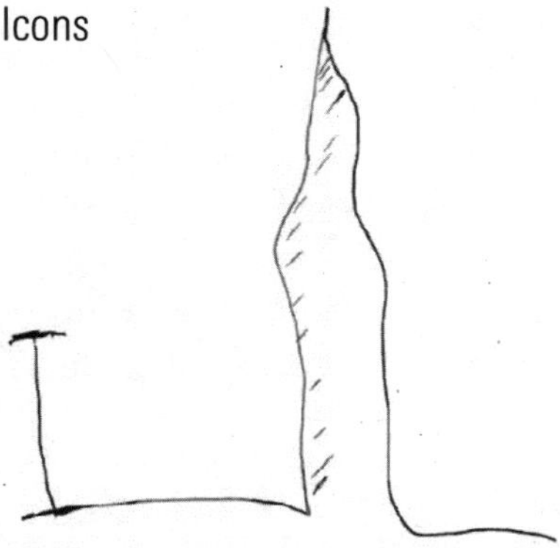

Icons used to be icons. You could spot them a mile off, maybe on a pedestal or accompanied by a brass band, touching the sky, with bird shit all over – not like shop and bank windows, shiny surfaces with stuff to buy on the other side, along with all the bellyaching that goes on these days for transparency. When the arcades were built early in the nineteenth century, which Walter Benjamin made the object of a study meant to rouse Europe from the death-sleep of capitalism, there were no shop windows in the streets, no display of things for sale. Icons were really icons in those days. You could spot them a mile off.

Effigy

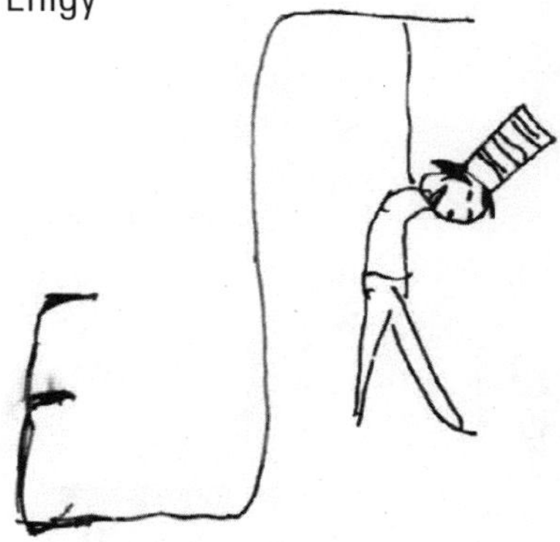

I recall in decades past seeing photos of effigies set alight in public protests in Third World countries, especially of Uncle Sam with a stovepipe hat and striped breeches. But that seems long ago. A strange-sounding word – *effigy* – it recruits magical powers through pronunciation as much as anything else, especially powers of hate and destruction that despoil the copy of what is to be hurt –

a process that Sir James George Frazer of *Golden Bough* fame called "sympathetic magic" (1922). A lot of what is called criticism has some of this going on too – copying the object in order to burn it up, like smashing the shop window.

Body

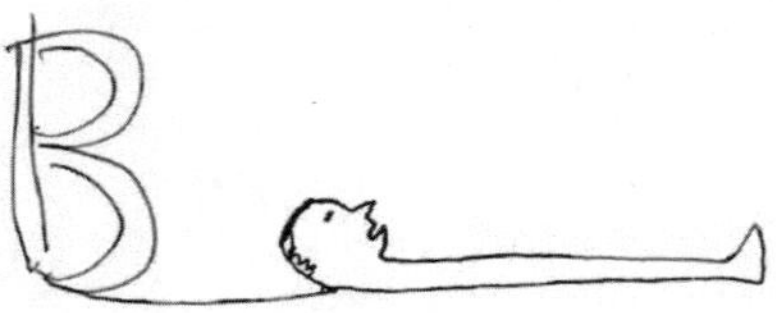

The human body can be an especially potent target of iconoclasm, as witnessed by the young vendor in Tunisia who set himself afire in December 2010, providing the spark that sent the dictator and his cronies scuttling. Before that this humble street vendor was not an icon. Before that he was anything but an icon. He needed self-immolation to make him one and he will be remembered for a while, maybe a year, maybe less, and songs will be sung and poetry recited and his photo held aloft. As I write in late January 2011 other Middle East dictators propped up by the US are in serious trouble because of this too. Egypt is tottering.

Wikileaks

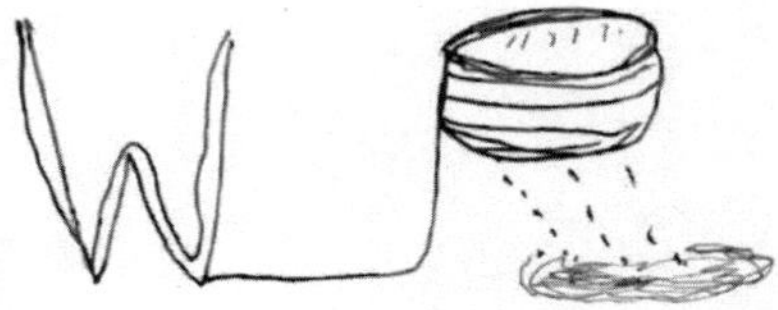

Is secrecy an icon and revelation iconoclasm? Is it not amazing that one of our best sources of insight into the background of what is happening in the Middle East comes from leaked diplomatic cables? Who or what is the icon here: Julian Assange; Private First-Class Bradley Manning[1] of the US armed forces, stewing in solitary confinement; or the US government? The rage on the part of the US government over the leaks and the baying for blood by some US congressmen testifies to the battle being fought over this question. These are nothing however compared with the real icon, which is the sacred nature of state secrets.

Suicide Bombers

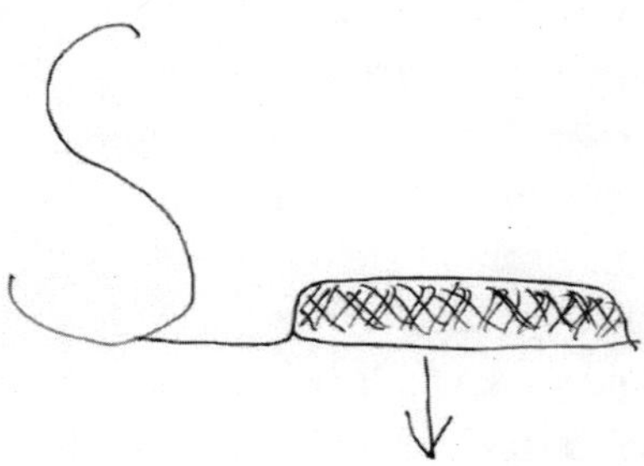

These are iconoclasts supreme. Yet it is strange how their action has become routinized and they are now seen more as bombers than suicide bombers. James C. Scott wrote a memorable book called *Weapons of the Weak: Everyday Forms of Peasant Resistance* (1985), making me ask whether suicide bombing is one such weapon, a sign of desperation in the face of a highly mechanized enemy such as the Israel Defense Forces or the US and Canadian armies in Afghanistan that put massive resources into protecting their bodies? But surely suicide bombing is not just another weapon of the weak, a matter of fox-like Brechtian cunning? The moral element in any act of iconoclasm is stupendously brought forth by self-immolation. It is thus extremely important that we in the West take note of how the media has set a de-iconoclastic tone such that suicide bombers are now just bombers.

Nietzsche

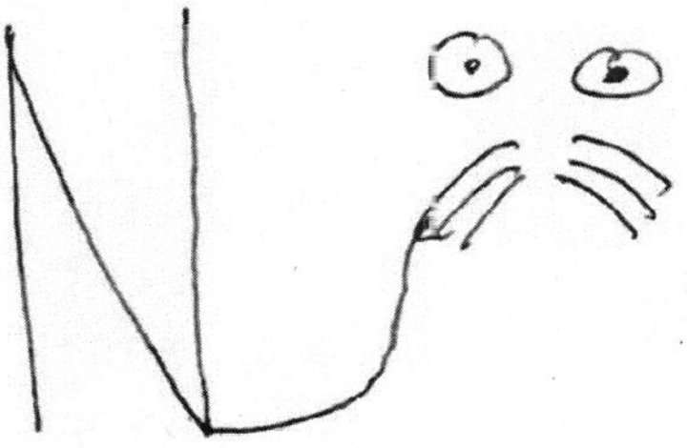

As for the moral element in any act of iconoclasm, how might we first think of the value of destruction that the larger-than-life mid-nineteenth-century Russian anarchist, Mikhail Bakunin, called a creative passion? In *The Gay Science* (1882), Nietzsche has a paragraph, "We Destroy Only As Creators," that seems like the other side of the same coin.

Sacrifice

This is confusing. Nietzsche calls attention to self-immolation as the weapon of the weak to dominate the strong. Think back again on the young man setting himself aflame in Tunisia. Christ is an archetype of humility, and *ressentiment* is the term Nietzsche uses for this performance of abjection. But on the other hand – and it is a very big hand indeed – sacrifice is the supreme act of prodigality, of giving for the sake of giving, that Georges Bataille, follower of Nietzsche, called *depense*, of which sex and sacrifice are the great examples. Sacrifice consecrates that which it destroys, writes Bataille, while Marcel Mauss and Henri Hubert emphasize that the victim becomes a god. How much greater does this become when self-sacrifice is involved?

Time

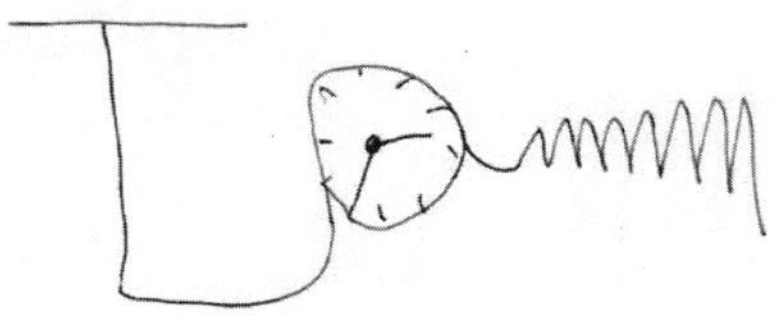

Time is iconic. Just try being iconoclastic by having your own time, like the Greek I met in Athens who boasted that he never kept appointments and turned up whenever he felt like it. Nothing would bring the modern world to a halt more quickly – certainly more quickly than torching police cars or breaking bank windows. In his "Theses on the Philosophy of History" (1940), Walter Benjamin distinguishes homogenous time from heterogenous time. The former belongs to clock-time and to the idea of progress. But heterogenous time, which he also calls the "time of the now," is a sudden rupture in time when something in the present leapfrogs unexpectedly so as to constellate with something in the forgotten past. There is a cessation of movement, a strange nothingness out of time, and here it is when the Messiah may return – in other words a revolutionary chance in the fight for the oppressed past. "Thinking involves not only the flow of thoughts, but their arrest as well." Benjamin refers us to holidays today as sad vestiges interrupting the flow of time with traces of this other time, the time of the now. He thinks of the calendar as a monument of such forgotten historical consciousness. During the July Revolution in France in 1830, one event showed this consciousness to be still alive. On the first day of fighting, several different clock towers were fired upon simultaneously. Time stood still.

Lightning

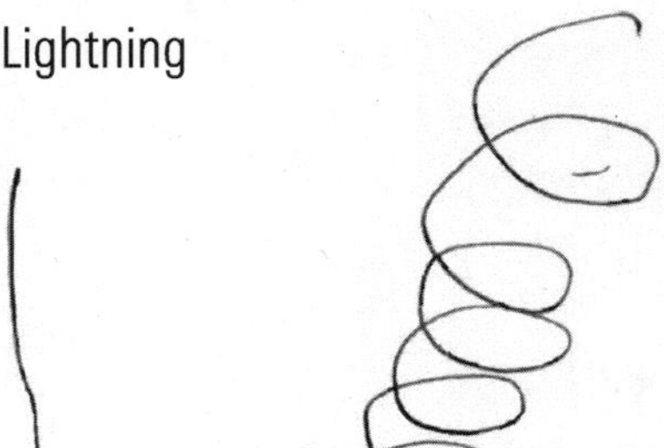

Foucault is fascinated by what I call the back-to-front logic of taboo and transgression of which iconoclasm is an example. Along with Bataille he is not fazed by the fact that transgression merely suspends the taboo. Both philosophers instead direct our attention to what Benjamin calls the "now time," the *nunc stans*, of the heterogenous time opened up, even if only momentarily, by iconoclasm. Neither of them mentions Benjamin, who actually attended some of the sessions of the College de Sociologie in Paris in 1938–39 where the taboo and the sacred came in for a lot of analysis. But there is a remarkable convergence of thought here. Along with Bataille, Foucault thinks language fails us at this moment. Bataille writes of thought jumping the rails, of how when the very heavens open we can speak in nothing but clichés. Foucault, however, becomes positively rhapsodic at this incapacity to speak and lets fly with a torrent of heightened language, a sort of hysteria in which the very impossibility makes the speaker redouble his or her efforts to express what is happening. There is first a lot of geometry in an effort to show how infinite is the experience, the experience of iconoclasm, meaning the experience of the paradox in which each step of rupture or of breaking the taboo results in yet another taboo and the effort multiplies, feeding on itself. Hence we hear a lot about spirals rather than breaks or ruptures: "the form of a spiral which no simple infraction can break" ("A Preface to Transgression," 1977). We hear of circles too, but not your typical smooth circle. Instead it is a circle made of "fissures, abrupt descents, and broken contours." It is a "misshapen and craglike language" folded back on itself and continuously questioning its limits. Then there are the cosmic and meteorological metaphors in which iconoclasm is likened to "the solar inversion of satanic denial," or to "a flash of lightning in the night which, from the beginning of time, gives a dense and black intensity to the night it denies … yet owes to the night the stark clarity of its manifestation." The reason Foucault writes in such a breathtaking manner in my opinion is because he is doubly stressed compared to Bataille. It is now maddeningly complex. Bataille may have been a proto-postmodernist, but Foucault is the real thing and for him there is, after the Death of God, no solid taboo to butt against such that transgression itself becomes the new god and as such takes the form of sex which, as he insists, has to be spoken about in order to remain a secret. Oh my God!

Death of the Author

They say you should always keep an author separate from his or her text, that it is wrong to allow biography into literary criticism. Some go further and talk of the Death of the Author and, as did Barthes, relate such deaths to the songs of shamans acting as mere vehicles for a sacred text. Yet I cannot not think about Foucault as not only gay but for much of his life in the closet, just as I cannot not think of an activist in Uganda as gay when he was beaten to death with a hammer in late January 2011 for being gay. Can we really say there are no more taboos? And what happens when gay sex becomes no less tabooed than straight sex? Sex is always taboo, right, even in marriage?

Wisdom

Why is it that wise-sounding people are quick to tell you that

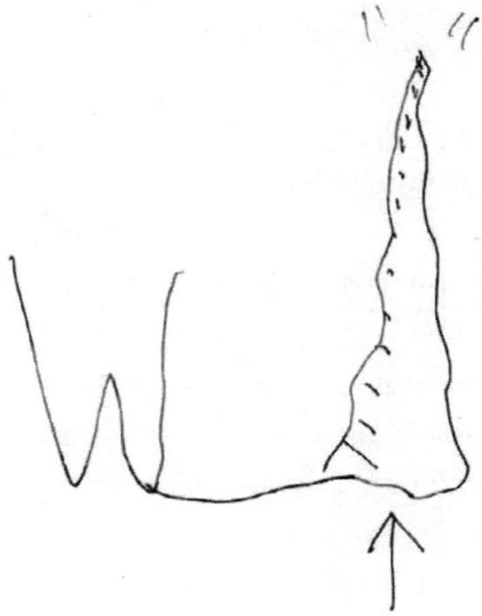

iconoclasm actually boosts the icon and thus betrays the iconoclast? There is so much joy in destroying the icon and even more, it seems, in destroying the joy the iconoclast enjoys.

Obelisk

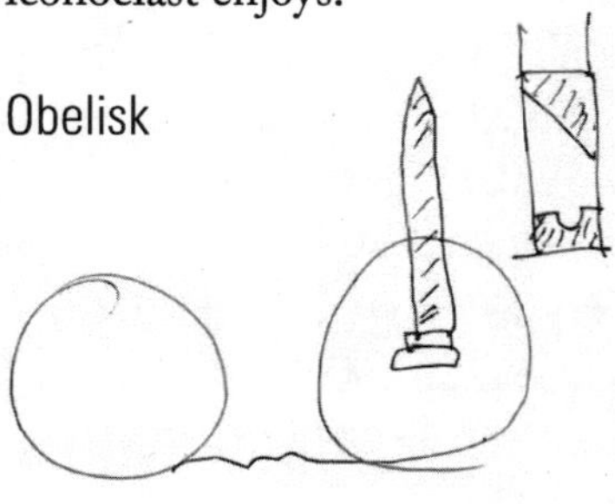

Some societies have permanent sites for iconoclasm. This is worth thinking about. Like the sea, iconoclastic waves batter against this Supreme Being, only to fall back again as the Supreme Being rises intact or stronger than ever. Such is the huge obelisk in what came to be called the Place of Concord in the centre of Paris.

But before it got that name of Concord it was the site of the guillotine during the French Revolution where Louis XVI and Marie Antoinette were beheaded. Now, that's iconoclasm for you! Perhaps we can call this sacrifice, but in any event what to me is eye-opening is the layering of history, from the guillotine to the obelisk, from the king to the republic, and in particular the unconscious or barely conscious manner by which myth and magic converge to create a permanent site for iconoclasm such that suddenly – like the human body set afire in Tunisia – the history and magical power of the obelisk can, on iconoclastic occasions, leap out at us. Weighing 250 metric tons and standing 75 feet high, there seems as much magic – technological and statist – entailed in its transport from its home in Egypt as there was in its original purpose there, which seems tied in with the worship of both the sun and the dead, mindful of the name given Louis XIV: "the Sun-King." Two mighty states, the theological state of ancient Egypt and the republican one of modern France, converged in forming what is surely the ritual centre of the French state and where the German army set up its headquarters during World War II. In 1993 the AIDS activists of ACT UP managed to unroll a gigantic pink condom covering the obelisk. We always knew the obelisk existed there, surrounded by snarling traffic. But once the pink condom was in place, the obelisk truly came into being. As an illustration of what he meant by the "dialectical image," Walter Benjamin in his *Arcades Project* (1999) cites Chateaubriand (born 1768), who wrote about the Obelisk de la Concorde: "The hour will come when the obelisk of the desert will find once again, on Murderers' Square, the silence and solitude of Luxor."

Animism

Is there a career or life history to an iconoclastic act? If so it might go like this. First the stage of invisibility or taken-for-grantedness of the icon. Then the stage of its destruction or humiliation, which automatically leads to the third stage, that of resurrection, as the icon explodes into visibility because of the aforesaid destruction or humiliation. It is no longer taken for granted. It has burst into consciousness, not only in its damaged, destroyed, or humiliated form, but also, in memory, at least – as it was before its disgrace when it existed in its noble, pristine, pretraumatized, form. Then comes sometimes a fascinating fourth stage, a moment of animation or animism in which the damaged icon comes alive in a most disturbing way (as objects are not supposed to have life like this), bred of violence and death now mixed with sacred or magical emanation. If this is true or true enough, then it seems a terrible simplification – an impoverishment – to say that iconoclasm paradoxically increases the power of the icon. Yes! Agreed. But so much more is going on. When Neil Roberts felt moved to pick up the damaged statue of the Queen of England, along with her consort, the Duke of Edinburgh, decapitated and amputated, and place them in his pick-up truck and take them to an undisclosed location, he seems to have felt that something unbearable had occurred. "It's gone beyond a bit of fun now," he said. It was as if in the depths of their destruction the statues had come alive.

Contagion and Proliferation

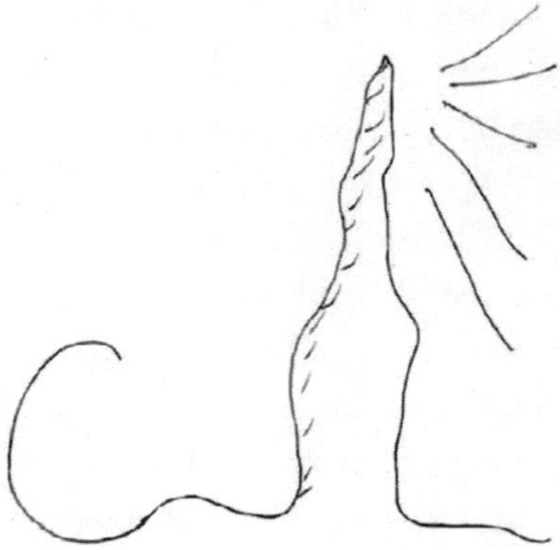

There is another stage as well, more like a flow, when once iconoclasm has occurred, it is like pulling a thread in a stocking: the whole thing can unravel. Foucault's spirals come to mind. A person who breaks a taboo, for example, is likely to be an object of dread, full of some evil toxin that can spread to other people. Freud specifically refers to this as "contagion" in his book on taboo. AIDS was exactly like this for the first few years, and still creates a chill, which is what is happening to Muslims in the US with the congressional hearings organized by an IRA militant, Republican party stalwart Peter King, who endorsed terrorism in Ireland and now endorses the use of state terrorism to spread the contagion of fear.

Castration

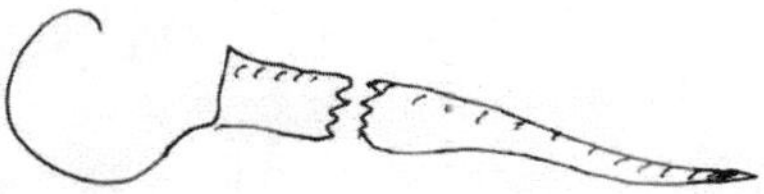

This is a quote from a news source:

> A phallic phenomenon was short-lived after police told a 16-year-old boy to remove a snow sculpture emulating male genitalia from his front yard on East River Street and Yale Avenue. Roman King said it took about 20 minutes to shape the 7-foot sculpture about two days ago. He said he created it "just to see what people would think," and he has gotten "car honks with people giving us the thumbs up," from drivers while it was standing.
>
> "My friends really like it," King said. But after police came by Thursday afternoon and told King to remove his interpretative model of the male sex organ, he said this was the last such sculpture he was likely to make (*Ohio Chronicle-Telegram*, 21 January 2011).

It is hard to say what is more iconoclastic here; building the phallus in the front yard or making the sculptor tear it down. Then we have to consider his name, Roman King. This quotation has some strange wording, such as "emulating" as in the "snow sculpture emulating male genitalia," and "interpreting" as in being made to "remove his interpretive model of the male sex organ." On the one hand it seems that the mere act of imitating is to run the risk of exceeding reality in a morally disturbing and even exciting manner, especially when it comes to the phallus. On the other hand we have the safe harbour of cognitive relativity with the introduction of the notion that any representation is merely an interpretation. Yet surely what is disturbing about the phallus is that it is the very model of the icon and of iconicity. What does it mean, then, to make an icon out of an icon, of the mother of all icons? I recall a brilliant colleague in Ann Arbor explaining to me many years ago Charles Sanders Peirce's trichotomization of the sign into the icon, the index, and the sign proper, or symbol.

As I recall his explanation, the icon is evoked when we speak of a phallic symbol such as a skyscraper – which is, he said, iconic on account of the shape. So why don't the police order skyscrapers razed? Why don't motorists honk when they drive past a skyscraper? Could it be because the skyscraper is actually an index and not an icon, an index meaning that there exists a cause-and-effect relationship between the building and an assumed phallic drive to dominate on the part of architects? As I recall further it all got dreadfully confusing because having trichotomized so neatly, Pierce then went to say that each category contained elements of the others. No such thing, therefore, as a pure icon? Where does that leave iconoclasm? Ask Roman King.

NOTES

The "Iconoclasm Dictionary" was originally presented as a keynote address at the "Iconoclasm: The Breaking and Making of Images" conference, University of Toronto, 17–19 March 2011. A video recording of Prof. Taussig's talk is archived and publicly available through the website of the Centre for Comparative Literature at the University of Toronto (complit.utoronto.ca). The "Iconoclasm Dictionary" was later published in vol. 56, no. 1 (2012) of ***TDR**: The Drama Review*, and in Michael Taussig, *The Corn Wolf* (University of Chicago Press, 2015).

1 Editors' note: In 2013, lawyers for Bradley Manning announced that she was a trans woman, and would be known as Chelsea Elizabeth Manning. On 17 January 2017, President Barack Obama commuted Manning's sentence, save four months; she was released on 17 May 2017. In 2018, Manning challenged Ben Cardin, a two-term incumbent, in the US Senate Democratic primary for Maryland; she placed second of eight.

KEYWORD

religion, n.[1]

Brit. /rɨˈlɪdʒ(ə)n/, US /rəˈlɪdʒ(ə)n/, /riˈlɪdʒ(ə)n/

Origin: Of multiple origins. Partly a borrowing from French. Partly a borrowing from Latin.

Etymons: French *religioun*; Latin *religiōn-*, *religiō*.

Etymology: < Anglo-Norman *religioun*, *religiun*, Anglo-Norman and Old French, Middle French *religion* (French *religion*). < *re-* re- *prefix* + a second element of uncertain origin; by Cicero connected with *relegere* to read over again (see relection *n.*), so that the supposed original sense of "religion" would have been "painstaking observance of rites," but by later authors (especially by early Christian writers) with *religāre* religate *v.*, "religion" being taken as "that which ties believers to God."

Religion is as old as at least a few Methuselahs,[2] and it seems fitting that its etymology would be shrouded in mystery. Religion is repetition and attention to detail. It means to reread, to be attentive to the very ceremonies that act as thresholds within its organization, its structure, its evolution. Movement forward and a sense of stagnation therefore occupy a similar space, where the repetitive or the cyclical meet the linear progression marked by solemn acts and rites. According to Gilles Deleuze, repetition, however, is anything but static: it is a reconfiguration of elements that constantly creates something new, whose limit is endlessly being pushed and drawn, constantly becoming.[3] Religion, one of the pillars of societal organization, along with politics and power – as "the opium of the people"![4] – would inevitably perform this repetition to the point of also becoming secularized and profaned, as the notion of being "tied" or "bound" to something – whether God, gods, Nature, the almighty dollar, sex – inexorably shifts, especially in a world with approximately 4,200 current organized religions to which many of us are tied, and which we constantly question, read, and "reread." Oh, the dangers of (re)reading!

Religion is…

I. A state of life bound by religious vows; the condition of belonging to a religious order.

It is first of all a "state," that is, a condition in which one finds oneself at a given moment due to a promise that binds one. It is neither inherent nor intrinsic, nor is it necessarily permanent. The polysemy of "state" allows us to tie religion to an organized community, an "order," not wholly unlike another state where, to echo the same etymology of "to vow," *votum* – for better or for worse – becomes to vote: the nation.

A sense of "belonging" for an individual within a community should not be underestimated in this context. There may be an "I" in "religion" – in fact, there are two. An "I" for an "I"? – but there is also an "us" in "religious" that cannot be ignored. Even the origin of "church" – *ecclesia* – signifies assembly.

However, when does one's "(re)reading" – either liberal, fundamentalist, or anything in between – become the responsibility of the community? Can and should one person be the icon of any religion? And how do we engage, socio-politically and spiritually, with the status of a religion's iconicity: from accepting the symbol around one's neck, to the forcible removal by the police of a burkini on the beaches of southern France, to the recognizability of a "type" that usually demands further "random" screening at the airport? Most countries in the West divide church and state (at least on paper); however, the way we engage with religions, out of respect or fear, participates in a nation's building of tolerance and sovereignty.

1.a. Action or conduct indicating belief in, obedience to, and reverence for a god, gods, or similar superhuman power.

How does one properly demonstrate belief or obedience? Many commandments, regardless of the scripture's religion, demand similar things: for example, to love only one (true) God, to avoid idols,[5] and to respect one's family. These are practically identical in the Abrahamic religions, as well as many others. Beyond following rules, however, other actions include prayer, (self-)sacrifice, fasting and feasting, pilgrimage, genital mutilation, and even suicide. In fact, the Church of Euthanasia's motto is "Save the Planet – Kill Yourself," and its only commandment is "Thou shalt not procreate" – a church whose goal is to fight planetary overpopulation by means of "suicide," "abortion, cannibalism, and sodomy."[6] Faith might move mountains, but self-proclaimed Reverend Chris Korda advocates jumping off one.

(Re)reading and education, proliferation and indoctrination, all play a key role in an individual's and a group's collective understanding of a particular religion as well as its guidelines and system(s). To understand when the codes of conduct are allegorical, metaphorical, or parabolic, and when there is no room for interpretation, is a complex, fundamental(ist) problem, in the name of any God.

2. A particular system of faith and worship.

This system has its own logic, hierarchy, and organization, whether based on calendars, gender, mono- or polytheism, a set of rules dictating what one can and cannot eat on particular days, how many wives/husbands one can take, as well as promises of enlightenment following the breaking of the life-and-death cycle, or how one will be rewarded in the afterlife. These systems can, in turn, become sacred cows themselves, metonymically replacing the spirituality at its original core with rules that may or may no longer have a place in contemporary societies, rules that decide who goes to hell in a handbasket, when it is acceptable to take an eye or a tooth, or to bear one's cross. There is an economy and politics of religion, which are very much exportable and imposable.

3. Belief in or acknowledgement of some superhuman power or powers (esp. a god or gods) which is typically manifested in obedience, reverence, and worship; such a belief as part of a system defining a code of living, esp. as a means of achieving spiritual or material improvement.

Religion, according to this definition, aids one in having a better life thanks to the previously acknowledged "system." Such a code might improve one's life, and, we would add, one's death as well, as in many religions the ethical choices – living a *good* life, at least according to that specific system – signifies a meaningful death or afterlife. In ancient

Egypt, for example, naturally preserving the dead via mummification became an essential part of their religion, particularly with regard to the desire for a cushy afterlife. This practice extends to Japan and China as well, with a unique form of ascetic self-mummification in Buddhism, described by Rambelli and Reinders: a person seals themselves in a cave in order to avoid the decomposition of the body. They prepare themselves by following a strict diet, including pine needles, and maintain a meditative state in order to assume a Buddha image: where "self-mutilation or self-immolation, in which the profane self is literally destroyed to leave only the subtle, pure body of a Buddha image," thus transforms their bodies into icons in death.[7] A body becomes iconic once something is done to it. Does sacrifice consecrate "that which it destroys," as Michael Taussig writes in this volume (echoing Georges Bataille), and what exactly are the consequences of victims becoming gods?

4. Strict fidelity or faithfulness; conscientiousness; devotion to some principle.

Fidelity and devotion have long since taken a leap of faith away from religion, setting their eyes on other matters to which people are now bound. Our present-day augury includes looking up to the stars, Hollywood trendsetters and entertainers, and following their styles, their selfies, and their tweets, as we devotedly check our feeds, chomping at the food porn and any glimmer of shine or hope that might give our lives more meaning, often immolating our time.[8] Some choose new idols, *American Idol*(s), or sports heroes, sporting their jerseys – their Sunday best – and cheering for a team on any given Sunday. Sex also enjoys an ambiguous relationship alongside and in contradistinction to religion, from supposed orgies in Satanist cults to atheists who exclaim "Oh my God!" during intercourse – cited as the most common exclamation during sex, according to Father Brendan (played by William H. Macy) in the film *The Sessions*. If religion is in part a tie or bond to something, then the plurality of subcultures within BDSM communities (or assemblies) – dominated by bondage and discipline, dominance and submission, as well as sadism and masochism – offer a fruitful example of a new devotion, and a different means to reach epiphanic bliss or enlightenment. Even the iconic abbreviation "OMG" has lost any direct spiritual resonance it once had. One example of bondage that subverts religious practices – apart from "religious play," in which participants dress as and enact religious relationships as sexual acts – is the practice of bondage mummification. Far from embalming an individual, this practice uses materials such as leather, latex, cellophane, and tape. If the purification of the body and preparation for the afterlife were elements inherent to the practice of mummification for several religions, then the arousal felt from (momentary) mummification on behalf of the sub or dom entirely transgresses the asceticism of religion, and challenges, as a different form of both abnegation and the Freudian death-drive, the recognizability and signification of the mummified body.[9]

NOTES

1 *Oxford English Dictionary Online*, s.v. "religion, n.," http://www.oed.com/ (accessed 14 December 2016).

2 According to the Hebrew Bible, Methuselah lived to the age of 969.

3 Deleuze, *Difference and Repetition*.

4 Marx, *A Contribution to the Critique of Hegel's Philosophy of Right*.

5 See Noyes, *The Politics of Iconoclasm*, xiii, for an excellent example of the polysemy of the term *shirk* in Islam, and, in particular, in the context of ISIS with regard to iconoclasm.

6 Grad, "Eat Me."

7 Rambelli and Reinders, *Buddhism and Iconoclasm*, 190.

8 The etymology of "immolation" is to "sprinkle with sacrificial meal." *Oxford English Dictionary Online*, s.v. "immolation, n." http://www.oed.com/ (accessed 11 January 2017).

9 Examples of mummified bondage can be found at: http://yumyumencasement.tumblr.com/ (accessed 11 January 2017).

BIBLIOGRAPHY

Deleuze, Gilles. *Difference and Repetition*. New York: Columbia University Press, 1995.

Grad, David. "Eat Me: Rev. Chris Korda Dines for Our Sins." http://www.churchofeuthanasia.org/press/david_grad.html (accessed 10 January 2017).

Marx, Karl. Introduction to *A Contribution to the Critique of Hegel's Philosophy of Right*. https://www.marxists.org/archive/marx/works/1843/critique-hpr/intro.htm (accessed 10 January 2017).

Noyes, James. *The Politics of Iconoclasm: Religion, Violence and the Culture of Image-Breaking in Christianity and Islam*. London: Tauris, 2013.

Rambelli, Fabio, and Eric Reinders. *Buddhism and Iconoclasm: A History*. London: Bloomsbury, 2012.

Christopher van Ginhoven Rey

2

An Aesthetics of Splendour

1. Introduction

Did the resurrected Christ have to ascend to heaven? Considering this question in the *Summa*, Aquinas points out that because Christ took on human flesh for the sake of our salvation, it could seem as though it would have been "more beneficial for men if he had lingered on earth among us."[1] The ascension, however, was an event of salvation history whose "expediency" (in the sense of "necessity," as when one speaks of a "necessary expedient") was underscored by Christ himself (John 16:7) – Aquinas's efforts to imagine why it would have been more beneficial for Christ not to disappear will thus give way to the argument that it was actually "fitting" for him to do so. Like Augustine and Anselm before him, the *Doctor Angelicus* contends that the "expediency" of Christ's departure must ultimately be explained by reference to the fact that, in disappearing, Christ ceased to be seen; in so doing, he created an opening for faith, a virtue that is necessarily concerned with "things unseen" (*non visis*).[2]

Contemplatives were particularly attuned to the problem posed by the final moments of Christ's time on earth. To be sure, late medieval currents of devotion, inspired largely in Anselm's meditations, had emphasized a form of prayer centred on the imaginative engagement with the events of salvation history and with the figure of Christ – the image's pertinence within contemplation was in this sense taken for granted, and it would remain a presupposition of the diffusion of the *devotio moderna* and of the transformation of the imitation of Christ (*imitatio Christi*) into a cultural imperative.[3] Contemplatives, however, were also the first to recognize that, if one was to insist on the exemplarity of Christ and his story, one could not ignore the implications of his passage into the *non visis*. Did Christ's disappearance not make it necessary to think of prayer as an experience oriented toward an iconoclastic climax, a moment in which the soul, having abandoned all images, would be able to exercise itself wholly in love?[4]

While this outcome would seem to mirror (in a way that dogmatically justifies it) the ecstatic descent of the Holy Spirit shortly after the ascension, the iconoclastic moment that functions as a sort of threshold leading to it posed a challenge to the kind of epistemological mediation associated with images of Christ and ultimately with the figure of Christ himself. The presupposition that God and his love must be made known to humans in ways that accord with their capacities (a central tenet of discussions of the incarnation) seemed to be undermined by the imperative to abandon all images and to flee into higher states of spiritual absorption. Indeed, the bishops gathered at Trent, in their famous decree against iconoclasm, went so far as to suggest that the Church's own mediation in matters of salvation followed from this epistemological mediation.[5] By the sixteenth century, the implications of an excessive emphasis on purely spiritual states in questions pertaining to the legitimacy of institutions like the Church were clear to contemplatives. And it was with these implications in mind that they confronted the tension between the mediated and embodied dimension of God's love, which found expression in a history one could memorialize in and through images, on the one hand, and the desire for states of absorption where this mediation and this embodiment would seem to have been transcended, on the other.

Saint Teresa of Ávila's *The Interior Castle* (1577), the text I will be considering in what follows, presents us with a remarkable attempt to reconcile the two polarities of this tension. Teresa's solution to the conflict outlined above consists in the institution of a *delay* that defers the iconoclastic climax, postponing without actually compromising the dissipation to which images are fated. This delay, which finds support in Aquinas's claim that the ascension itself presupposed a delay, since it did not happen immediately after the resurrection but only after forty days, is a twofold one. It initially takes the form of a commitment to remain with the images one meditates upon as long as possible, up until the point in which Christ's physicality proves to be an overwhelming and unbearable sight. Past this threshold, as one opens oneself up to the spirit, the delay takes the form of a proliferation of visionary images that, themselves a gift of the Holy Spirit and thus the way in which the spirit announces itself, serve to postpone the climax they would seem to announce. What interests me about this delay – and ultimately about the theological problem to which it refers – is the manner in which it relates to the opening, within Teresa's narrative, of a transitional space between medieval and modern aesthetics. Teresa's critique of iconoclasm in *The Interior Castle*, I will argue, is the condition of possibility for the emergence of a concept of beauty that, foreshadowing Hegel's insights on the nature of art, insists on beauty's localization in contingent and concrete entities rather than in the totality of the cosmos. The image that resists its own dissipation in the purely spiritual reality of love presents us, that is, with the theological correlate of the work of art, that "sensuous concrete thing" (in Hegel's words) that posits its own contingency not only as a legitimate and autonomous site of beauty, but as that site of beauty whose delimitation and identification makes aesthetics, understood as a discourse about art, possible in the first place.

As my title announces, these concerns are worked out in the course of a reflection on a "splendour" that is said to accompany the images of which Teresa speaks, and which appears as a necessary correlate of the concept of beauty she develops in the course of their defence. Indeed, the distance between a work like *The Interior Castle* and the medieval system of aesthetics epitomized by Albert the Great and Aquinas makes itself felt in what Teresa has to say about this radiance, a necessary concomitant, I argue, of what one could refer to as the "majesty of contingency," an expression that refers to the way in which the concrete and sensuous individual thing asserts itself as such, over and against its dissolution in a diffuse totality. The epistemological and institutional implications of the exaltation of this majesty have already been sketched. *The Interior Castle*, however, manages, as I hope to show, to go beyond a defence of mediation that is invested in granting legitimacy to the existence and work of institutions. It does so on account of an emphasis on beauty that gestures, I argue, in the direction of aesthetics as an autonomous domain of experience and of value. In considering this question, I hope, in the pages that follow, to elucidate what modern aesthetics owes to the critique of iconoclasm and to some of the theological questions raised in the course of this critique.

2. Meditation

With the aim of presenting us with an exhaustive account of the soul's progress in prayer, Teresa appeals to the familiar allegory of the soul of the Christian as a stronghold, "a castle made of a single diamond or of a very clear crystal, with as many rooms as there are abodes in heaven."[6] Leading us into this structure, which she declares to be incessantly assailed by the forces of temptation and vice, she then invites us to follow the soul as it moves through seven of these abodes or *moradas* – the book's original title is *Las moradas del castillo interior* – from the one closest to the courtyard to the one at the centre, "the place where the most secret things between God and the soul are said to unfold."[7]

While Teresa's parable of the contemplative ascent emphasizes the soul's progress, it subjects the soul's approach to the central chamber to continuous delays. ("Parable," from the Greek *parabola*, is in this regard an apt word, since the soul's journey takes the form of an asymptotic approach, with the destination becoming more unattainable the closer it lies.) Contributing to these delays are those lizards, toads, and snakes that creep around the outskirts of the castle, and which threaten to drag the soul along with them. Then, once inside, the soul is prone to feel weak and intimated by the majesty of the castle's Lord, or else to fall into sin and find itself, once again, in the outskirts, where the journey began. Further cause for delay is found, finally, in what Teresa refers to as the castle's great capacity: "Around the central room," she writes, "there are many chambers, and there are also many more above it." For this very reason, the soul must be permitted "to roam through the castle's chambers, through those below, above, and on the sides."[8] The admonition recurs throughout the book, all the way down to the epilogue, where Teresa writes that even though she has spoken only of seven chambers, "in each there are many more, below and above and around, with gardens and fountains and mazes and things so delectable that you will want to lose yourselves in praise of the great God who created it in his image and likeness."[9] Teresa concludes by suggesting that this garden of earthly delights – to echo the title of Bosch's famous painting – may even furnish the nuns under her care with a means of forgetting the hardships of confinement: "Considering how strictly cloistered you are, and how few opportunities you have of recreation and how few in number are the rooms in some of your convents, I think it will be a great consolation for you to take your delight in this interior castle, for you can enter it and wander around in it at any time, without having to ask leave from your superiors."[10] If the injunction to enjoy what the castle has to offer is accompanied by the dispensation to circumvent the superior, it is because the profusion of delectable things constitutes an authority of its own. This profusion requires the soul to go in search of the delights it holds in store for it and, once in their presence, to take delight in them. Overflowing with delectable things, the castle itself can be said to interpose more than one distraction in the way of the soul anxious to draw closer to the castle's Lord – enjoyment of what this *locus voluptatis* has to offer requires the soul not to rush forward, and to linger instead around what it finds most pleasing.[11]

The images which the soul can expect to project while praying are among the things worth delaying its progress through a sequence, as becomes apparent in the third of the three modalities of meditation that Teresa discusses early on: "We begin by thinking of the favor that God bestowed upon us by giving us his only Son, and we do not stop there but proceed to consider the mysteries of his whole glorious life. Or we begin with the prayer in the Garden and our understanding does not stop until he is placed upon the cross. Or we take one step of the Passion – Christ's arrest, for example – and go over this mystery in our mind, meditating in detail upon the points which we need to think over and feel deeply, such as Judas' treason, the flight of the apostles, and so on and so forth."[12] A movement that finds itself inexorably thrust toward its own culmination (what Teresa herself refers to, in relation to the first two examples, as a refusal to stop) contrasts with the delay that ensues when, as we can see in the third example, one embarks on a circumspect consideration of an individual step independently of any kind of diachronic drift: one's "taking a step" (*tomamos un paso*) implies, in this case, no movement forward – the right expression, in that case, would be *damos un paso* – but an effort to extract the step from the sequence to which it belongs. Fittingly, Teresa mentions, by way of example, the "arrest" (*prendimiento*) of Christ, a step of the passion in which Christ undergoes what the step as such can be said to undergo: the *pasión*, as process, disappears behind a *paso*, an individual moment captured by the one meditating, much like Christ allows himself to be captured as the apostles flee. This reference to the apostles' "flight" (*huída*) is particularly significant – it comes right after Teresa has voiced her refusal to believe that after one has accumulated enough experience in prayer, "it is better to occupy oneself with matters pertaining to the divinity and to *flee* from corporeal things."[13] One should actually strive to *remain* with those things, Teresa suggests, to side with Christ's captors and to arrest the corporeal thing (*cosa corpórea*) that Christ is.

Instead of searching after an immediate experience of the divinity, to be found beyond the memorialization of Christ's life and passion, one should therefore strive to capture Christ through those images that allow one to ponder specific episodes of salvation history in detail – only angels, Teresa writes in connection with this, are permitted "to remain permanently enkindled in love."[14] In order not to sound, however, as though she were accusing those who wish to be so "enkindled" of a faulty loyalty or even of treason, she wonders whether the desire to flee from corporeal things might be symptomatic of a deeper understanding of the mysteries considered during meditation. The more experience one has with prayer, she writes, the more these mysteries become engraved in one's memory, "in such a way that the mere sight of the Lord on his knees in the Garden, drenched in that awful sweat, suffices us not merely for an hour, but for many days."[15] Could it be that if some would counsel fleeing from the corporeal things one imaginatively evokes, they do so out of a sense that such evocations have the power to *overwhelm* the imagination? In raising this question, Teresa suggests that, ideally at least, the corporeal thing one imaginatively arrests will be endowed with an *arresting* corporeality, as indicated by the reference to Christ's "awful sweat" (*espantoso sudor*). The very Christ one refuses to arrest is thus himself arresting, and it is for this reason that some might not want to remain with his image in the same way that one should remain with the other things that the castle has to offer for one's consideration.

3. Visions

Meditation in its third modality – the attempt to arrest Christ in his arresting features – constitutes only one instance of the soul's relation to the image. Another important instance is found in those visions with which the soul begins to be graced in higher states of mystical absorption.

Teresa's discussion of visions follows the threefold typology established by Augustine in his commentary on Genesis, which distinguishes between corporeal, imaginary, and intellectual visions. Her focus is on the last two, imaginary visions being those that, as their name indicates, have their locus in the imagination, the capacity by which, as Augustine writes, we see "heaven and earth and the visible things in them when we are in the dark."[16] This kind of vision, in which God causes an image to appear in the imagination, differs from intellectual visions, which refer to things that "have no images resembling them which are not identical with them."[17] This last bit may seem redundant – as likenesses, images are never identical to what they are like – yet it helps to foreground the fact that intellectual visions concern conceptual, and thus self-identical, entities.[18]

Stuart Clark writes in his analysis of vision in early modern Europe that Augustine's "hierarchy of supernatural seeing" allowed for "the cultivation … of visionary experiences at levels of certainty and purity far above those of mundane sight." Clark then mentions, as an example, "the kind of imageless devotion often aimed at by mystics."[19] Teresa was well aware of Aquinas's claim that "it is impossible for our intellect to understand anything actually except by turning to phantasms," and her devotion is in fact anything but "imageless."[20] Thus it is that, even if she begins her discussion of imaginary visions by acknowledging the risk they entail – the imagination is the capacity most prone to demonic interference – she then writes that "they seem to me in some ways more profitable, because they are in closer conformity with our nature." Culminating in an indubitable certainty about essences rather than in a knowledge of things in their corporeal qualities, intellectual visions do not conform as well to the soul's union with a body. Teresa also recognizes that they are extraordinary and thus extremely rare occurrences, and for that very reason cherishes those she has been gifted with – for a while, she writes, she could intuit and be certain of Christ's presence by her side, even if she could never see him. Ultimately, though, she suggests that they were a propaedeutic for the imaginary visions in which, in opposition to an intellectual certainty, God grants the soul "a clear revelation of [Christ's] most sacred humanity, either as he was when he went around the world or after his resurrection."[21]

As Teresa notes, the image of an imaginary vision differs radically from those that the soul may itself conjure during meditation, even if these, too, show a body. "Truly alive," the imaginary vision speaks to the soul and instructs it, even though the soul's lowness can barely suffer what is nothing short of an "awful" (*espantosa*) sight.[22] That this "awfulness" presents something in excess of the "awfulness" that marks images like those of Christ's "awful" sweat is made clear when Teresa writes that an imaginary vision, "while being the most beautiful and delightful kind of vision imaginable … is of such an exceeding majesty that it fills the soul with a great terror."[23] Close examination of *The Interior Castle* reveals, indeed, that the excess that sets the image of a vision apart from its meditative counterpart resides in the "beauty" mentioned in the above description – it is indeed in the discussion of imaginary visions that we have the first reference to Christ that takes account not merely of Christ's overwhelming corporeality, but also of what we may call his *corporeal beauty*. Perhaps what is most crucial about this beauty is that it sets the image of an imaginary vision apart not only from the images conjured in meditation, but also from intellectual visions. It is in relation to an imaginary vision, indeed, that Teresa can speak passionately of "the Lord's eyes, so beautiful, tender, and kind," and also of how the soul that sees this image can later "remember his most meek and beautiful face," when not long before the same Christ, intuited in an intellectual vision, was said to be "faceless," and thus without any eyes of which anything like beauty, tenderness, and kindness could have been predicated.[24]

In the end, then, the beauty that imaginary visions bring to the fore might be nothing but the name of a twofold disjunction, between an imaginary vision and the images conjured in meditation and between a knowledge of specific corporeal attributes and the intellectual intuition of an essence. Teresa's approach to the second disjunction is especially worthy of note, more than anything else because she seems as interested in specifying its nature as she is in exploring the continuities that undermine it, and to do so in ways that might reveal a further dimension of the visions' characteristic beauty. This is most clearly apparent in the analogy she deploys to explain the manner in which the imaginary vision experientially confirms the intuition bestowed by the intellectual vision. The occurrence is likened to the opening of a reliquary:

> It is as if in a gold reliquary there were hidden a precious stone of the highest value and the choicest virtues. Although we have never seen the stone, we know for certain that it is there, and if we carry it about with us, we can have the benefit of its virtues. We do not prize it any the less for not having seen it, because we have found by experience that it has cured us of certain illnesses for which it is a sovereign remedy. But we dare not look at it, or open the reliquary in which it is contained, nor are we able to do so. For only the owner of the jewel knows how to open it, and though he has lent it to us so that we may benefit from it, he has kept the key and so it is still his own. He will open it when he wants to show it to us, and will take it back when he sees it fit to do so, as he certainly does. Now let us suppose than on some occasion the owner of the reliquary suddenly wants to open it, for the benefit of the person to whom he has lent it. Obviously this person will get much greater pleasure from it if he can recall the wonderful splendour of the stone, and it will remain the more deeply engraved upon her memory. This is what happens here. When our Lord is pleased to bestow greater consolations upon this soul, he shows with great clarity his most sacred humanity in whatever way he thinks best … And even though this happens so quickly that we could compare it to a flash of lightning, this most glorious image is so engraved in the imagination that I do not believe it can disappear until it is where it can be enjoyed for all eternity.[25]

The imaginary vision embodies the intuition, and its appearance is announced by a "splendour" (*admirable resplandor*) intended to elicit in the soul the desire for a vision as everlasting as the beatific vision.[26] Teresa suggests in her discussion of the analogy that the very occurrence of the vision hints that the soul is edging closer to the most exalted form of rapture, an experience that she equates with a dissolution of the kind of sensuous concreteness that an image like that of Christ's humanity can capture. Equating the experience to the passage into the castle's last chamber, she will write that it requires those eager to proceed "to set aside everything corporeal and to leave the soul in a state of pure spirituality."[27] Imaginary visions can thus be said to foreshadow a dissolution in the spirit not unlike the one demanded by salvation history, where Christ's disappearance from the world is a condition for the events of Pentecost. Their content, however, denies this very dissolution, since they show Christ as he existed prior to that moment. Their very occurrence serves, then, to delay the iconoclastic climax at which the journey aims. This is perhaps most clearly attested in narrative terms. Intended as an illustration of the soul's journey, Teresa's book is divided into seven sections, each of them corresponding to one of the castle's *moradas*. Of these, the sixth *morada*, the place where imaginary visions are discussed, is by far the longest. A reflection of the difficulty of the matters treated in them, their length (eleven chapters in total) evokes, too, the postponement of the consummation that imaginary visions foreshadow.[28] It is as if the narrative, in distending itself and postponing its own conclusion, were enacting the postponement that the discussion of meditation associated with the consideration of Christ's humanity. In the case of this image that is given by God himself, however, the beautiful displaces the merely arresting. What the delay allows Teresa to grasp thematically is beauty and – as a dimension that exceeds the twofold disjunction associated with it – the *splendour* that accompanies it.

4. The Splendour of the Image

The passage to the seventh *morada* cannot be postponed indefinitely, and just as Teresa cannot avoid affirming the necessity of Christ's disappearance – and, along with it, the very closure of revelation – the delay represented by the sixth *morada* is bound to come to a close. How are we to account, then, for the fact that the first time that God grants the soul the favour of crossing an iconoclastic threshold, "his Majesty is pleased to show himself to the soul through an imaginary vision of his most sacred humanity, so that it may clearly understand what is taking place and not be ignorant of the fact that it is receiving so sovereign a gift"? Speaking about her own experiences as if they were those of somebody else, Teresa writes of a time when "the Lord revealed himself to this woman, not long after she had received communion, through a form of great splendour and beauty and majesty, just as he must have looked after his resurrection, and told her that it was time she took upon his affairs as if they were her own."[29]

Is this splendour similar to that which, as Lacan eloquently puts it, "all those who have spoken worthily of beauty have not omitted from its definition"?[30] One such figure would have to be Albert the Great, a theologian whom Robert Ricard, in a now classic essay, numbers among those with whom Teresa is in dialogue.[31] In the second article of the first, primarily the expository *quaestio* of *De Pulchro et Bono*, his commentary on Pseudo-Dionysius's reflections on beauty in *The Divine Names*, Albert defines beauty as "the splendour of the substantial or actual form which is found in the proportioned parts of a material thing" (*splendorem formae substantialis vel actualis supra partes materiae proportionatas*).[32] The term "form" has a specific technical sense in Albert's system, and we must be careful not to think of it as a designation for the "shape" of a thing, even if it is qualified as "actual." The form of a material thing is rather "actual" in a substantial sense – the conjunction *vel* is crucial in this respect – and it designates the principle of a thing's being or, more exactly, the principle of the actualization responsible for a thing's emergence as a distinct thing within being: this emergence (or "entelechy") is very likely what Albert has in mind when he writes elsewhere that "splendour is by its nature a kind of manifestation."[33] But neither should we think of the splendour of the form that manifests itself as emanating exclusively from the consonance of the parts that constitute it, even if Albert speaks of the "proportioned" parts of a material thing. Proportionality functions, instead, as the necessary correlate of actuality: if something is, it has a form, and this form is found, in turn, in the proportioned parts of what is, proportion being here the name for a law of distribution that issues from the form itself. Proportionality and actuality are virtually synonymous, and so we would do well to think of the splendour found in the proportioned parts of a material thing as the mark of the thing's actuality, a state which, in the Scholastic system, is commensurate with perfection. It is, indeed, the movement away from the privation of potentiality that is seen to emit a kind of radiance – the beauty that Albert speaks is thus metaphysical, a beauty that has everything to do with the event of being itself, seized as it is in things as they come to be and as they, by so doing, attain perfection.[34]

One may ask whether the "splendour and beauty and majesty" (*resplandor y hermosura y majestad*) of the image that Teresa encounters at the threshold of the iconoclastic climax are the correlate of its own actuality, of the perfection implied by its emergence against the indifferentiation that characterizes the state of pure spirituality associated with the seventh *morada*. In order to answer this question, however, it is necessary to take a closer look at what is, without a doubt, the distinguishing characteristic of Teresa's relation to the imaginary visions she confronts: namely, her obstinate attachment to the parts of an image, often to the expense of the whole. Recounting her experience with visions in the *Book of Her Life*, the autobiographical account she wrote at the request of her confessors, Teresa writes that initially Christ revealed himself to her gradually – the first thing she saw were his hands, and only after some time did she see his face.[35] Teresa writes that, to her surprise, she would remain interested in such individual features so strongly that even after Christ appeared to her whole she longed to focus on them. She explains that even though Christ appeared in front of her and spoke to her, she was fixated on "his most beautiful and divine mouth" and on "the color of his eyes." This longing for detail had calamitous consequences: "I was never worthy enough to see them, nor was my trying to do so any good. On the contrary, these efforts lost me the vision altogether."[36]

Teresa's yearning for such details marks a clear departure from the purely "objective" character that Albert assigns to beauty. To be sure, the definition of beauty in *De Pulchro et Bono* speaks of a splendour that is the correlate of the actuality of a thing: any individual thing can be said to be beautiful to the extent that it is. Things are beautiful in and of themselves, simply because they are, and hence outside of any *encounter* with them. Teresa's yearning, however, directly implicates the one who confronts the beautiful thing in such a way as to introduce a "subjective" dimension to the consideration of beauty. This subjective dimension will turn out to be the dimension whose theorization Umberto Eco regards as Aquinas's most significant departure from the work of Albert, as well as his greatest contribution to medieval aesthetics. Eco notes that, as that which bears witness to the perfection of the beautiful thing – a perfection that has everything to do with the thing's actualization – the splendour Albert considers is ultimately nothing but "a figure of speech"; it does not refer to anything that is not already implicit in the concept of form itself, serving only to underscore, in a kind of pleonasm, what is already considered to be essential to it.[37] Aquinas, Eco suggests, distances himself from this conception by considering beauty to be dependent not only upon a *confrontation* with the beautiful thing, but also upon a *judgment* pertaining to its beauty; the purely objective splendour, an emphatic but ultimately redundant assertion of the fact that the beautiful thing is in existence, becomes the subject of a *visio*: for something to be beautiful, it must give pleasure when it is seen.[38]

The phenomenology of visions developed by Teresa can be shown to present a coded formulation of the problem of early modern Catholicism as concerning a whole's heretical division (*kata*, "with respect to" + *holos*, "the whole") into parts.[39] In a way, though, this phenomenology might also have something to say about of the status of the vision itself and of the image in which it consists. The image that comes forward against a spiritualization that intends to do away with every definite form resembles its parts, which come forward against the emptiness precipitated (almost like a punishment) by the very yearning they elicit. The paradox captures, in a condensed form, the relation between the image and the iconoclastic limit that Teresa places at the end of her narrative. What remains to be seen is whether it also constitutes a contribution to the reflection on beauty's splendour inaugurated by Albert. On the one hand, the yearning for the detail would seem to point to an intensification of the subjective component discussed by Aquinas. But the part comes forward and imposes itself against a whole that, as a result of the very focus on the part, is "altogether lost." The desire that confronts the part, too, should be lost as a result of this, in such a way as to mark, perhaps, a return to a position like Albert's, who ascribes a sovereign objectivity to the beautiful thing. In this case, though, this sovereignty resides in the part. The dynamic alluded to in this question resonates with what Hegel writes in his *Aesthetics*: "However much the particular aspects, parts, and members of the beautiful object harmonize with one another to form an ideal unity and make this unity appear, this harmony must nevertheless be only so visible as to ensure that they still preserve an appearance of independent freedom over against one another." The beautiful thing, Hegel elaborates, must bear the mark of that necessity which only a certain harmony can bestow, but this necessity must remain "hidden behind an appearance of undesigned contingency. For otherwise the particular real parts lose their standing as existing on the strength of their own reality."[40]

5. The Edge of Glory

To speak "worthily" of beauty (following Lacan) one must not omit a reference to the splendour that accompanies its manifestation. Is it possible to conceive, however, of a splendour whose function is to convey the strength of the *contingent* reality of the beautiful thing, its standing *as a part*? It is worth asking whether Teresa has such a splendour in mind when, already within the realm of the spiritual, she mentions the imaginary vision's *resplandor y hermosura y majestad*. Like the "particular real parts" of the ideal unity that, in Hegel's view, shines forth in those objects through which art fulfills its aim, the imaginary vision, too, presents us with a singular entity that, coming forward against the indifferentiation of the spiritual, aspires to exist on the strength of its own contingent reality.

This insistence on beauty's contingent localization evokes, of course, the condition of art in the sense that Hegel himself understands it, namely, the "sensuous concrete thing" that the *Aesthetics* considers the work of art to be.[41] It is also, one may say, the condition of art in the sense in which this word is understood in the modern age, and more decisively since the articulation of aesthetics as an autonomous field of inquiry. Hegel, as we know, regards the "sensuous concreteness" of the work of art as the reflection of the "concreteness" of its ideal content, a concreteness that rests on the content's capacity to avail itself of "the determinate character of advancing to particularization and phenomenal manifestation and to unity with itself in these."[42] By way of example, he singles out the proposition that God "is simply *one*, the supreme being as such." The God of that proposition, Hegel argues, can provide no content for art, given that he has not been apprehended "in his concrete truth." Only the Trinity, and hence the Christian God, makes this apprehension possible, for it makes explicit what God is as Spirit, that is, as that medium which reconciles God's essence with his particularization (Christ) and in so doing guarantees a self-awareness of his oneness: Hegel writes that "only such unity" (in other words, the unity that results from a difference that is dialectically overcome) "is the concrete."[43] A genuinely concrete content, then, demands an equally concrete manifestation – content and its manifestation coincide and correspond in their concreteness, and in the case of the Trinity (to continue with Hegel's example), it is the human body that emerges as the concrete content that Spirit demands.

Hegel nevertheless considers the sensuous concrete thing to exist, in the final instance, "solely for our mind and Spirit." He insists on this existence *for* the mind because only the reflective operation of thought can turn the particular, sensuous concrete thing into a "moment" of the dialectically constituted unity of Spirit: following the particularization of the essential – he writes in reference to the Trinity – there must be a *return* to Spirit. The human body that is the particular manifestation of the God of the Trinity (and who exists not as simply one but as Spirit) demands to be known, precisely, as Spirit, for that is after all the concept's genuine content: "His medium of existence is therefore essentially inner knowledge and not the external natural form through which he can be represented only imperfectly and not in the whole profundity of his nature."[44] To speak of art as Hegel speaks of it, then, the contingent thing has to come forward; Hegel himself recognizes that it is "presentation" rather than inner knowledge that constitutes the "primary" aim of art. But primary has also the connotation of elementary and, hence, of unfulfilled: there must also be a return to Spirit, in the absence of which one ends up simply with "illustration."[45]

If, as an example of a localization of beauty on the strength of its own contingency, the image discussed by Teresa comes to illuminate the category of art, the fact that it is set against the indefiniteness that marks the iconoclastic climax would seem to entail a sacrifice of the "profundity" that, in Hegel's own words, only the spiritual can confer. It is precisely this sacrifice that is at stake in the refusal of glory exhibited, as Teresa explains, by the souls transformed by the mystical experience. The souls that make it to the last chamber of the castle, she writes, will care very little for "the glory that belongs to the saints – they do not desire as yet to attain this." She concedes that there might be times when they "turn with their tender longing to the thought of enjoying God and of desiring to escape from this exile," but very soon they will "turn back and look within themselves, and remember that they have him with themselves continually."[46]

Hegel explicitly notes that the moment of particularization must advance toward a reconciled unity in the reflective apprehension of the sensuous concrete thing: thought emerges as the mirror of spirit, but only in the encounter with the particular manifestation of a concrete content. In terms of the schema that Hegel presents, we can say that the claim that Christ is a "concrete personality" but also "*pure* spirituality," and that he thus demands to be known "as *Spirit* and in Spirit," posits the necessity of his disappearance; this return to the Spirit, this refusal to remain in the domains of illustration, is the moment of *thought*. This is precisely what is foreclosed by the refusal of glory of which Teresa speaks, the last in a series of delays that defer the definitive dissolution of everything in the spiritual. The refusal of glory keeps the soul within the very space in which the image has been arrested. The soul remains in this world, at the very edge of glory, deriving strength from the strength of the contingent thing that comes forward on the strength of its own reality. This strength, or *fortaleza*, is in a certain sense present in the very *fortaleza*, or fortress, that Teresa's castle is. In coming forward on the strength of its own contingency, the image emerges as the place of beauty, as does the castle to which it is linked through a metaphorical relation to the "jewel" in the reliquary – made of diamond, the castle is nothing but this jewel. Of course, along with this castle, one must also consider the castle that, by virtue of a felicitous eponymy, designates Teresa's book. When in the epilogue Teresa writes to the nuns under her care that, given the restricted conditions in which their life unfolds, "it will be a great consolation for you to take your delight in this interior castle," the boundary between the allegory as a didactic device and the book that explicates it is suddenly blurred. The deictic inflection that marks the interior castle as *this* interior castle can indeed be taken to mean the manuscript one has read and now holds in front of one. And this, too, has often been regarded as a beautiful thing in its own right.[47]

NOTES

1 Aquinas, *Summa Theologiae*, III, q. 57, a. 1.

2 Ibid., III, q. 57, a. 1, ad. 3.

3 Beyond such historical and cultural factors, one finds further theological support for the image's pertinence in Christ's status, as Saint Paul had first written and as Augustine had underscored in his treatise on the Trinity, as *imago Dei*. See: Augustine of Hippo, *On the Trinity*, XIV.3.11.

4 This argument was at the heart of the *alumbrado* heresy that swept through Spain in the sixteenth century. One thinks here in particular of the practice of *dejamiento*, a form of interiorized prayer that sought a purely spiritual experience of God's love through a complete surrender to his will. As the edict condemning the heresy makes clear, *alumbrados* were critical of forms of prayer that expressed too much interest in images of Christ and notably in images of his humanity. Interestingly, despite the heresy's condemnation, the question concerning the benefits of meditating on this humanity would remain a matter of dispute. For a discussion of the alumbrado heresy and of the edict more specifically, see: Márquez, *Los alumbrados*, 276–8.

5 The Catholic challenge to iconoclasm – and, more broadly, to the exclusive focus on the private encounter with Scripture championed by Protestants – can be found in the second decree of the Council of Trent's twenty-fifth session, which speaks of the need for bishops to "instruct the faithful diligently" in all matters concerning "the legitimate use of images." See: Waterworth, *Canons and Decrees*, 233–4. Condemning the destruction of images as anathema, the Council explicitly states that images are valid means for people to be "confirmed" in their faith and that the mysteries of Christ's life, "portrayed by paintings or other representations," can serve as powerful reminders of God's love for humanity. Images, the decree concludes, are effective means for the faithful "to cultivate piety" (Ibid., 235). Images had become a heated topic of debate in light of the resurgence, throughout Reformed territories, of a polemic that had taken centre-stage during the Byzantine period. Were images worthy of honour, or were they to be banned as idols? Calvin, Zwingili, and Karlstadt were much less welcoming of the use of images in worship than Luther was, and it is mainly in response to the uncompromising nature of their iconoclasm that the bishops at Trent set out to legitimize and then to regulate the use of images. For an overview of the debate, see: Dillenberger, *Images and Relics*, 3–21.

6 Teresa of Ávila, *The Interior Castle*, 28.

7 Ibid., 29.

8 Ibid.

9 Ibid., 234–5.

10 Ibid., 234. The relation between Teresa's vindication of the soul's right to lose itself in the delectable things that her "garden" has to offer and Bosch's marvellous rendition of paradise in *The Garden of Earthly Delights* has not escaped the attention of critics. Eduardo Subirats speaks of this garden as the embodiment of a "splendid vision of sensuality and beauty" intended to lend voice to "a mystical and heretic conception of the realization of paradise on earth." Teresa's depiction of a locale teeming with *cosas deleitosas*, he writes, presents a vision of

a *locus voluptatis* that functions first and foremost as "an artistic place, the place of the sensual pleasure elicited by color, nature, and life," all the while offering a place, also, to the "nostalgia for a lost paradise so central to the culture of the Renaissance." See: Subirats, *El alma y la muerte*, 155–6. One is also reminded here of what in the opening pages of *The Mystic Fable* Michel de Certeau regards as the unique way in which Bosch's garden manages to open and simultaneously to close a multiplicity of "pathways of meaning." *The Garden*, Certeau explains, "offers a multiplicity of possible itineraries, the traces of which, as in a labyrinth, would constitute so many stories, until one comes to a dead end that marks a forbidden meaning." Certeau, *The Mystic Fable*, 51.

11 That such a delay would seem indispensable should come as no surprise, signalled as it is in the very title of the book: Covarrubias's *Tesoro* explains that *morada* is the word for "one's ordinary room." Noting that "it is in our house that we stop and are the most," Covarrubias thinks it natural that the word would originate in a verb (*morar*) whose Latin predecessor means, precisely, "to slow down and to stop." Covarrubias, *Tesoro de la lengua castellana o española*, 814.

12 Teresa of Ávila, *Interior Castle*, 175.

13 Ibid., 171. The emphasis is my own. Here Teresa suggests that there is a model of apostleship which rests not on deserting Christ, but on remaining with him and ultimately on delaying his departure. Her discussion of images gestures in the direction of this other model.

14 Ibid., 172.

15 Ibid., 176.

16 Augustine of Hippo, *The Literal Meaning of Genesis*, 185.

17 Ibid., 186.

18 Thus, in contrast to men, who might be seen in body or in spirit, either as things out there or as representations one makes in their absence – for example, when they are shrouded in darkness, or while contemplating their hypothetical existence – Augustine mentions love, asking if it is seen "in one manner when present, in the form in which it exists, and in another manner when absent, in an image resembling it." Love, he answers, is seen only in one way, and that way involves nothing corporeal – its vision admits only of a difference of clarity, which can vary from person to person. Augustine of Hippo, *The Literal Meaning of Genesis*, 186.

19 Clark, *Vanities of the Eye*, 204.

20 Aquinas, *Summa*, 1, q. 84, a. 7.

21 Teresa of Ávila, *Interior Castle*, 185.

22 Ibid.

23 Ibid., 186.

24 Ibid., 187, 190. Teresa notes that, unlike what follows the reception of the intellectual vision, "it is unnecessary to ask here how, without being told, the soul knows who it is." This may seem obvious, since in the imaginary vision one is seeing what previously one intuited. One must remember, however, that the evidence signalled by the phenomenal element is tainted by the possibility of deception, to which imaginary visions remain by nature open. If Christ, as Teresa writes, "reveals Himself quite clearly as the Lord of heaven and earth," and if the imaginary vision comes with an unshakable certainty regarding its authenticity, it is because it carries with it its own criterion: the Lord of heaven and earth, Teresa has written, reveals himself quite clearly, "which is something that the kings of the earth never do, for they would be thought very little of were they not accompanied by their suites, or were heralds not to proclaim so" (186). The flight of the apostles that in the first modality of meditation prepared the stage for the *prendimiento* of Christ reappears here in the certainty that greets Christ's self-authenticating image: the earthly king's entourage fails to disperse, and in so doing contributes to his mystique. Earthly majesty feeds on secrecy rather than on disclosure, whereas the image of Christ presents Christ in his sovereign self-sufficiency.

25 Ibid., 185.

26 It is largely in view of this splendour that the image deserves to be called a gem or a jewel, or, as Teresa puts it, *una piedra preciosa de grandísimo valor y virtudes*. This, of course, is not the first time that the text of *The Interior Castle* speaks of a precious stone: the jewel bestowed with such value and such virtues in fact answers, almost in every respect, to the description of the castle itself, which from the outset has been said not only to be made "of a single diamond or of a very clear crystal," but also to emit and to be enveloped, being made of such material, in a refined luminosity.

27 Ibid., 216.

28 The longest of the other *moradas* – the fourth, the fifth, and the seventh – span no more than four chapters each. The first and the third *moradas*, in turn, consist of two chapters, while the second *morada* comprises one chapter only. Teresa is well aware of this, and even aligns this delay with a purgatorial economy: "It is well that great things should cost a great deal," she writes, "all the more so because, if the soul can be purified by suffering and enabled to enter the seventh *morada*, just as those who are to enter Heaven are to be cleaned in Purgatory, this suffering is no more than what a drop of water is to the sea" (199).

29 Ibid., 212.

30 Lacan, *The Ethics of Psychoanalysis*, 248.

31 Ricard, "Quelques remarques," 187–98. Ricard refers specifically to Albert's sermon for the first Sunday of Advent.

32 Albertus Magnus, *De pulchro et bono*, 1, 2c. Albert's treatise was until recently wrongly attributed to Aquinas; hence its inclusion in the complete works of the *Doctor Angelicus*. For my discussion of Albert's theory of beauty, and of his understanding of the splendour that accompanies it, I have relied on Umberto Eco's excellent summary in *The Aesthetics of Thomas Aquinas*, 20–121.

33 Albert defines splendour in this way while commenting on the opening hymn of Pseudo-Dionysius's *Mystical Theology*. In reference to the Areopagite's invocation to the Trinity to "direct us to the more than unknown, more than resplendent and highest peaks of the mystic oracles," Albert writes that "manifest" is the opposite of "unknown," and hence that to speak of the resplendent oracles implies a paradox. See: Magnus, "Commentary on Dionysius' Mystical Theology."

34 As with the elucidation of Albert's definition of beauty, the nuances of the Scholastic concept of form are lucidly clarified by Eco in his *Aesthetics*, 45–6, 66–71.

35 Teresa of Ávila, *The Life of Saint Teresa of Avila*, 196.

36 Ibid., 205.

37 A look at the larger context of the assertion might help clarify Eco's point: "In its purely formal aspect – the aspect which is of interest in aesthetics – a perfect object is an object which has integrity and proportion, and nothing more is required. Its form is complete, ontologically ready to be judged beautiful. To speak of the 'resplendence' of the form is simply a figure of speech for referring yet again to integrity and proportion, the wholeness which saturates and coordinates the constituent parts." Eco, *Aesthetics*, 118–19.

38 Ibid., 56. In support of this understanding of Aquinas's definition of beauty, Eco points to the passage where Aquinas writes that "those things are called beautiful which please us when they are seen" (*pulchra enim dicintur quae visa placent*) (*Summa*, 1, q. 5, a. 4, ad. 1). Aquinas, Eco suggests, rescues the resplendent quality of beauty from a purely ornamental function: the splendour of the substantial or actual form (*splendorem formae substantialis vel actualis*) cannot be fully accounted for by reference to a proportionality (*partes materiae proportionatas*) that in the final instance refers to the actualization of the thing. Instead, Aquinas appends, to the splendour of the beautiful thing, what he calls *claritas*, a word designating a radiance, which, in excess of the metaphysical, comes forward as an expression of "the fundamental communicability of form, which is made actual in relation to someone's looking at or seeing of the object. The rationality that belongs to every form is the 'light' which manifests itself to aesthetic seeing" (119).

39 Van Ginhoven Rey, "The Hermeneutic Image," 165–8.

40 Hegel, *Aesthetics*, 115.

41 The phrase occurs repeatedly in the *Aesthetics*, but it figures prominently in Hegel's discussion of the division of his subject in the introductory section (69–90).

42 Hegel, *Aesthetics*, 71.

43 Ibid., 70–1. Hegel goes so far as to claim that it is for this reason that Christians have been more successful than "the Jews and the Turks" in representing their God.

44 Ibid., 72.

45 Hegel writes that illustration "is not a matter of chance" – in terms of the Trinitarian analogy he is working with, that would amount to saying that the incarnate Christ, prior to his death, was himself a matter of chance – but it is also "not the highest way of apprehending the spiritually concrete." Ibid., 71.

46 Ibid., 220–1.

47 It would be instructive, in this regard, to think of the history of the manuscript of *Las moradas* itself, also encased, like the living image, in a reliquary. María Mercedes Carrión includes a vivid description of it:

> Vale la pena destacar el estuche relicario que alberga el manuscrito del propio *Castillo interior* en Sevilla. Esta arca representa un castillo con fundamento de mármol de color azul verdoso sobre el cual se alza una estructura de plata que le hace las veces de cuna al castillo, el cual reposa sobre un entallado cojín de terciopelo rojo y dorado. Sobre éste a su vez descansa una tapa de cristal muy grueso coronada con una masa vítrea que en virtud de su transparencia hace las veces tanto de cúpula como de monte para su valioso habitante. Gracias a las mismas propiedades que establece Teresa a propósito del material de base para el castillo, el manuscrito se encuentra protegido y es capaz de "ver" el exterior; por otro lado, sin embargo, ve sus lujosas portadas carmesí inevitablemente reveladas.

Carrión, *Arquitectura y cuerpo en la figura autorial de Teresa de Jesús*, 235–6, n. 6.

BIBLIOGRAPHY

Albertus Magnus. "Commentary on Dionysius' Mystical Theology." *Albert and Thomas: Selected Writings*. Edited by Simon Tugwell. New York: Paulist Press, 1988.

– *De pulchro et bono*. Edited by Roberto Busa. Vol. 7. Sancti Thomae Aquinatis Opera Omnia. Stuttgart: Frommann-Holzboog, 1980.

Aquinas, Thomas. *Summa Theologiae*. Cambridge: Blackfriars, 1963.

Augustine of Hippo. *On the Trinity*. Edited by Gareth B. Matthews. Translated by Stephen McKenna. Cambridge: Cambridge University Press, 2002.

– *The Literal Meaning of Genesis.* Translated by John H. Taylor. Mahwah, NJ: Paulist Press, 1982.
Carrión, María Mercedes. *Arquitectura y cuerpo en la figura autorial de Teresa de Jesús.* Barcelona: Anthropos, 1994.
Certeau, Michel de. *The Mystic Fable: The Sixteenth and Seventeenth Centuries.* Chicago: University of Chicago Press, 1995.
Clark, Stuart. *Vanities of the Eye: Vision in Early Modern European Culture.* New York: Oxford University Press, 2009.
Covarrubias, Sebastián de. *Tesoro de la lengua castellana o española.* Edited by Martín de Riquer. Barcelona: Alta Fulla, 1998.
Dillenberger, John. *Images and Relics: Theological Perceptions and Visual Images in Sixteenth-Century Europe.* Oxford University Press, 1999.
Eco, Umberto. *The Aesthetics of Thomas Aquinas.* Translated by Hugh Bredin. Cambridge, MA: Harvard University Press, 1988.
Van Ginhoven Rey, Christopher. "The Hermeneutic Image." *Journal of Spanish Cultural Studies* 12, no. 2 (2011): 155–76.
Hegel, G.W.F. *Aesthetics. Lectures on Fine Art.* Oxford: Clarendon, 1988.
Lacan, Jacques. *The Ethics of Psychoanalysis.* New York: Norton, 1997.
Márquez, Antonio. *Los alumbrados: orígenes y filosofía (1525–1559).* Madrid: Taurus, 1972.
Ricard, Robert. "Quelques remarques sur les 'Moradas' de Sainte Thérese." *Bulletin Hispanique* 47, nos 1–2 (1945): 187–98.
Subirats, Eduardo. *El alma y la muerte.* Barcelona: Anthropos, 1983.
Teresa of Ávila. *The Interior Castle.* Translated by Edgar A. Peers. New York: Image Books, 1961.
– *The Life of Saint Teresa of Avila by Herself.* Translated by J.M. Cohen. New York: Penguin Books, 1957.
Waterworth, James, ed. *Canons and Decrees of the Sacred and Ecumenical Council of Trent.* London: Dolman, 1848.

Beth Saunders

3

Visionary Camera: The Polaroid SX-70 and Marian Apparition Photography

Could it be that the power of icons, like the power of iconoclasm, depends on this presence made intimate?
– Michael Taussig, "Iconoclasm Dictionary"

This essay explores the meeting of two icons: the Virgin Mary and the Polaroid. Within the past decade, there has been a wave of literature surrounding the use of photography at Marian apparition sites. Numerous scholars from fields such as anthropology, folklore, and religious studies have examined how photographs made at these sites represent a technological transformation of traditional Marian veneration, establishing an innovative popular religious practice. Existing literature emphasizes aspects of photography that have made it an appealing (and perhaps inevitable) choice for pilgrims to apparition sites, noting in particular its perceived objectivity in recording truth, and its ability to render things unseen by the naked eye visible – in other words, its status as proof. Yet, surprisingly little attention has been paid to the practice within histories of photography. Surprising, when we consider that also within the past decade such formerly marginal vernacular practices as snapshots and spirit photography, which are both highly relevant to Marian apparition photographs, have been the focus of numerous publications and exhibitions.

Through close examination of the Marian apparition Polaroid, this paper considers the genre's significance within contemporary culture. Since Polaroid instant cameras are particularly prevalent at apparition sites, an analysis of the specific qualities that have contributed to its adoption within this religious practice reveals the motivations and desires of pilgrims. The "instant" production of the Polaroid and its unique materiality results in a performative or ritualized relationship between pilgrims and photography that challenges the prevailing emphasis scholars have placed on its evidentiary qualities. I argue that the Polaroid as a medium is particularly suited to the visionary experiences associated with Marian apparitions. The fact that the Polaroid has continued to be used at these sites into the twenty-first century suggests that the photograph's evidentiary qualities are subsidiary to other concerns such as intimacy and presence. This shift in emphasis may help us better understand the status of photographic images (and our relationship to them) in the digital age. The afterlife on the Web of many Marian apparition Polaroids complicates the perception that the digital represents a form of iconoclasm enacted by the destruction of photography's relationship to reality and, thus, its nature as a medium. Instead, it serves as powerful evidence of photography's unwavering ability to reflect our own desires back to us. As icons for a digital age, Marian apparition Polaroids embody the paradoxical archaism of photography's material presence in cyberspace, and proclaim an age of iconolatry.

The Photograph as Icon

In 1867, Cardinal Pecci, the future Pope Leo XIII, penned the Latin poem *Ars Photographica*, proclaiming in verse the virtues of photography. A decade later, he commissioned a ceiling painting for the Vatican's Galleria dei Candelabri that depicts the camera alongside the traditional arts, indicating the Catholic Church's blessing over the medium.[1] This papal sanction aligned photography's representational authority with the earlier interpretation that photography is a mechanical means by which nature reproduces itself through the agency of sunlight, or God's creation representing itself though divine agency. Nineteenth-century discourse surrounding photography frequently invoked the spiritual, mystical, magical, religious, and otherworldly qualities of the medium. This discourse, which promotes photography not as a socially constructed medium of representation created by human labour, but as a mechanical, divinely authored fragment of reality, helps us to understand the conditions that make possible a practice like Marian apparition photography. It also links the genre to its proto-photographic examples: the Mandylion, the Veil of Veronica, and the Shroud of Turin.

An icon is considered the one true likeness of the divinity that it depicts. Icons are distinguished from other images representing divine figures because an icon also demonstrates, "a manifestation or appearance of its prototype."[2] In other words, icons are apparitional; they are both the image and the divinity. Cynthia Freeland has established a number of connections between the icon and photography, one of these being the icon's "causal origin," which refers to the *acheiropoietic* (not handmade) or mechanical production of icons.[3] In commonly used photographic terms, this causal relationship can be likened to the photograph's indexical quality: a photograph is both an image of and the result of the light touching its subject – both icon and index.[4] The early Christian justification for the veneration of images relied on the understanding that they were of supernatural origin and thus possessed miraculous powers. While icons represent a divine prototype, they also continue to produce miracles, and therefore become an extension of the divinity they represent.[5] Similarly, Freeland writes, "photographs continue to serve the manifestation function that was facilitated in earlier time periods by a wide succession of types of images (icons, funeral portraits, death-masks)."[6] These aspects have led especially to the medium's use within memorial practices. Indeed, the memorial and ritualized uses of photography reflect earlier interactions with icons, and attest to belief in the power of images.

An early example of the supernatural origin of icons is the Mandylion: a cloth allegedly imprinted with the face of Christ. According to legend, in the first century AD, King Agbar of Edessa asked for a portrait to be painted of Christ, but instead was given a cloth with the imprint of Christ's face. During the period of iconoclasm in the Orthodox Church, the Mandylion became an example of God's approval of images in religious practice. The Veil of Veronica, or Sudarium, another miraculous image, was produced when St. Veronica (her name is translated as *ver icon*, or "true image") used her handkerchief to wipe Christ's face when he fell on the way to the crucifixion.[7] The most famous example today of these miraculous images is that of the Shroud of Turin, believed to be the burial shroud imprinted with Christ's crucified body.

While each of these proto-photographic examples relates to photography's indexical and mechanical qualities, the case of the Shroud of Turin is of particular interest to a discussion of photography. The image of Christ's face is not fully visible on the linen alone, but became visible when Secondo Pia photographed the shroud and then developed the negative plates in his darkroom in May 1898.[8] Like the Mandylion and the Veil of Veronica, the shroud is a miraculous image produced by the imprint of Christ's body, and thus became a photographic negative from which the likeness of Christ can be printed in its positive form. Georges Didi-Huberman writes of this photographic proof as a kind of miracle: "The holy shroud became the negative imprint of the body of Christ, its luminous index miraculously produced and miraculously inverted in the very act of resurrection, henceforth to be conceived of in photographic terms."[9] Marian apparition photographs unite earlier traditions of religious icons with photography's contemporary uses; the photograph represents a desire on the part of the beholder to reach a connection with something much greater than oneself. As manifestations of desire, in a sense, all photography is about faith, and each photograph is a resurrection.[10]

Photographic Faith: Photography at Marian Apparition Sites

In seeking to define miraculous photography as a popular religious practice, scholars have pointed to its uses by pilgrims to a variety of twentieth-century Marian apparition sites.[11] That century saw a vast increase in Marian visitations throughout the Western world. Mary has been sighted approximately 21,000 times since the fourth century, reaching a high in the 1990s.[12] Significantly, the use of photography within visionary experience is restricted to pilgrims, who otherwise do not see the visions themselves. For example, outside California City in the Mojave Desert, Maria Paula Acuña has reported visions and conveyed messages from Mary to believers on the thirteenth of every month since 1990. Acuña promotes photography as a means by which Mary's divine messages may be received by the world.[13] Use of photography in recording and conveying apparitions is so prevalent among pilgrims to apparition sites that in Conyers, Georgia, one in four visitors arrives with a camera – the same percentage that brings rosaries.[14]

As these examples suggest, photography has become an essential element of pilgrimages to Marian sites. Within this community, photography serves in particular to affirm religious belief, to attest to visions, and to communicate the experience to others as a form of witnessing. As Lisa Bitel notes, "Christian denominationalism, the competing claims of non-Christian visionary traditions, and a daily tidal wave of electronically-delivered images and virtual realities, along with pervasive postmodern disillusionment about media objectivity and accuracy, all help to undermine the truth claims of both visionaries and their critics."[15] Current scholarship like Bitel's suggests that it is in the wake of such challenges – not just to religion, but to photography's authenticity – that the medium's historical claims to evidentiary representation of reality are paradoxically called upon to shore up its authority. For the faithful, photography provides powerful, tangible evidence of the enduring presence of divinity in daily life despite increasing "postmodern disillusionment" with its digital incarnation.

W.J.T. Mitchell identifies this "iconoclash," or war of images, as a major feature of contemporary culture, but demonstrates that belief in the power of images is typically considered naïve, and associated with lower classes and the uneducated.[16] Marian apparition photography is a popular religious practice, not a Church-sanctioned one, underscoring Mitchell's claims. This essay takes up Mitchell's call to "critical idolatry,"[17] and recognizes Marian apparition photography not as a marginal religious belief practiced at the fringes of modern-day Christian culture, but rather as indicative of more widespread ideas regarding photography and belief in contemporary culture. In this context, the strategic use of the Polaroid to record divine presence is an important aspect of the practice, and deserving of further inquiry. Specifically, I am interested in examining how the use of Polaroid cameras not only bolsters claims to evidentiary proof, but also, more significantly, extends the revelatory experience beyond visionaries to the pilgrims themselves. I will then broaden this line of thought to examine how those features that have led the Polaroid to become the favoured photographic medium at apparition sites have also been adapted to the digital age. The advent of the digital age did not signal the destruction of photography's evidentiary value, because the medium does not shape our understanding of reality so much as the opposite: photography's capacity as evidence is shaped by our own beliefs and desires.

The folklore historian Daniel Wojcik has written extensively on Marian apparitions in Flushing Meadows, Queens, on the site of the 1964 World's Fair Vatican Pavilion, which then housed Michelangelo's *Pietà* and where visions appeared to Veronica Lueken, a housewife from Queens, beginning on 5 June 1968, the day that Robert F. Kennedy was shot. Through Lueken, Mary communicated the directive that believers record Lueken's visions with Polaroid cameras.[18] Because they are instantly developed, Polaroid photographs were less likely to draw accusations of darkroom tampering from non-believers – a complaint lodged against Secondo Pia's evidence of the Shroud. While some of the resultant Polaroids (easily accessible on several pilgrims' websites) contain likenesses of Mary herself, others depict deceased family members, or simply balls and beads of light, glowing shapes, and double exposures of shrine objects. Such common motifs are interpreted as various heavenly signs and messages by visitors to apparition sites, and the addition of scripture verses, captions, and personal narratives begin to shape their "afterlife" as documents of singular visionary moments recorded and shared for posterity.

Textual elements and processes of display and interpretation function as a crucial part of the devotional practice associated with apparitions, allowing a singular experience to be re-enacted through subsequent viewings of the photograph, and inspiring further visits to the sites (which in turn inspire the creation of more photographs). In a 1984 study, for example, the sociologist Edward Berryman reported that not only did his subject, a Canadian visionary named Susan, see apparitions, but she also took pictures of them, awaking from her trances to find the Polaroid snapshots surrounding her on the ground. These Polaroids were then organized into a thirty-nine-page photo album, accompanied by extensive explanatory texts and drawings, which she could consult after the visionary experience had passed.[19] Polaroids are also frequently displayed at apparition sites, used in literature on pamphlets and websites, and placed in albums to be venerated just like the sacred images they contain. I would argue that this interpretive function is as significant as the Polaroid's claims to proof, since it establishes a ritual relationship with the photograph that is repeated by subsequent visitors to the apparition site and through virtual pilgrimages enacted by visitors to the many websites that display such photographs. The textual accompaniments framing the photographs on these websites guide virtual pilgrims in their interpretations of the images, and reconstruct narratives of the visionary experience in acts of witnessing. The interpretive and narrative function served by these photographs, which amounts to a performative or ritualized interaction, is closely tied to the specific characteristics of the Polaroid medium and have yet to be articulated in existing literature on Marian apparition photography.

Visionary Medium: The Polaroid SX-70 Instant Camera

In a blurred monochrome blue photograph (see figure 3.1) a man stands in the foreground, his back turned to the camera (and me) with his head down. Beyond, two geometric fields of light appear on the ground, one circular and one rectangular. They give the impression of space receding into the distance, where trees on the horizon create a haze of dark, blurred shapes. The man's head cuts slightly above the outcropping of indistinct forms at the horizon and into a field of blue sky, which takes up half of the image. Above him and to his left is a ghostly figure, a nearly transparent woman in white robes: the Virgin Mary, her arms outstretched, head and face indistinct. Surrounding her are chemical splotches and shadows of what seem to be the branches of trees layered over the original snapshot in double exposure.

What one might easily interpret as amateur play with the medium of photography is presented on several Baysiders' websites as evidence of a miraculous appearance by the Virgin Mary on 26 November 1978. It was taken seventy yards from the site of the Vatican Pavilion in Flushing Meadows, Queens, by Tom Bachor of Little Neck, New York, using a Polaroid camera. The website text informs me not only of the location in which the photograph was taken, but explains the image in closer detail. What I had interpreted as chemical splotches is given form. To Mary's left is the hand of God, pointing for us to "behold!" Mary, and to the left of her neck is the outline of a light bulb, indicating that she is light of the world.[20] The image appears in literature circulated by the shrine organization, Our Lady of the Roses, Mary Help of Mothers Shrine.[21] Dis-

Figure 3.1 | Tom Bachor, untitled Polaroid, Flushing Meadows, Queens, 26 November 1978.

tinguished among other apparition photographs, this image has become an iconic Marian apparition Polaroid, a new sacred prototype – though nonetheless a typical Polaroid snapshot.

Literature on Marian apparitions suggests strong similarities among visionary phenomena across geographical locations. For example, women and children are most likely to experience the visions, and descriptions of Mary closely adhere to traditions of her representation in Western art. In photographs, Mary frequently appears life-size or smaller (thus resembling a sculpture) and wearing flowing blue robes like those seen in traditional religions iconography.[22] Both traits are pertinent to Bachor's Polaroid of Mary, whose form is similar to that of the sculpture of Mary that had adorned the Vatican Pavilion shrine near where the photograph was taken. The unique qualities of the SX-70 relate the image to earlier representations of Mary: rather than flowing pale-blue robes, she materializes out of the blue-green chemical of a Polaroid.

The Polaroid SX-70 camera, favoured at apparition sites, was unveiled to the public in 1972, introducing instant photography to the existing practice of taking family snapshots. The family or personal snapshot is the most ubiquitous form of photography, with recent statistics indicating that, for example, in 2010 Americans took 550 snapshots every second, and that in 2017, 1.3 trillion digital photographs were made.[23] We can expect that this number will only increase, as phones and portable electronic devices outfitted with cameras ensure that the average person has a camera in hand wherever she goes. This hardly conceivable mass of amateur snapshots was made tangible in a 2011 installation at Foam Photography Museum, a photo-art gallery in Amsterdam, The Netherlands. In *Photography in Abundance*, photographer Erik Kessels printed out a single day's worth of digital images uploaded to the online photo-sharing website Flickr, and flooded entire rooms with these million photographs. Kessels's emphasis on the saturation of digital photography, in which an infinite quantity of photographs overrides the significance of a single image, both contradicts and elucidates the recent valorization of the snapshot within museum exhibitions. Frequently, these exhibits emphasize snapshots with unique formal characteristics or surprising subjects over the more commonplace images familiar from one's own family albums. While this paper does not intend to provide a history of the snapshot or its entry into the museum, subjects which have been treated elsewhere,[24] the context and characteristics of the family snapshot are significant to the practice of Marian apparition photography, and share many of the same features as well as theoretical issues, which will be outlined below.

The SX-70 camera was specifically created with the amateur snapshooter in mind. It was the first commercially successful instant camera. A folding, single-lens reflex camera, it produces unique photographs that develop immediately upon automatic ejection after exposure. The emphasis on instantaneity reflects the snapshooter's desire to quickly capture a fleeting moment, and to preserve its memory against the threat of time and forgetting. Kodak, Polaroid's largest competitor at the time, most successfully articulated this motivation for family snapshots in its many

Figure 3.2 | "Forget one detail of your girl's face? Never ..." Kodak advertisement, 1930s.

successful advertising campaigns over the course of the twentieth century. One ad that appeared in the 1930s (see figure 3.2) featured such text and slogans as, "Forget one detail of your girl's face? Never ... (*that's what you hope*)," and "The snapshots you'll want Tomorrow – you must take Today." These statements emphasize the fear of forgetting a loved one, and the swift passage of time; the face you might forget is a child's and children grow up fast! The ominous "that's what you hope" plants the seed of doubt that memory alone will be sufficient to hold onto an image of a loved one. In this advertisement, the fear of forgetting (and, the ad hints, mortality) can only be assuaged by the Kodak snapshot.[25] By the time the SX-70 came onto the market, the importance of the snapshot to preserving images of family life had already been fully accepted.

The instant nature of the Polaroid SX-70 was made possible by combining the act of taking the photograph with the development process. Rather than wait to send a roll of film to be developed, the two actions were united in a single apparatus. The photosensitive and developing chemicals of the Polaroid SX-70 are contained in a 3⅛-inch square panel held in place by a thin, protective, blue-green chemical film. Daniel Wojcik has noted that the language used in an October 1972 *Life* magazine article about the SX-70 proclaimed the camera to be a magical device, capturing precious memories in an instant.[26] Entitled "Dr. Land's Latest Bit of Magic," it began: "Push the button and less than two seconds later, with a buzz, a clunk, and a whir, the oddly folded machine ejects a blank card. In 30 seconds an image slowly appears, emerging out of a blue-green fog and becoming within minutes a fully developed color photograph."[27] The article's text is surrounded by a close-up of Edwin Land, the inventor and head of Polaroid, snapping a photograph with the SX-70, and a series of four Polaroids of the same small child, each illustrating a time-lapse step in the development process (at one-, three-, five-, and ten-minute intervals) (see figure 3.3).

The girl sits in a small chair in front of a brightly coloured Asian wall hanging. She wears a pastel-patterned apron-front dress across which her arms are folded. Her mouth is turned down. It is a representative image that stands in for any other family snapshot of a child forced to sit for the camera. This two-page spread creates a narrative demonstrating the "magical" instant process of the SX-70 for the reader, placing emphasis on the major type of subject for which the camera was intended: amateur images of family. The article amounts to an "advertorial" for Land's new Polaroid camera, and evokes the same concerns of the earlier Kodak advertisement. What was implicit there – the fear of an important moment passing unremembered – is the operative principle of the SX-70, enabling a form of technological transcendence that limits mediation. The new process unites the moments of experience, capture, development, and interpretation in a then-unprecedented way. The picture almost takes itself, is nearly acheiropoietic.

Regarding this aspect of the SX-70, photography collector Jim McKeown has noted, "the miracle was watching the coloured photo slowly appear in broad daylight after being automatically ejected from the camera."[28] McKeown points to the phenomenology of the Polaroid

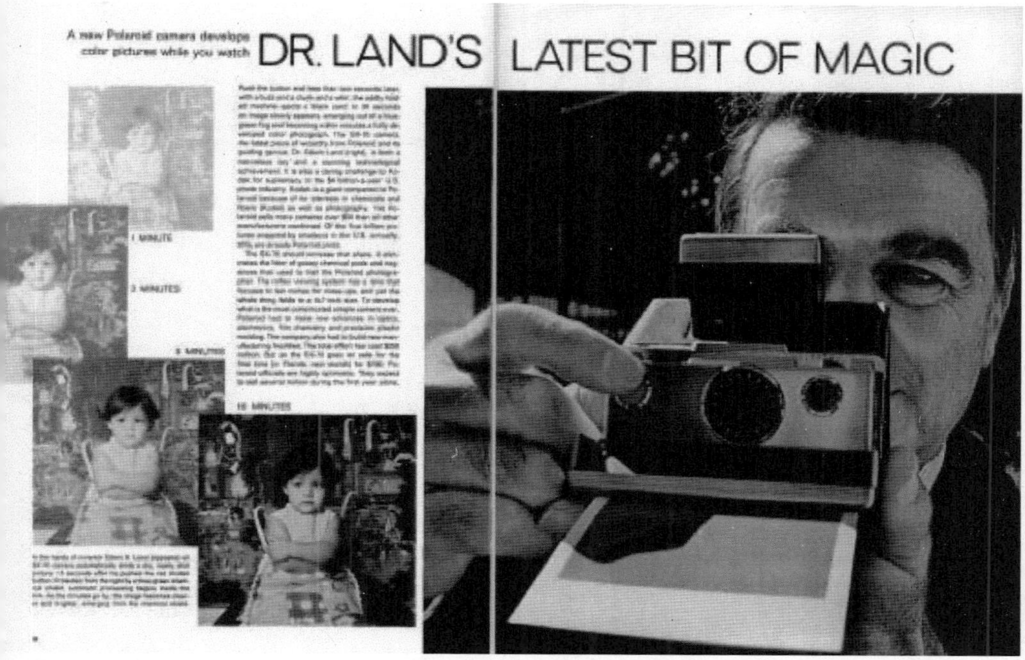
A new Polaroid camera develops color pictures while you watch

DR. LAND'S LATEST BIT OF MAGIC

1 MINUTE

3 MINUTES

10 MINUTES

Figure 3.3 | Co Rentmeester photo spread in "Dr. Land's Latest Bit of Magic."

SX-70, which is especially relevant to the practice of Marian apparition photography in that the miraculously "instant" photograph is almost but not truly instantaneous. This results in the viewer's captivation by the process. Depending on temperature and lighting conditions, the image takes up to one minute to appear, with the colour continuing to develop thereafter. As anyone who has ever taken a Polaroid snapshot will be aware, that minute can seem particularly long. The photographer, and frequently her subject, holds onto the white border in anticipation of the image's appearance (sometimes shaking it in hopes of speeding along the process), watching different colours slowly reveal themselves as the chemicals give form to the image. McKeown calls this experience miraculous, and he is but one of many to evoke magic in explaining the unique qualities of the Polaroid.

Historically, the use of metaphoric language to describe photography's supernatural capabilities co-existed alongside scientific accounts. This duality reflected both a lack of knowledge about the medium's technological makeup among amateurs, and a widespread desire to explain photography's revelatory relationship to reality. Scholars have previously discussed photography's use within the context of nineteenth-century spiritualism as a precedent for Marian apparition photography.[29] This is a natural comparison, given that both practices appear to rely on the camera's perceived scientific objectivity to legitimate its seemingly supernatural ability to capture invisible beings in photographs. However, distinctions between these two practices must be articulated. By the time Polaroid introduced the SX-70, photography's claims to truth were culturally diminished. Leaving aside the court trials that highlighted the fraudulent nature of spirit photographs, even amateur photographers were aware of the "tricks" that could be created through clever lighting, photomontage, and double exposure. What is more interesting is to question why, in the face of this knowledge, does photography, and the Polaroid in particular, appeal to pilgrims at apparition sites?

While most spirit images were captured in professional photographic studios, pilgrims to Marian apparition sites are amateurs. The promotion of Polaroid technologies among professionals and artists was an important motivation for the development of many of the company's products. Land even employed Ansel Adams as a creative consultant. Adams experimented with Polaroid products, advised Land on hiring other photographers, and made early purchases for Polaroid's own collection of art photographs.[30] The 1972 *Life* article summed up Land's personal ideas about the medium's creative potential as expressed in the text via a two-page photo spread by *Life* photographer Co Rentmeester. This series, captioned "A Professional Shows What the Camera Can Do," illustrates the artistic and documentary capacity of the camera in images indicative of professional practice, such as a fashion model and an action shot of dancers. Shortly after its introduction, artists began to explore the SX-70's potential themselves, submitting Polaroids to double exposure, rubbing, and reworking with a pencil or stylus to produce distortions to the human body captured on film.[31] In the nineteenth century, studio photographers like William Mumler captured spirits chemically at the same time that art photographers, like Henry Peach Robinson and Oscar Rejlander, were manipulating the medium through multiple negatives and exposures.[32] This reveals that professional photographers were easily capable of manipulating reality as it is presented in photographs, and this knowledge was readily available to amateurs and public alike through photographic literature and at photography exhibitions. These examples are not intended to disprove the practice of Marian apparition photography, but rather to show that amateurs using the SX-70 were aware of its capacities and chose it among other types of photography for its particular qualities and despite its capacity for manipulation.

Aiding artists and amateurs alike, a number of publications from the 1970s and 1980s served as how-to guides for "special effects," with detailed pictorial demonstrations. In his introduction to one such publication, *SX-70 Art*, a 1979 book of Polaroid art photographs by the likes of André Kertész, Hans Namuth, Helmut Newton, and Paolo Gioli, the critic Max Kozloff muses on the eerie qualities inherent to the SX-70 medium, noting that "the photographs reproduced in this book could be considered as a series of miniature apparitions. They not only present, they affirm the dream-like space, the abrupt contrasts, and the mute, inorganic color of the medium as special, transforming agents of reality."[33] For Kozloff, the signature blue-green tone, the distortions to depth of field caused by the relatively shallow optical range, and the experience of watching the development process take place before one's eyes all contribute to the Polaroid's super-natural qualities, in which each record of reality appears as an apparition. While literature from pilgrims to apparition sites shows that they did prize the SX-70 for mechanically producing fragments of unmediated truth through its instantaneous operations, the otherwise "magic" and apparitional qualities of the Polaroid outlined in contemporary publications and in artistic practice also contributed to articulating the SX-70's nature as a medium. Furthermore, the unique process of development and the common aesthetic characteristics of the Polaroid aligned with pilgrims' desires for visionary experiences.

Holy Family Snapshots

To return to the Polaroid of Mary, consider now the experience of awaiting with anticipation the possibility of seeing divinity appear within the Polaroid's white frame at a Marian apparition site. The use of Polaroid film in particular serves an additional ritual function, allowing the visitor to perform the visionary experience herself. In other words, even though visitors to apparition sites such as those in Flushing Meadows or

California City cannot see Mary with their naked eye like the visionaries Veronica Lueken and Maria Paula Acuña, the process of the SX-70 allows them to recreate the sense of anticipation and divine mystery revealed as Mary's presence takes form on the chemical surface of the Polaroid. More than the camera's ability to see what the naked eye cannot, the Polaroid is a visual and physical manifestation that the beholder can interact with on intimate terms. The signature shape of the photographic square within a white border creates a space ready-made for both holding and captioning the photograph. The Polaroid is looked at, touched, inscribed with holy names or divine messages, and returned to the apparition sites in albums propped up in shrines. The Polaroid becomes a visual and tactile object of devotion, the singularity of its process giving it special significance for the beholder, since it stands as a unique and personal object. Every pilgrim with a Polaroid camera is a potential Veronica.

The particular materiality of the Polaroid means that within Marian practice the photograph itself is an embodiment of divine presence and contact. Peter Buse has deemed the Polaroid a photo-object, and the experience of its "instant" development a "photography of attractions."[34] Descriptions of the clicking of exposures, the buzz of film being ejected, and flashes going off amidst the crowds at these apparition sites support this notion. Amongst these crowds, the fervent interest in one another's images also reinforces the social capacity in which the cameras are deployed.[35] Buse argues that in this "photography of attractions," the Polaroid and its content are less important than the mode of its creation – the semiotic and narrative potential of photography thus devalued in favour of technological spectacle. This emphasis on the attraction of SX-70 technology is in many ways accurate; at apparition sites, however, the Polaroid is not an end in itself but a means by which the spectacle of a heavenly vision is miraculously revealed to the faithful. It is the physical trace of divine contact, and the means of its communication to others.

The notion of contact might also be extended beyond the spiritual presence of Marian apparitions to the physical presence that is manifested by the Polaroid as well. Buse has argued that because the experience of the technology is more important than the resultant image, the Polaroid is often seen as ephemeral – easily given away or simply discarded.[36] Within the practice of Marian apparition photography, the Polaroid is clearly held in higher regard than a typical snapshot, and the physicality of the medium is another aspect that characterizes its ritual use at apparition sites. The close range at which Polaroids must be taken makes the human body an ideal subject for the SX-70. It is not surprising that among the earliest uses of the Polaroid were family snapshots and art photography. In particular, pioneers of SX-70 art frequently turned their lenses on the human body. Lucas Samaras, widely regarded as the first artist to employ the medium, created a series of photo-transformations in which he altered his body's physical attributes, revealing emotional depths beyond the skin's surface.[37]

The Polaroid was introduced at a time when artists were increasingly using their own bodies in work informed by the feminist, gay, and civil-rights movements – work that engaged with issues surrounding the cultural construction of gender and sexual identity. Polaroids by artists such as Andy Warhol, Mark Morrisroe, and Nan Goldin point to the intimacy of the medium and its capacity to capture shifting personal identities, as well as familial and sexual relationships. The Polaroid's associations with the family snapshot, as well as its small format (frequently held or annotated), reinforce the intimacy of the subject matter contained within these artists' works. Furthermore, the skin-like film that makes the Polaroid's instant development possible imbues them with a fragile sensuality, an almost human tactility.[38] At vision sites, Mary's presence is recorded as a physical and sensory manifestation. Pilgrims frequently report that when Mary appears, a faint scent of roses fills the air, and a calming sensation takes hold even if she is not visible. The skin-like surface of the Polaroid thus extends Mary's heavenly reach to the hands of her followers. The close associations between the Polaroid snapshot and the intimacy of human contact are ultimately reflected in the preciousness of Marian apparition Polaroids, which are incorporated into albums, shrines, and reproduced – the marks of a true icon.

I have attempted to outline the numerous ways that the iconic SX-70 Polaroid was particularly suited to the needs and desires of pilgrims to apparition sites. Whereas previous scholarship on the topic has focused on photography's relationship to belief – in particular the interest in providing instantaneous proof of miraculous presence – I argue that this is a secondary concern for pilgrims who desire their own visionary experience. In the case of Marian apparition photography, the medium of the Polaroid represents a different relationship to belief, one that is founded less on proving the existence of divinity among skeptics than on providing tangible evidence of personal beliefs about Mary's continued active presence in the world. Marian apparition Polaroids could be likened to Holy Family snaphots: often strange, ephemeral, or even banal to those who lack familiarity with the subject, but precious, enduring, and affirming for believers.

The Marian Apparition Polaroid's Digital Afterlife

Of course, we must acknowledge that the Polaroid is now an antiquated technology and that more widespread interaction with Marian apparition Polaroids in fact appears in the form of virtual pilgrimage on the Internet. This aspect of Marian apparition photography has implications for understanding the status of belief in photography in the digital age. Polaroid ceased production of instant cameras and film in 2009, turning its focus toward digital technologies after filing for bankruptcy protection. Nonetheless, some pilgrims to apparition sites continue to use the Polaroid, although others have turned to digital cameras.[39]

Digital cameras replicate many of the functions that the SX-70 had previously served, including instant visibility of the photograph and its claims to evidentiary proof. The turn to digital photography also allows for quicker dissemination of visionary images. However, the persistent use of Polaroid technology underscores that this medium holds specifically desirable characteristics. The power of the Polaroid to convey intimacy without mediation is central. The persistent desire to interact with a tangible, physical, chemically based photographic process highlights the fact that photographs remain physical objects that continue to hold a unique position, even in the digital age. In this context, flooding a room with hard copies of digital pictures is an act of idolatry; while the aim may be to show that these images saturate our culture and overwhelm any personal relationship with them, printing each one and giving it a physical form in fact reveals the opposite: that each image has a tangible place for the true believer. Marian apparition Polaroids reveal the physical, emotional, and spiritual associations we have with photographs, transforming otherwise banal images into icons. The recent scholarly interest in them suggests that we are motivated to define this religious practice because we see reflected in it the fact that our belief in the power of images is eternal.

NOTES

This essay arises from a paper presented as a PhD student at the twenty-second annual conference of the Centre for Comparative Literature, at the University of Toronto, in March 2011.

1 Henisch, *The Photographic Experience*, 433.
2 Freeland, "Photographs and Icons," 59.
3 Ibid., 58–9.
4 For indexical relationship of photography, see: Barthes, *Camera Lucida*; and Krauss, "Notes on the Index."
5 Belting, *Likeness and Presence*, 48-57.
6 Freeland, "Photographs and Icons," 69.
7 Belting, *Likeness and Presence*, 53.
8 Didi-Huberman, "The Index of the Absent Wound," 41.
9 Ibid.
10 In his essay "Rhetoric of the Image," Roland Barthes writes, "the image is re-presentation, which is to say ultimately resurrection." Barthes, *Image, Music, Text*, 32.
11 Some of the best-known sites include those at Lourdes, France (1858); Fatima, Portugal (1917); Necedah, Wisconsin (1950s); Garabandal, Spain (1960–65); San Damiano, Italy (1964–81); Bayside and Flushing Meadows, Queens, New York (1968–95); Medjugorje, Bosnia and Herzegovina (1981); Conyers, Georgia (1990–98); and California City, California (1990–present).
12 Boles and Davis, "Pilgrim Apparition Work," 372.
13 Bitel, "Looking the Wrong Way," 74–7.
14 Boles and Davis, "Pilgrim Apparition Work," 378.
15 Bitel, "Looking the Wrong Way," 81.
16 Mitchell, *What Do Pictures Want?*, 7–12.
17 Ibid., 26.
18 Wojcik, "Polaroids from Heaven," 130.
19 Berryman, "Taking Pictures of Jesus," 433.
20 "Miraculous Photos."
21 "Jesus and His Mother."
22 Bitel, "Looking the Wrong Way," 72.
23 Heyman, "Photos, Photos Everywhere"; Batchen, "Snapshots," 123; Ritchin, *After Photography*, 11.
24 See Batchen, "Snapshots."
25 Such guilt-inducing reminders of mortality in Kodak advertisements were first pointed out to me by Geoffrey Batchen in a lecture on snapshots, part of a course on twentieth-century photography at the CUNY Graduate Center in spring 2008.

26 Wojcik, "Spirits, Apparitions, and Traditions," 128.
27 Callahan, "Dr. Land's Latest Bit of Magic."
28 Quoted in Hitchcock and Crist, *The Polaroid Book*, 368.
29 See: Harvey, *Photography and Spirit*; Perez, *Revelation*; Wojcik, "Spirits, Apparitions, and Traditions."
30 Hitchcock, "When Land Met Adams."
31 Ibid., 28.
32 Kaplan, *The Strange Case of William Mumler*, 33.
33 Kozloff, Introduction to *SX-70 Art*, 11.
34 Buse, "The Polaroid Image as Photo-Object," 192.
35 Bitel, "Looking the Wrong Way," 79–81; Wojcik, "Polaroids from Heaven," 132.
36 Buse, "Polaroid Image," 198.
37 Kao, "Edwin Land's Polaroid," 115.
38 Trotman, "The Life of the Party," 10.
39 Lyons, "Polaroid Abandons Instant Photography."

BIBLIOGRAPHY

Barthes, Roland. *Camera Lucida: Reflections on Photography*. Translated by Richard Howard. New York: Hill and Wang, 1981.

– *Image, Music, Text*. Translated by Stephen Heath. New York: Hill and Wang, 1977.

Batchen, Geoffrey. *Each Wild Idea: Writing, Photography, History*. Cambridge: MIT Press, 2001.

– *Forget Me Not: Photography and Remembrance*. Amsterdam: Van Gogh Museum, 2004.

– "Snapshots: Art History and the Ethnographic Turn." *Photographies* 1, no. 2 (2008): 121–42.

Belting, Hans. *Likeness and Presence: A History of the Image Before the Era of Art*. Translated by Edmund Jephcott. Chicago: University of Chicago Press, 1993.

Berryman, Edward. "Taking Pictures of Jesus: Producing the Material Presence of a Divine Other." *Human Studies* 28, no. 4 (2005): 431–52.

Bitel, Lisa. "Looking the Wrong Way: Authenticity and Proof of Religious Vision." *Visual Resources* 25, nos 1–2 (2009): 69–92.

Boles, Jacqueline, and Phillip W. Davis. "Pilgrim Apparition Work: Symbolization and Crowd Interaction When the Virgin Mary Appeared in Georgia." *Journal of Contemporary Ethnography* 32, no. 4 (2003): 372–3, 378.

Buse, Peter. "The Polaroid Image as Photo-Object." *Journal of Visual Culture* 9, no. 2 (2010): 189–207.

Callahan, Sean. "Dr. Land's Latest Bit of Magic." *Life*. 27 October 1972.

Chéroux, Clément. *The Perfect Medium: Photography and the Occult*. New Haven: Yale University Press, 2005.

Didi-Huberman, Georges. "The Index of the Absent Wound (Monograph on a Stain)." In *October: The First Decade*, edited by Annette Michelson et al., 39–57. Cambridge: MIT Press, 1987.

Freeland, Cynthia. "Photographs and Icons." In *Photography and Philosophy: Essays on the Pencil of Nature*, edited by Scott Walden, 50–69. Malden, MA: Blackwell Publishing, 2007.

Harvey, John. *Photography and Spirit*. London: Reaktion Books, 2007.

Henisch, Heinz. *The Photographic Experience, 1839–1914: Images and Attitudes*. University Park: Pennsylvania State University Press, 1994.

Hitchcock, Barbara, and Steve Crist, eds. *The Polaroid Book: Selections from the Polaroid Collections of Photography*. Cologne: Taschen, 2005.

Kao, Deborah Martin. "Edwin Land's Polaroid: 'A New Eye.'" In *Innovation Imagination: 50 Years of Polaroid Photography*, 13–19. New York: H.N. Abrams in association with the Friends of Photography, 1999.

Kaplan, Louis. *The Strange Case of William Mumler, Spirit Photographer*. Minneapolis: University of Minnesota Press, 2008.

Kessels, Erik. *Photography in Abundance*. Catalogue to "What's Next? The Future of the Photography Museum," curated by Lauren Cornell, Jefferson Hack, Erik Kessels, and Alison Nordstöm, 5 November–7 December 2011. Amsterdam: FOAM, 2011.

Kozloff, Max. Introduction to *SX-70 Art*, by Ralph Gibson. New York: Lustrum, 1979.

Krauss, Rosalind. "Notes on the Index, 1 and 2." In *The Originality of the Avant-garde and Other Modernist Myths*. Cambridge: MIT Press, 1986.

"Miraculous Photos Taken at Our Lady of the Roses Shrine Gallery #1." Our Lady of the Roses, Mary Help of Mothers Shrine. n. d. https://www.tldm.org/photos/skyjp.htm (accessed 15 December 2011).

Mitchell, W.J.T. *What Do Pictures Want? The Lives and Loves of Images*. Chicago: University of Chicago Press, 2005.

Morgan, David. *The Sacred Gaze: Religious Visual Culture in Theory and Practice*. Berkeley: University of California Press: 2005.

– *Visual Piety: A History and Theory of Popular Religious Images*. Berkeley: University of California Press, 1999.

Pagliaroli, Jessy C. "Kodak Catholicism: Miraculous Photography and Its Significance at a Post-Conciliar Marian Apparition Site in Canada," *Historical Studies* 70 (2004): 71–93.

Perez, Nissan. *Revelation: Representations of Christ in Photography*. London: Merrell, 2003.
Ritchin, Fred. *After Photography*. New York: Norton, 2009.
Sheehan, Tanya. *Doctored: The Medicine of Photography in Nineteenth-Century America*. University Park: Pennsylvania State University Press, 2011.
Trotman, Nat. "The Life of the Party: The Polaroid SX-70 Land Camera and Instant Film Photography." *Afterimage* 29, no. 6 (2002): 10.
Wojcik, Daniel. "Polaroids from Heaven: Photography, Folk Religion, and the Miraculous Image Tradition at a Marian Apparition Site." *Journal of American Folklore* 109, no. 432 (1996): 129–48.
– "Spirits, Apparitions, and Traditions of Supernatural Photography." *Visual Resources* 25, nos 1–2 (2009): 109–36.

KEYWORD

pop art, *n.*[1]

Brit. /ˌpɒp ˈɑːt/, U.S. /ˈpɑp ˈɑrt/

Frequency (in current use):

Origin: Formed within English, by compounding. **Etymons:** pop *adj.*, art *n.*1

Etymology: < pop *adj.* + art *n.*1; apparently coined by the British art critic Lawrence Alloway, although with a different original meaning; compare:

1967 L. Alloway in L. R. Lippard *Pop Art* 27 The term 'Pop Art' is credited to me, but I don't know precisely when it was first used. (One writer has stated that 'Lawrence Alloway first coined the phrase "Pop Art" in 1954'; this is too early.) Furthermore, what I meant by it then is not what it means now. I used the term, and also 'Pop Culture', to refer to the products of the mass media, not to works of art that draw upon popular culture. In any case, sometime between the winter of 1954–55 and 1957 the phrase acquired currency in conversation, in connection with the shared work and discussion among members of the Independent group.

The Independent Group was a circle of young artists, architects, and critics, associated with the Institute of Contemporary Arts, London, in the1950s.

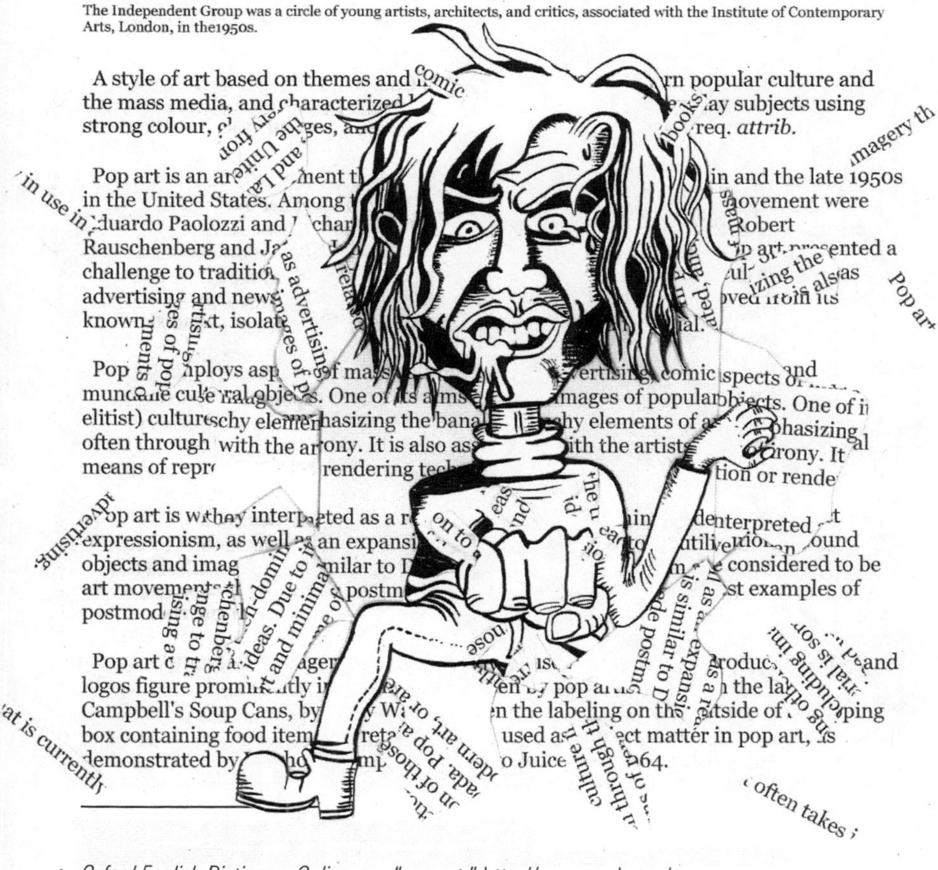

1 *Oxford English Dictionary Online*, s.v. "pop art," http://www.oed.com/ (accessed 14 December 2016).

JUST...
SHAKE
WIPE
LEMME JUST GIVE A FORM TO THINGS!
GRUNT
NOW, WHERE WERE WE? RIIIIIIGHT! POP ART!
SO-
UH ANDY?
HUH? YES MARILYN?
THE FACTORY
WHAT WOULD YOU LIKE FOR LUNCH?
A BOWL OF CAMPBELL'S TOMATO.
SO, POP AR-
HEY ANDY?
GAH! WHAT IS IT ELVIS?
WHERE ARE THE BANANAS?
IN MY WIG CLOSET.
GOTCHA!
POP ART. WELL, IT'S WHEN YOU TAKE SOMETHING THAT YOU BOUGHT FOR FUN CONSUMPTION—AND REDO IT AS ART.
I GUESS I DIDN'T NEED
THIS WHOLE PAGE.
NBP

Emily Hoffman

4

The Bluest Eye: Paul Newman, Iconoclasm, and the Shameless Exploitation of Beauty

BEAUTY! Say it! Say it! What you had was beauty! I say it, with pride …
– Tennessee Williams, *Sweet Bird of Youth*

"And why are you entering Canada?" asked the fifty-something customs agent from her high stool at a high counter, deep in the grey-blue bowels of Lester B. Pearson International Airport.

"I'm presenting a conference paper at the University of Toronto," I said.

"What conference?"

"The Centre for Comparative Literature's conference."

"What is your paper about?"

"Paul Newman."

"They let you talk about Paul Newman at a literature conference?"

Until this point, the woman had simply been doing her due diligence, making sure that I posed no national security threat, that a literature conference where academics talked about movies and movie stars was not a dull, and thus clever, front for my true, nefarious intentions. That last answer of mine, though, those two simple but evocative words – *Paul Newman* – transformed the tone of her voice. The words not only transformed her voice but altered her face. The practised sternness, as much a part of her uniform as her red vest and ID badge, softened. Now she was genuinely curious. After I indulged her with a broad and not terribly eloquent overview of my paper, she asked, "so you're really talking about his movies?"

"Partly. Movies and the salad dressing."

Seeming somehow younger than she had when I stepped up to her counter, she smiled, wished me luck, and waved me through. As I wheeled my suitcase in the direction of the arrows on the wall behind her, she called after me.

"Will you talk about his eyes?" she asked. Her voice had become strangely desperate.

"Yes," I said, turning back.

"Oh, good. You *have* to talk about his eyes."

Indeed. I have to talk about his eyes. Since that encounter, I have wondered what that customs agent would say if she knew that Newman would have considered her parting words to me an ignorant, frustrating insult, one he would be inclined not to forgive.

"*But why? They're beautiful eyes!*" I imagine her saying with distress and sad indignation. Naïve but inquisitive, she is, to my mind, like the Old Lady, that foil Hemingway creates for himself in *Death in the Afternoon*. She keeps asking simple yet incisive questions, though the answers alternately perplex and displease her.

But why did Paul Newman hate his beautiful blue eyes? The answer to this question is a gateway to better understand Newman's contradictory status as both an icon and an iconoclast, as well as our own distanced yet collaborative relationship with celebrities. It reinforces Michael Taussig's contention, presented in this volume's flagship essay, that iconoclasm is inextricably linked to close encounters with the body. Newman resented his fame and status as an icon because he believed both depended more on the tastes of a superficial public that appreciated his physical beauty rather than his inner beauty, as represented by his acting talent and his efforts as a citizen. He is not wrong about this, but he is not entirely right, either. He was, after all, "cast for nearly every part he tried out for" because "he looked like a Greek god."[1] Nevertheless, his transformation from mere movie actor to icon results from a more complex interplay between his physical appearance, his career decisions, and the cultural climate of the late 1950s and early 1960s. Uncomfortable with his iconic status, Newman does a rather amazing and, perhaps, unprecedented thing. At first, he positions himself as an iconoclast determined to burn his own image, to strategically and metaphorically self-immolate, to use one of Taussig's central images. When that is not successful, he exploits it to construct a second, enduring iconic persona. And, in a very real way, it all depends on those beautiful blue eyes …

The Iconic Iconoclast

If we are to understand how Newman constructs this second iconic persona, we must first go back to its origins, and those origins reside in the movies that evoked a wistful, almost girlish nostalgia in my customs agent. Think – as she no doubt did – of the most beloved Paul Newman characters, the career-defining characters like Ben Quick, Chance Wayne, Brick Pollitt, "Fast" Eddie Felson, Hud Bannon, Luke Jackson, Butch Cassidy. Throw in some of the less acclaimed roles – ones like Alfred Eaton in *From the Terrace* or Ram Bowen in *Paris Blues*. With few exceptions, the characters Newman played from the late 1950s through the 1960s were all of a type: clever, smooth-talking, enterprising, risk-taking, vaguely dangerous if not mildly criminal, occasionally self-destructive, angry, stubborn, rebellious, and always the personification of cool. They were that new breed of man: the brooding but charismatic antihero, the iconoclastic antidote to the seemingly outmoded, simplistic, do-gooding heroism embodied by the characters of John Wayne.

Throughout his career, Newman perpetuated the myth that there were two of him: a private persona, and the public persona of the actor playing a coterie of fictional men with lifestyles and psychologies that shared nothing in common with his own. "They have nothing to do with me personally,"[2] Newman once told an interviewer for *Playboy*, who had asked if he had anything in common with the "cool studs" he played. Fans' failure to grasp and respect the difference between the two Paul Newmans irritated him. Nevertheless, they recognized what he either did not see or refused to recognize. When it came to core personality traits and motivations, he had *everything* in common with the characters he played. Like

Figure 4.1 | Newman in *The Hustler* (1961) as Fast Eddie Felson, one of the many alluring but dangerously defiant iconoclasts he played throughout his career.

Luke Jackson and Hud Bannon, the young Newman was a wild drinker. At Kenyon College, Newman and some of his football teammates got themselves arrested for brawling at a bar. Several years later, he would be arrested again for a drunk-driving rampage through a section of Nassau County, Long Island. Also at Kenyon, he made money selling corsages before dances and opened an off-campus laundromat that served customers free beer, an ingenious enterprise that foreshadows the more corrupt machinations of Ben Quick, "Fast" Eddie, Hud, and Chance Wayne. An economics major, he ultimately rebelled by choosing a career in acting rather than one in his father's large and very successful Cleveland sporting goods store. Once he became a working actor, he often butted heads with directors and screenwriters. In other words, "he developed a reputation as an uncooperative smart-ass."[3] His willingness to brazenly challenge or defy authority made him "cool," that nebulous but coveted quality Dick Pountain and David Robins define "as a *permanent* state of *private* rebellion"[4] and "an expression of a belief that the mainstream mores of your society have no legitimacy and do not apply to you."[5] In truth, Paul Newman was a real life antihero. He was a handsome antihero playing handsome antiheroes with convincing ease and swagger.

Newman's inability to acknowledge the parallels between himself and the characters that made him an icon is curious. How, one wonders, could he not see them? He was, after all, a devoted student of Stanislavsky's Method and part of the Actors Studio at the zenith of its influence. To convincingly play a character, Method actors learn to excavate their memories, searching for moments that would help them connect with the character's circumstances and guarantee a realistic portrayal. Newman succeeded as a Method actor because he did not have to dig very deep to uncover the emotional and psychological essence of his characters. They were convenient mirror images. In her essay "How Method Actors Create Character Roles," Nina Bandelj contends that "those events, which are more salient to an actor's personality or were acquired in more emotionally intense circumstances, are more potent and will be selected more often than the less emotionally charged ones."[6] If Bandelj is correct, then Newman did not rely on some insignificant set of hazy recollections. Rather, he tapped into the core of his identity. Choosing acting over the family business was, for Newman, a defining decision in his life, one that indisputably established him as a rebel uninterested in a traditional workaday life and earned him his father's disapproval. Here is just the sort of emotionally intense circumstance that Bandelj describes, and for a young actor like Newman, it would likely have been his default source of insight and inspiration. Bandelj goes on to explain how the method actor's creative process is, in part, a collaboration with the audience. Because "verisimilitude is the ultimate goal,"[7] Method actors must portray characters that affirm the audience's perception of reality. Newman, therefore, had to take into account not only the audience's understanding of a "real" antihero, but their understanding of one played by Paul Newman. In a character like Hud Bannon, for instance, audiences had to sense an aggressive sexual charisma that recalled an earlier role like Ben Quick or the strutting cockiness of Eddie Felson.

By simply doing what the Method required of him – being himself, albeit often in an exaggerated way – he unwittingly created, at least in his own mind, a monster. In a sense, his close identification with his roles allowed him to play them too well. As a Korean War veteran in an episode of *Goodyear Television Playhouse*, "he is believable first as an overeager glad-hander, then as a conniving huckster … and finally as a young man riddled with guilt and shame."[8] Newman himself viewed it as a turning point: "'I felt comfortable in the part … It was the first part I'd ever played that I found the character for.'"[9] From that point forward, he gravitated to parts that made similar sets of demands on his abilities, parts that allowed him to return to that comfort zone. He entered into an unusual three-picture partnership with Martin Ritt, a director also drawn to stories about roguish outsiders. That agreement led to the acclaimed anti-Western *Hud*, an adaptation of Larry McMurtry's *Horseman, Pass By*, significantly re-imagined by screenwriters Irving Ravetch and Harriet Frank Jr especially for Newman. As Ravetch said, "we were specifically trying to create material that would interest Paul … So we enlarged the character of Hud and wrote with Paul in mind."[10] In other words, they knew Newman would have an affinity for a virile, dynamic pariah like Hud. To truly write "with Paul in mind" means that Ravetch and Frank had to write not only with an awareness of the types of characters Newman enjoyed playing – those with some level of kinship to the Korean War veteran from *Goodyear Television Playhouse* – but with an awareness of Newman himself, because he would eventually utilize the memory-searching strategies of the Method actor to locate the identifiable reality of Hud. They had to shape Hud in ways that would make him easy for Newman to access if he was to play the part successfully. Otherwise, the film would fail as a compelling narrative. Of course, that did not happen. Ravetch thought that "Paul completely understood that role, and … completely embodied the character."[11]

Not content just to entertain moviegoers, Ravetch and Frank wanted to use *Hud* as a catalyst for the audience's critical engagement with the culture's growing affinity for "cool jerk[s]."[12] According to Harriet Frank Jr, "there's something in the American psyche that's sadly attracted to the dangerous, the flamboyant, and the immoral. And that's exactly what we were trying to show in that film."[13] However, the American public read the film and the character of Hud in an entirely different way. Ravetch describes the painful discovery of their miscalculation: "Then, at the first screenings, the preview cards asked the audiences, 'Which character did you most admire?' and many of them answered, 'Hud.' We were completely astonished. Obviously, audiences loved Hud, and it sent us into a tailspin. The whole point of all our work on that picture was apparently undone because Paul Newman was so charismatic."[14] Ravetch and Frank failed to realize that to tell the story they wanted to tell in a way that would provoke the reaction they desired of the audience was a rhetorical impossibility so long as Newman played Hud. Pauline Kael exposes the folly of casting Newman as a "bad" man. "The audience would never believe in his meanness" because Newman "project[s] such a traditional heroic frankness and sweetness that the audience dotes on [him]."[15] She partially attributes Newman's rapport with audiences to his physical beauty. Referencing his role in *The Long Hot Summer*, she argues that, "with enough close-ups of his blue, blue eyes and his hurt, sensitive mouth, Newman's Ben Quick could have burned barns all right, and audiences would have loved him more for it."[16] Newman's body had more rhetorical power than any screenwriter's words. He becomes an icon of mainstream iconoclasm because on screen he seems to be, in the words of Chance Wayne to Alexandra Del Lago in *Sweet Bird of Youth*, "a nice monster."[17] From the audience's perspective, Kael argues, no one who looks that good could possibly be that bad. The assumption that outward beauty corresponds to goodness and morality is a myth deeply ingrained in Western culture, articulated in such disparate places as Plato, Aquinas, high school textbooks, and James Bond novels.[18] Physical beauty cancels out the threat Newman's characters pose, makes the threat more attractive by association, or is so potent that it convinces the viewer something equally beautiful must exist inside him even if the movie offers no evidence of it.

Newman's popularity skyrocketed because, as iconoclastic antiheroes, his characters in general, and Hud especially, can be understood in diverse ways that appeal to practically any moviegoer. On the one hand, young people can look to Hud as a role model who shares their hostility toward the rigid and outdated ethics of Homer Bannon. This is a true counterculture iconoclasm, one associated with the inevitably violent ripping of the social fabric. On the other hand, Newman and Hud exemplify a comparatively safe iconoclasm because of Newman's appearance and because, while his characters may not be admirable or uphold a virtuous moral standard, their values align with traditional American ones as articulated by the country's founding fathers. Audiences responded positively to Hud because, as Gabriel Miller says, he has "precisely what [they] admire in classic Western heroes, their individualistic bravado. Hud exemplifies this glamorous American persona in his dislike of the government and the law."[19] In a paradoxical way, an unrepentant antihero like Hud stands as a powerful emblem of the rugged individual standing alone in a society increasingly concerned with the group. The 1960s signalled a shift from an obsession with personal success, identified with men in grey flannel suits, to a concern for community welfare. As passionate about limited government as he is about women and sex, Hud is a dissenter in a time when President Kennedy's New Frontier policies prompted the federal government's rapid expansion. It expanded through legislative programs designed to assist groups such as the impoverished and the unemployed. As a result, whether they wanted to or not, taxpayers assumed greater responsibility for their fellow citizens. Moreover, the decade featured other group-centred trends, like the increased popularity of communal living and public protests, like sit-ins, which depend in part on the spectacle of a large crowd for their effectiveness. *Hud* roared into movie theatres just when the viability of the individual seemed socially and politically tenuous, and the merging of Newman's charisma and America's political climate made Hud irresistible – and his portrayer miserable.

The Iconoclastic Icon

Paul Newman most certainly was not was a passive bystander to his own career. Regardless, he tended to portray himself as a victim in danger of losing his soul to Hollywood, as "the only guy in America who doesn't want to be Paul Newman."[20] So, the reluctant icon did what came naturally: he resorted to being a relentless, unabashed iconoclast.

At the start of its wide-ranging 1968 interview with the actor, *Playboy* unequivocally declares that "Paul Newman now stands as the male sex star of American films."[21] In the interview, however, Newman is at his most iconoclastic, actively undermining his iconic heartthrob status. He rails against Hollywood and the movie-going public for objectifying him, for failing to see him as anything other than a man with an uncommonly beautiful face. Like the billboard advertising Dr T.J. Eckleburg in *The Great Gatsby*, he has been reduced to nothing more than an arresting pair of eyes: "You break your ass for 18 years working at your craft and a lady comes up and says, 'Please take off your dark glasses so I can see your blue eyes.' … It's really awful. I'd like to think there's a mind functioning somewhere in Paul Newman, and a soul, and a political conscience, and

Figure 4.2 | Paul Newman at the Black March on Washington for Jobs and Freedom, 28 August 1963.

a talent that extends beyond the blueness of my eyes."[22] Here Newman's rhetoric echoes that of 1960s feminism, and, as a sex object valued for his body, he occupies a traditionally feminine space. As Ericha Reischer and Kathryn S. Koo explore, he is demanding the right to define beauty on his own terms without the collaborative input from society.[23] Newman explicitly identifies himself with women, crassly claiming that being asked to uncover his eyes is akin to saying to a woman, "open your blouse, I want to see your tits."[24] His own mother once said: "In a way it was a shame to waste so much beauty on a boy."[25] One cannot help but wonder if Newman resisted his iconic status because it originated in his feminized beauty, an unwelcome reminder of his youth, when, as a scrawny teenager, he longed to take part in the masculine rituals of high school and college football.[26]

Newman's decision to hide behind the mask of sunglasses is a political one. In an article primarily devoted to the construction and meaning of female beauty, Reischer and Koo contextualize Newman's actions: "If maintaining a 'beautiful' body ... is a symbol of cultural and social cooperation, then striving for a body in direct opposition to that ideal is tantamount to civil disobedience."[27] Newman had made his face "a battlefield between contending groups asserting different values and interests."[28] Through his stubbornness and antagonism, he demanded a renewal of "the interior-exterior debate," which asks: "is beauty a matter more of the soul or the body?"[29]

Indeed, more than anything, Newman's agenda seems to be establishing himself as a political thinker while distancing himself from the shallow movie industry. In the *Playboy* interview, he is, ironically, casting himself – again – in the role of outsider. The interview begins with his analysis of Democratic presidential candidate Eugene McCarthy and what, in Newman's mind, makes him preferable to the incumbent, Lyndon Johnson. This evolves into a highly critical assessment of Johnson's handling of Vietnam. Newman goes on to pointedly discuss the merits of legalizing marijuana, the reasons for granting amnesty to draft dodgers who fled to Canada, and the best strategies for ensuring meaningful progress in African Americans' struggle for civil rights. He takes unambiguous stands on all of these controversial issues knowing – and, he claims, not caring – about the damage they could potentially do to his acting career. To those who think he should stifle his opinions, he snaps, "kiss off!"[30] By flaunting his radical opinions, he seems determined to sully his beauty, to make himself "ugly" in the eyes of a large segment of mainstream society. He portrays himself as a rude ideologue and dangerous activist intent on crushing the status quo.

At the time, comments Newman made in the *Playboy* interview were the latest in a series of iconoclastic gestures that separated him from the expectations fans and the Hollywood establishment had for a star of his magnitude. Instead of a sleek sports car or a chauffeured limousine, Newman drove himself around in what amounted to a Volkswagen Beetle on steroids. The *Playboy* interviewer asks Newman if he, like others in Hollywood, sees the car as an "irreverent thumb of the nose at Hollywood status symbolism."[31] Newman replies that, yes, he does. Without further prompting, Newman steers his reply about the car into a more general discussion of the aspect of Hollywood culture he finds most unsavoury: the neverending effort to stay relevant through public relations stunts. "I don't want to be part of supporting that fraud," he says defiantly. "That's why I've never made a personal appearance to promote a picture."[32] To emphasize his philosophical distance from Hollywood, he had also established a bucolic domestic existence with his wife, Joanne Woodward, and their children in an eighteenth-century farmhouse in Westport, Connecticut, which he discusses at length.

Moreover, Newman expends a great deal of energy distancing himself from acting and from his own abilities as an actor. "But let's not talk about me and my roles," he insists.[33] He shifts to praising his wife's abilities, which he believes are superior to his own. Specifically, he marvels at her nuanced work in *Rachel, Rachel*, the film that marks his directorial debut. At every opportunity he resists his identity as an actor, daring his fans to accept him as someone other than an amalgam of the cool, clever rebels he played in all of his most successful movies. When the interview finally turns from the politics of Washington and Hollywood to the twin subjects of his movies and his acting, he makes a claim sure to leave moviegoers puzzled. "I think the best work I've done was in *The Outrage*," he says,[34] referring to the ill-conceived, poorly executed adaptation of *Rashomon*. This sounds like a deliberately contrarian assessment, especially because Newman's portrayal of Carrasco, the Mexican bandit/rapist, relies on cartoonish ethnic stereotypes that rival those of Mickey Rooney's Mr Yunioshi in *Breakfast at Tiffany's*. By singling out this role as his greatest achievement on screen, Newman implicitly devalues both the classic roles largely responsible for transforming him from a movie actor into an icon and the importance his physical appearance played in landing and successfully portraying them.

Though he does not explicitly say so, Newman's affinity for his work in *The Outrage* is surely rooted in the stark contrast between Carrasco and the other rogues and rascals who populate the gallery of vivid Newman characters. Carrasco does not possess a mere hint of danger. He *is* dangerous. He is not the rapist conveniently interrupted, like Hud. He *is* a rapist. He is a one-dimensional criminal devoid of charm or even a modicum of repressed sensitivity. Perhaps more importantly, it is an iconoclastic gesture, an act of civil disobedience, that renews the cultural battle over his face. His skin is darkened by makeup, his fair hair covered by a floppy dark wig, his smooth face marred by a scratchy goatee, his blue eyes camouflaged by cinematographer James Wong Howe's use of infrared film. His character's villainy, combined with the discomfiting sight of Newman in an unartful disguise intended to coarsen his "'Greek god'" features, contributed to the film's box-office failure. The lesson to be learned from *The Outrage* was this: Newman could indulge in these iconoclastic career moves, but he could not expect them to be embraced by the public. They did not want to be witnesses to this intimate act of cinematic self-destruction.

The Iconic Iconoclast Reborn

The *Playboy* interviewer confronts Newman about the "redundancies"[35] in the roles he has played. Newman, of course, had noticed them. Such similarity is unavoidable, he claims, but it frustrates him. "Wherever I look," Newman complains, "I find parts that are reminiscent of Luke or Hud or Fast Eddie."[36] Although the sameness became tiresome and diminished his enthusiasm for acting, it would prove essential as he embarked on his most successful exercise in iconoclasm, the one that would result in a second iconic persona, that of the humanitarian entrepreneur.

When Newman and his friend A.E. Hotchner decided to make the transition from bottling large batches of Newman's salad dressing for their neighbours to an actual company in the early 1980s, they hit a marketing roadblock. They had to figure out how an upstart food company could convince consumers its product was superior to all the other options currently on the shelf. Since its inception, every Newman's Own product has featured the actor's face on the label, a marketing decision he, at first, vehemently opposed. As Newman and Hotchner explain in *In Pursuit of the Common Good*, new products tagged with a celebrity's name succeed over the long run not because of the celebrity but because of the product's quality. However, a customer has to notice a product on the grocery store shelf before she can decide to buy it. This is the point a New Jersey grocery store owner impressed upon the two at the company's outset. "Paul Newman's blue orbs popping out at [a female shopper] would stop her in her tracks,"[37] he says, capturing the reaction I'm sure my customs agent has had at least once in the aisle of some Ontario supermarket. Newman agreed to use his image on the condition that the company donate all its profits to charity. "To go the low road – shameless exploitation for charity, for the common good – now there's an idea worth the hustle," he decided.[38] He could use the copy of himself on the label as the merchandising equivalent of Taussig's burning effigy. He could exploit external beauty to cultivate inner beauty. What's notable, but not terribly surprising, is that the image of the actor adorning Newman's Own products does not match his appearance in the early 1980s – the more weathered and somewhat harder Newman of *Absence of Malice* or *The Verdict*. And it is absolutely not the Newman of *The Outrage*. Instead, the likeness is eternally youthful. Situated between Newman's unwrinkled brow and his slightly uneven, vaguely mischievous smile are those intensely aquamarine eyes that contrast the neutral beiges and browns of the label and arrest the roving glances of shoppers. This likeness, then, most closely resembles the Newman of his most recognizable early roles, the ones he saw as an albatross and creative obstacle.

Newman's willingness to use his image on the labels has been essential to the success of Newman's Own and the new iconic persona he created from it. In his analysis of celebrity endorsers, Grant McCracken explains how consumers interpret a celebrity as "a composite of his fictional roles."[39] These roles carry with them a myriad of meanings that celebrities "have created ... on the public stage by dint of intense and repeated performance."[40] The best celebrity endorsers, then, are those who, over time, embody a consistent set of meanings. For an actor, a consistent set of meanings comes most easily through typecasting. McCracken asserts that, "without typecasting, actors are unable to bring clear and unambiguous meanings to the products they endorse."[41] Newman cleverly exploited decades of playing the charismatic, rebellious outsider to turn his company into a major force in the food industry. He was able to do so because meanings consumers associated with the iconic Newman on the product labels perfectly mirrored the company's unorthodox philosophies.

The decision to use his image on the company's label marked a turning point for Newman. In doing so, he endorsed the public's role in defining his identity and realized that he could, to use his word, "hustle" them, manipulate them stealthily into helping him achieve recognition for the kind of socially conscious values he felt were ignored earlier in his career. He makes the public his partner rather than his adversary, and, through the representation of his physical beauty on the product labels, Newman offers consumers the opportunity to nurture their own inner beauty. This collaborative act, as McCracken explains, is no different than the one Bandelj describes in her analysis of Method actors: "the final act of meaning transfer is performed by the consumer, who must glimpse in a moment of recognition an essential similarity between the elements and the product in the ad. The consumer suddenly 'sees' that the cultural meanings contained in [the endorser] ... are also contained in the product."[42]

By entering the food industry, Newman seemingly created for himself the challenging role he struggled to find in the scripts that came his way. Out of his element, Newman did what any committed Method actor would do: he mined past experiences for behaviours that suited the new role. But the role was only new on the surface. He had cast himself as the brash outsider yet again. Not only, then, did Newman use an image of himself that recalled his most iconic roles, but, as *In Pursuit of the Common Good* illustrates, he relied heavily on the attitudes exemplified by those characters to navigate his way through an unfamiliar environment. Newman brought to the partnership rebelliousness and stubbornness, imbuing the fledgling company with an identity that differentiated it from its competitors. "When the experts said that something was 'always done' a certain way, we'd do it our way, which was sometimes the very opposite," he and Hotchner say proudly.[43] For instance, they refused to add common chemicals used in the majority of salad dressings as preservatives and refused to hire a chemist to perfect the recipe. Despite being told it could not be done, and despite "'having no marketing survey, no business plan, no organized strategy for [its] introduction'"[44] they claimed to have "'revolutionized spaghetti eating in America'"[45] by producing a fresh, preservative-free sauce. At one point, Newman and Hotchner even overtly compared their approach to business with Newman's approach to his movie roles. They characterizes themselves as fearless risk-takers, "like Butch and Sundance jumping off a cliff into a business and marketing canyon."[46] Their willingness to get back up each time a botched trial or other glitch knocked them down made them less like Butch and Sundance and more like Luke Jackson absorbing punches from the merciless Dragline. Still, the comparison has merit because Newman's signature roles are all uncompromising risk-takers and underdogs. Audiences' unexpectedly favourable reactions to a character like Hud become, in an endorsement context, an invaluable asset. Newman is the perfect pitchman for such an unconventional enterprise for the reasons Kael identifies in her *Hud* analysis. Specifically, Newman's Own offered movie-going grocery shoppers a delayed payoff, a confirmation that they were right to sense goodness beneath the cruelty, selfishness, and rule-breaking of characters like Hud and "Fast" Eddie.

With the public's help, Newman successfully used the company to transform himself from an outwardly beautiful cinematic icon to an in-

Figure 4.3 | Newman's Own salad dressing.

wardly beautiful philanthropic icon. The transformation is evident in a *Nation's Restaurant News* headline from 1994: "Salad Dressing King Conducts Recipe Contest in Manhattan."[47] The article does not identify Newman as an actor, as someone whose successes depended, in large part, on his physical appearance. *In Pursuit of the Common Good* provides even more poignant evidence in a brief chapter titled "From the Campers," which includes eight letters from seriously ill children and their parents who attended the Hole in the Wall Gang Camps started by Newman and Hotchner with profits from Newman's Own. The letters are heartfelt testimonies expressing gratitude for the positive, life-affirming experiences Newman helped make possible. Again, not one of the letters calls attention to his movie career, his handsome face, or his blue eyes. Instead, they unanimously attest to an inner beauty born out of generosity and empathy.

Theoretically, Newman's Own should have enjoyed a meteoric rise followed by a dignified decline mirroring that of its co-founder. Today's consumers are not like the speaker in Doris E. Abramson's poem, "I Eat Paul Newman Daily," who says:

> I eat
> in memory of the youth we shared,

> Paul and I, he on the screen and me
> eating popcorn, bad popcorn, at the Cinema
> in our little town.[48]

The company's own research showed that in 1998 only 40 per cent of the college students surveyed knew who Newman was. More than a decade later, this percentage has undoubtedly declined, yet the company continues to flourish. Why? It is because the blue-eyed face on the label is now synonymous with doing good. Newman himself made this point in 2003 to the *New York Times*: "'The younger generation doesn't buy the stuff because of me … They don't even know me. I think they buy it because of the charity.'"[49] In Timothy P. McMahon's opinion, consumers buy Newman's Own products because they "are concerned about not only how food tastes but also how it is grown, who makes money off of it and what's in it," not to mention "the values [the company] holds or not."[50] McMahon cites Newman's Own as a company that connects with consumers because "the brand is in tune with an emerging social consciousness."[51] Jon Gertner's *New York Times* profile of Newman's Own quotes an executive from another food company with a similar ethos who says that to succeed, "the strategies of companies with social goals need to be subversive,"[52] arguably Newman's Own's defining trait. The subversion extends to the consumers, who get to participate in a transaction that does not have profit as its end goal. They get to break with tradition and support an underdog challenging the food industry giants. In other words, buying a Newman's Own product is *cool*. It is cool because the product itself is cool. As Pountain and Robins argue, "Cool … is intrinsically judgmental and exclusive: it can ultimately define itself only by excluding what is uncool."[53] Newman's Own products are both judgmental and exclusive. They exist because Newman judged the products on the market as inferior to the ones he could make and manufacture himself. They are exclusive because they are made with fresh ingredients and without preservatives. Newman, the philanthropic icon, and Newman's Own, the beloved food brand, owe their status to this cool consumerism that has replaced Newman's personal cool, which launched both the actor and the salad dressing. Newman's Own illustrates perfectly Pountain and Robins's belief that "cool can drive new … and more discriminating modes of consumption" so that "everyone is a rebel."[54]

Paul Newman may not have wanted fans like my customs agent to ask him to remove his glasses, but he did need them to ask. He needed them to make the demand. He needed them to want his blue eyes. That, after all, is simple, beginner's capitalism. And in his clever, devious way, he exploited not only his own beauty but their desire for it. He assumed that shoppers would be seduced by and contented with a static blue stare. In reality, it is a terribly cynical, unflattering – you might even say *ugly* – portrait of average consumers. Yet, his assumption proved correct, and, in pursuit of the common good, he made of them unwitting iconoclasts in his own image.

NOTES

1 Levy, *Paul Newman*, 86.
2 Newquist, "*Playboy* Interview."
3 Levy, *Paul Newman*, 93.
4 Pountain and Robins, *Cool Rules*, 19.
5 Ibid, 23.
6 Bandelj, "How Method Actors Create Character Roles," 398.
7 Ibid., 395.
8 Levy, *Paul Newman*, 96.
9 Ibid.
10 Baer, "*Hud*," 261.
11 Ibid., 272.
12 Pountain and Robins, *Cool Rules*, 140.
13 Baer, "*Hud*," 264.
14 Ibid., 260.
15 Kael, "*Hud*," 16.
16 Ibid.
17 Williams, *Sweet Bird of Youth*, 15.
18 Synnott, "Truth and Goodness," 58–9.
19 Miller, *The Films of Martin Ritt*, 56.
20 Levy, *Paul Newman*, 10.
21 Newquist, "*Playboy* Interview."
22 Ibid.
23 Reischer and Koo, "The Body Beautiful," 302.
24 Ibid., 156.
25 Ibid., 29.
26 Ibid.

27 Ibid., 302.
28 Synnott, "Truth and Goodness," 64.
29 Ibid., 71.
30 Newquist, "*Playboy* Interview."
31 Ibid.
32 Ibid.
33 Ibid.
34 Ibid.
35 Ibid.
36 Ibid.
37 Newman and Hotchner, *In Pursuit of the Common Good*, 38.
38 Ibid.
39 McCracken, "Who Is the Celebrity Endorser?," 312.
40 Ibid., 315.
41 Ibid., 316.
42 Ibid., 314.
43 Newman and Hotchner, *In Pursuit*, 19.
44 Ibid., 83.
45 Ibid., 87.
46 Ibid., 23.
47 "Salad Dressing King," 32.
48 Abramson, "I Eat Paul Newman Daily," 566.
49 Gertner, "Business; Newman's Own."
50 McMahon, "Social Values of Food Companies," 42.
51 Ibid.
52 Gertner, "Business; Newman's Own."
53 Pountain and Robins, *Cool Rules*, 166.
54 Ibid.

BIBLIOGRAPHY

Abramson, Doris E. "I Eat Paul Newman Daily." *Massachusetts Review* 40, no. 4 (1999): 566.

Baer, William. "*Hud*: A Conversation with Irving Ravetch and Harriet Frank, Jr." *Michigan Quarterly Review* 42, no. 2 (2003): 255–72.

Bandelj, Nina. "How Method Actors Create Character Roles," *Sociological Forum* 18, no. 3 (2003): 387–417.

Berman, Karen. "Building Brand Recognition on Fairfield Univ. Campus." *FoodService Director* 11, no. 2 (1998): 52.

Kael, Pauline. "*Hud*, Deep in the Divided Heart of Hollywood." *Film Quarterly* 17, no. 4 (1964): 15–23.

Levy, Shawn. *Paul Newman: A Life*. New York: Three Rivers, 2009.

McCracken, Grant. "Who Is the Celebrity Endorser? Cultural Foundations of the Endorsement Process." *Journal of Consumer Research* 16 (1989): 310–21.

McMahon, Timothy P. "Social Values of Food Companies Can Guide Consumer Choice." *Nation's Restaurant News* 38, no. 26 (2004): 42.

Miller, Gabriel. *The Films of Martin Ritt: Fanfare for the Common Man*. Jackson: University Press of Mississippi, 2000.

Newman, Paul, and A.E. Hotchner. *In Pursuit of the Common Good*. New York: Broadway, 2003.

Newquist, Roy. "*Playboy* Interview: Paul Newman." *Playboy*. July 1968. https://archive.org/stream/USPlayboy196807/US_Playboy_1968_07_djvu.txt (accessed 15 July 2018).

Pountain, Dick, and David Robins. *Cool Rules: Anatomy of an Attitude*. London: Reaktion, 2000.

Reischer, Erica, and Kathryn S. Koo. "The Body Beautiful: Symbolism and Agency in the Social World." *Annual Review of Anthropology* 33 (2004): 297–317.

"Salad Dressing King Conducts Recipe Contest in Manhattan." *Nation's Restaurant News* 28, no. 43 (1994): 32.

Synnott, Anthony. "Truth and Goodness, Mirrors and Masks Part II: A Sociology of Beauty and the Face." *The British Journal of Sociology* 41, no. 1 (1990): 55–76.

Williams, Tennessee. *Sweet Bird of Youth*. New York: New Directions, 1959. Reprint, New York: New Directions, 2008.

Brendon Wocke

5

Q Is for Queer: Banksy, Iconoclasm, and the Queering of British Traditional Authority

Banksy is one of the most widely known "post-graffiti"[1] or "street artists," emerging from his home city of Bristol and coming to prominence in 1993 with a particularly interesting blend of socially and politically critical image construction, which remains a hallmark of his work. Given that he (or she) remains anonymous, and given the popular cultural references that he deploys, Banksy has come to represent an "everyman" akin to what Michael Taussig refers to in his essay "Iconoclasm Dictionary" as the manner in which "free speech and free markets allow everyman to be an iconoclast." At once accepted and rejected by the established art world, Banksy's work now features in the collections of several renowned institutions (among them the British Museum), as well as in private and temporary collections, including a 2009 Bristol City Museum exhibit. While his work has not enjoyed the critical success and academic recognition as contemporary British artists such as Jeff Koons and Damien Hirst, public auctions of his artworks nevertheless generate much interest and command prices indicative of his growing status as an artist in his own right. From his early graffiti work on walls and trains in and around Bristol to the appearance of his stylized signature, first in London and then as far afield as Vienna, San Francisco, Barcelona, Paris, and the Holy Land, Banksy has become part of the British contemporary and popular art landscape. More recently branching out from his traditional stencilled spray-paint style, Banksy has also produced a number of interesting installations, nevertheless maintaining a deeply subversive sense of irony throughout all of his works to date. One of his greatest recent achievements, and a measure of the recognition he increasingly enjoys in the art world, was the aforementioned exhibition in 2009 of some hundred of his works (of which seventy-eight were new) at the Bristol City Museum,[2] following similar exhibitions in New York and Los Angeles.

Banksy's increasingly varied production, ranging from "street art" stencilling (both on and off the wall) to "sculpture," installation, "performances" (such as his surreptitious placement of his artworks in international museums), and animation (in 2010 he produced the introductory sequence for an episode of *The Simpsons*), illustrates a keen understanding of subversion as an art form and a more general socially critical gaze, which, as we shall see, underlies the iconoclastic nature of his work. This paper focuses on two pieces of his graffiti, which offer insight into the manner in which his iconoclastic appropriation of visual icons can be seen in terms of queering and, ultimately, as the production of a critical "queer idiom" within these works. In considering the particularly queer and iconoclastic manner in which Banksy portrays both Queen Victoria and a pair of British policemen, we can furthermore consider the more general mechanism of visual and iconic appropriation at work. Moreover, and essential to the task, is a consideration of the underlying socio-political critique that is particularly important to Banksy's work, both here and more generally. An understanding of this is central to our analysis of what is at stake in the (queer) iconoclastic treatment of these two figures of traditional British authority. Finally, our study traces the passage of both the "queer critical idiom," evident in the works here under consideration, and Banksy's socio-political critique as his images move from icon to iconoclasm, becoming, in their iconoclasm, representative of an iconic visual resistance to the orthodoxies of power.

Urban Graffiti: The Art and Semiotics of "Savage Writing"

Now, before considering the work of Banksy in particular, it may be pertinent to consider the predisposition of graffiti in general to both iconic and iconoclastic expression and the semiotic considerations thus implied. This is insofar as the medium of graffiti, through which Banksy here expresses himself, impacts the theoretical and practical structures of his work and its interpretation. Graffiti in general, by virtue of its nature as essentially outlawed (even if prosecuted to varying degrees), and by virtue of the general environment in which it is "exhibited" (in the street), readily lends itself to surprisingly complex semiotic and iconic representations. This arises out of two general necessities: first, the general prerequisite speed of production (at least for graffiti produced in the open) means that the use of colour and image complexity are relatively limited and that the resulting images must thus be relatively simple. Second, the placement of the works (in the street) means that the public would not normally be afforded the leisurely contemplation that would be possible (or required, or expected) in a gallery or museum. Simplicity can thus be seen as the one of the primary characteristics required for the successful production of a work of graffiti and the subsequent propagation of the intended message – for the both the limited time of production and the limited time of contemplation demand the simplification of the visual message in order to ensure its efficient propagation. In turn, a high degree of semiotic compression is required, a notion which we can understand as the compression of a central concept or argument in visual terms. This translates into the use of readily recognizable iconic symbols in order to structure the visual argument of the graffiti and to reference particular socio-political and cultural touchstones. The visual referencing of easily recognizable socio-cultural icons allows works of graffiti to structure a particular argument around a given set of references. Moreover, this visual argument, at least in terms of the manner in which it can be structured, lends itself heavily toward the subversion of the icons quoted. Certainly, forms of graffiti that make use of text and typography, or are produced in an area that affords the artist a greater freedom and productive time can be seen as exceptions to this. However, one can nevertheless consider that the fundamental movement of visual socio-politically aware graffiti (of which we take Banksy to be a prime example) is that of the compression of the semiotic message and its consequent expression in terms of icons and their subversion. That is to say that graffiti can essentially be seen to express itself in terms of iconoclasm, in terms of what one could call a "savage writing," which undercuts and subverts popularly recognizable icons as a fundamental part of its structural expression.

In "The Urban Revolution," Henri Lefebvre speaks to the savage nature of this form of expression:

> Revolutionary events generally take place in the street. Doesn't this show that the disorder of the street engenders another kind of order? The urban space of the street is a place for talk, given over as much to the exchange of words and signs as it is to the exchange of things. A place where speech becomes writing. A place where speech can become "savage" and, by escaping rules and institutions, inscribe itself on walls.[3]

Graffiti is precisely this revolutionary "savage" writing, which, quite literally by ignoring the rules of public order, is inscribed upon walls, representing a certain barometer of popular opinion, which, insofar as the artists' names are generally unknown, allows a greater level of freedom of expression than could perhaps otherwise be enjoyed. While Lefebvre doesn't specifically reference graffiti, one can immediately see the implication for graffiti of the manner in which the street is given over to the exchange of *signs* and images. In this reading, we can consider not only the revolutionary nature and subversion of the icons and the subtle violence of their iconoclastic representation (as we shall see), but also the manner in which this subversion of both the space and the subject matter reflects the inscription upon the walls of Banksy's critical flight from orthodox representations and structures of power. The compressed message carried in Banksy's "street art" arguably expresses the *zeitgeist* of the post-industrial era, playing with an antiauthoritarian mood that expresses itself with humour and sarcasm. And while not all graffiti can be seen to serve a critical role in the urban environment, the "street art" produced by Banksy (among others) most certainly serves a deeper civic function than simple "tagging," a form of graffiti that amounts to little more than signing one's name. Examples of the civically motivated subject matter of Banksy's work abound; one need only look as far as Banksy's 2005 work on the Palestinian side of the Israeli West Bank wall in order to see the manner in which the strategic use of graffiti can contribute to a civic dialogue.

In semiotic terms, we can consider that the compression and seeming visual simplicity of graffiti as a medium of expression is essentially undercut by the degree to which the coded iconic and iconoclastic images are visually at work in parallel. That is to say that subversive works of graffiti, in their iconoclastic subversion, evoke a representative parallelism, which can be described in terms of the concept of a visual metaphor. The initial iconic image – a point of cultural reference and even reverence – is, through the visual subversion of its constituent attributes, related to concepts that it would normally not necessarily be associated with. The metaphoric structure of the iconoclastic image, which introduces a parallel consideration of the icon, is underlined by Charles Sanders Peirce, for whom the representation of what he terms "a parallelism in something else"[4] is the essential characteristic of the visual metaphor. Further important implications of the semiotic nature of the visual metaphor at work within iconoclastic representation include what can be referred to as the "under-specification" of the base and target domains. That is to say that, as Lakoff and Johnson emphasize, the metaphoric parallelism consists of two domains: a base domain and a target domain. The "under-specification" of the metaphor is the manner in which the parallel representation of the domains permits only the *partial* representation of each. The base (or source) domain is defined in terms of the reasoning at work within the metaphor and "provides the source concepts used in that reasoning."[5] In providing the source material for the iconoclastic representation, we can consider the base domain to be largely equivalent to the initial iconic representation of the subject in question. Following this, the target domain is that which is mapped upon the base domain and modifies the understanding of the base domain as such. The target domain is constituted by the "immediate subject matter."[6] The resultant sign is thus a restricted compound representation, which brings the base and target domains into a parallel and, as we shall see, potentially iconoclastically subversive relation. The concept of "under-specification" refers to the fact that the image produced by the parallel combination of the base and target domains in semiotic metaphor cannot contain all of the visual elements common to both domains. That is to say that the resultant image (the sign) is restricted insofar as it contains sufficient visual cues in order to evoke both the base and target domains without fully representing either of the two. The "under-specification" or compression of the base and target domains is thus an essential consequence of the metaphoric nature of the images and is, in no small part, a result of the limitations of graffiti as a medium of expression. The structure of the visual metaphor as exemplified in graffiti more generally and, more particularly, in the work of Banksy, can thus be

Figure 5.1 | "Two Policemen Kissing," Banksy.

seen to invite an analytic approach that privileges full consideration of the "under-represented" base and target domains and the implication of the parallel relationship that is drawn between them.

Icons, Iconoclasm, and Banksy's Subversion of Authority

The first of the images here considered is that of "Two Policemen Kissing,"[7] a work that has become one of the most iconic of Banksy's images. While the work made its original debut as a lithographic mural or stencil in Banksy's hometown of Bristol, it has been reproduced in his 2005 book *Wall and Piece*,[8] and has been widely disseminated on the Internet as a clear example of the subversive nature of his work. "Two Policemen Kissing" depicts two typical, or even stereotypical, British policemen ("bobbies") in a passionate embrace. One could, given the shape of the badges and the conical custodian helmets that they wear, quite possibly identify them as part of the London Metropolitan Police Service, although this is not necessarily clear. One can furthermore, over and above the obviously homosexual overtones of the encounter, note the life-sized nature of the image (one can judge this from the positioning of the bicycle) and the colour scheme of the work, which, reflective of the black-and-white uniform worn by the policemen, together offer a degree of lifelikeness to the work. It is thus immediately clear that both the form and the content of the work function together in order to attract the attention of passing pedestrians and motorists, thereby propagating the message contained within. The natural, almost romantic, yet unexpected posture of the kissing policemen is indicative of the underlying parallelism which structures the image and which considers the stereotypical masculinity and authority of the policemen as undercut by what could be perceived as their homosexual deviance. That is to say that the base domain of the stereotypical masculine, authoritative British policemen, as representative of traditional British values and ultimately representative of the moral and legal authority of Britain itself, is placed in an incongruous parallel relationship with what in the target domain can be seen in terms of the popular perception of homosexual deviance. The iconic status of the base domain, which is constituted by the cultural reference point of the British policeman, provides us with the underlying concepts of morality and authority of which the policemen are symbolic. The target domain, symbolically evident in the (homosexual) kiss enjoyed by the policemen, constitutes the subject matter at hand. That is to say that the target domain consists of the symbolic deviance which undercuts the authority of the policemen, who, in their deviance from perceived social norms, lose their exemplary nature and thus their authority. One can, however, propose an alternative reading of the work, which would underline a normalization and legitimization of homosexuality: considering that the normality of the subjects as common to the British socio-cultural milieu and the legitimacy of their authority illustrate a socially permissive acceptance of homosexuality, while nevertheless retaining the iconoclastic nature of the image. However, given the generally subversive and antiauthoritarian tone of Banksy's work, an analysis placed in a more general thematic context would tend toward the former interpretation. The essential critical movement is nevertheless one of queering, the use of the homosexualization of the subjects as an

Figure 5.2 | "Queen Victoria," Banksy.

implicit critique of the underlying deviance of societal and state authority (represented by the "bobbies"), or of the underlying unjustness of the society at large. The movement is one from icon (the stereotypical policemen) to iconoclasm (their passionate embrace), subverting their symbolically representative authority.

The second image is that of Queen Victoria, depicted as seated on the face of what can be described as a highly sexualized female figure.[9] The iconic representation of the queen includes immediately recognizable elements such as her crown, sceptre, and profile, and, at least in terms of these elements, closely mirrors popular depictions of the queen in public circulation – an example being the depiction of Queen Victoria in profile on the 1897 two-and-a-half-cent Canadian postage stamp. It is at this point that Banksy's depiction of Queen Victoria departs from the iconic and enters the realm of iconoclastic depiction. Over and above the iconic elements that allow her identification, Queen Victoria is here portrayed as wearing a short skirt, garters, and knee-high boots, which, in sexualizing the queen, seeks to undercut her moral authority. The queen is furthermore, and perhaps more unexpectedly so, seated upon a second figure, who, by the shape of her legs, can be judged to be female. She too wears garters, as well as heeled shoes; her dress is pulled up, her face hidden by the seated queen. It is relatively clear that the base domain is here defined by the iconic representation of Queen Victoria, or rather, in terms of the upper half of her figure as portrayed. That is to say that the iconic representation of Queen Victoria corresponds to the popular cultural image of the queen, recognizable by her profile and royal regalia. As in "Two Policemen Kissing," the symbolic nature of the base or source domain is that of traditional Britannia. Queen Victoria is representative of both the legislative and social authority of the realm, and is, furthermore, a figure of (relative) social normativity. This can be contrasted to the target domain, which, as in "Two Policemen Kissing," introduces the notion of deviant homosexuality as the subversive alternate, which undercuts the moral and social authority traditionally accorded to the queen. The target domain problematizes the base domain, queering the iconic representation of the queen – resulting in a sexualized and iconoclastic representation. It is the strikingly incongruent nature of the parallelism between the queen's moral authority and her homosexuality that can be seen to be at the heart of her iconoclastic representation. However, as in "Two Policemen Kissing," a second interpretation, again less well supported by the general body of Banksy's work, is nevertheless possible. Insofar as Queen Victoria represents a paragon of British traditional cultural life, her homosexuality can be seen to be normalizing rather than critical. Her portrayal, which remains iconoclastic, as engaging in homosexual acts can be seen as a tacit endorsement or normalization of lesbianism, similar to the manner in which the kissing policemen can be seen to normalize homosexuality. Nevertheless, the central antiauthoritarian thrust of Banksy's artistic production would seem to preclude this interpretation, favouring an interpretation critical of the queen's moral, social, and legislative authority, which, in his portrayal of her, is seen as essentially deviant. The depiction of the queen furthermore evokes a popular cultural reference: Queen Victoria is believed to have considered that "lesbianism does not exist," refusing to accept section 11 of the 1884 Criminal Law Amendment Act, which criminalized homosexual conduct, unless all references to women were removed, as she did not believe women were capable of such acts. This is, however, as reported in a 2008 article by Gary Slapper for *The Times*, a misconception.[10] Nevertheless, this popular misconception can be seen to be part and parcel of the iconicity of Queen Victoria – part of her popular cultural and idealized footprint – and is thus part of that which essentially forms the base or source domain of the compound image.

Now, while "Two Policemen Kissing" and "Queen Victoria" share many similarities and, as we shall see, a similar argumentative structure in the manner in which they consider homosexuality in terms of a "queer critical idiom," there are, however, significant differences. Whereas the policemen, as depicted, engage in an almost romantic and near egalitarian kiss, the depiction of Queen Victoria's lesbian encounter emphasizes the role of her power in the exchange. Where the policemen are essentially face to face, Queen Victoria is seated upon the face of her female companion, raising questions regarding the equality of the encounter. This is underlined by the near romanticism of the kiss *shared* by the policemen, which can essentially be opposed to the manner in which Queen Victoria appears to be serviced by her companion, and seems to dominate and oppress her. One can furthermore note that the queen's companion is in an essentially passive position; legs and arms outstretched, she is pinned to the floor despite "servicing" the queen. The evident power differential between the queen and her companion illustrates the relationship between power and sex, which metaphorically can be seen to express the underlying difference between the power of the queen, in her moral, social, and legislative authority to oppress, and that of the people, who exist in order to serve. In this manner, Banksy's image can be seen to double down, so to speak, on its critique of authority – calling not only the hypocrisy of the queen into question, as per her supposed moral authority, but also illustrating the flagrant manner in which the queen dominates her population. It is significant that she *sits on* her female companion in the manner in which she would be seated upon the throne, sceptre in hand. She not only dominates the physical actions of her companion but also acts seemingly in repression: can lesbianism be said to exist if it is hidden (if it has no face)? This repressive injunction also functions in moral terms; in upholding a conservative moral order, Victoria would be complicit in the general repression of homosexual desire. One can furthermore consider that – insofar as her authority is grounded on social, moral, and legislative control and regulation – her depiction as having been caught in the act is evident of the degree to which she can be seen as having lost her self-control, consequently undermining her authority. It is interesting to note the manner in which the socially oppressive and morally restrictive aspects of the queen's relationship with her subjects can be seen to be part of a cynical view of the queen's iconic status. Yet this problematic relationship, structured by power and repression, is brought to the fore precisely as part of her queering. It is the movement from the iconic to the iconoclastic – the queering of the queen – which ultimately emphasizes what is perhaps a cynical view of the structure of her relationship to her subjects.

It is precisely the manner in which both "Two Policemen Kissing" and "Queen Victoria" move from the iconic to the iconoclastic in queering their subjects that is of particular interest. Indeed, in terms of the iconoclastic nature of these two images, it is evident that "street art," as practiced by Banksy, trades in highly recognizable icons in order to ensure their visibility and ease of comprehension. These icons carry a symbolic value, which is, as we have seen, visually undercut in order to make a more general political and critical point regarding, in this case, the British socio-cultural milieu. One can easily identify the iconoclastic element within these works, in terms of the target domain that, in deploying an element of homosexuality can be seen to "deconstruct" the icons (the base or source domain). This is one of the prime characteristics that run throughout Banksy's work: the "destruction" or critical questioning of a given icon and its representation through its incongruous and often iconoclastic depiction. In these two images, the iconoclastic element of homosexuality is essentially one of queering – that is, the deployment of a critical idiom of queerness in order to make an overarching point about the (perceived) relationship of authority to deviance. This critique of the underlying hypocrisy of traditional forms of authority within the British socio-cultural milieu is interesting in terms of the question of graffiti as a critical movement within the built environment, as well as in terms of the question of homosexuality and homophobia, both within this movement and in the more general population. The essential movement is, however, toward the emergence of a concept of "critical queering" as indicative of the changing social, moral, aesthetic, and popular philosophical approaches to queer theory and queerness per se.

It is in this dialogue that the iconic and iconoclastic elements of "street art" are most effective insofar as an iconoclastic representation, such as the depiction of the policemen kissing or of Queen Victoria as a lesbian, introduces a parallelism between the *ideal* icon and the icon as "deconstructed." That is to say that the depiction of the icon is queered and thus rendered iconoclastic, representing the parallelism at work between the base and target domains. The level of sophistication of the iconoclastic images that are produced belies their nature as "street art"; yet this can, however, be reconciled insofar as these images found in the street compete – successfully – with advertisements carefully and painstakingly structured for the attentions of passers-by. Nevertheless, the most striking feature of the two images here under discussion, as compared to Banksy's more general body of work, is the fact that despite the perceived masculine and hetero-normative nature of "street art," these two images deploy a strategic "queerness-as-critique" in order to push home Banksy's socio-political message. To begin with, in contrast to the most common association of homosexuality with deviance – where the accusation of homosexuality is in fact the sum total of the message and the identification as homosexual is the social punishment – the images here use the theme of homosexuality as a strategic tool in order to draw out the parallelism between deviance and authority. Granted, it must be noted that the images do not necessarily uplift the notion of queerness per se, but if we consider that the point of queerness is to assert an otherness in respect to the heterosexual norm, the parallelism that associates queerness with deviance does not do as much harm as one would think. Second, the critique does not simply end with the condemnation of the characters portrayed in the images as queer; that is not the point of the exercise. Rather, the socio-political critique takes precedence, unlike forms of graffiti that exist only as slurs, where the insults themselves are, in effect, the only currency. "Street art" can thus be seen to reflect elements of its artistic heritage in the consideration and the dissimulation of latent themes as opposed to the rash expression of a slogan. The fact that homosexuality is employed in these images is in fact less indicative of the homophobia of the "street artists" than of their awareness of the attention that these issues hold in the popular imagination, and is therefore essentially a reflection of a certain strategic awareness. Furthermore, the images of the policemen kissing and of Queen Victoria invite a reading that, as we have seen, could be considered as a normalization of homosexuality insofar as these figures of authority are presented as homosexual, or engaged in homosexual acts, thus making these acts permissible through their own actions. While it is clearly obvious that the personalities depicted do not directly endorse the actions (these are, after all, graffiti stencils), the images can nevertheless be taken (if obliquely) as homo-normalizing, reinforcing an understanding of Banksy in particular, and "street art" in general, as being less conservative than they may have been considered with regard to homosexual iconography. Interestingly, both Gilbert & George and Pierre et Gilles, artist duos whose main interest lies in the production of homosexual iconography, exhibit in their work many of the ambiguities regarding the critical use of homosexuality that has been discussed in relation to Banksy's use of "queer" as a "critical idiom." The treatment of the queer idiom in a manner similar to that of these established, openly gay artists points to the maturity of, at the very least, Banksy, but also of the "street art" community more generally – and to the evolution and maturation of graffiti from the aesthetics of the slur and of the scrawl into something more akin to true artistry, and to the poetics of social and artistic engagement, nevertheless retaining elements of radicalism lest the art form be tamed and rendered uninteresting.

The use of "queer" in these images by Banksy can be considered as the deployment of a critical idiom, rather than a critique of homosexuality in and of itself. The queerness, which marks the movement from the iconic to the iconoclastic, allows the socio-political critique to gain attention, rather than merely calling attention to itself. Accordingly, the "queer critical idiom" could be defined in visual terms, describing the use of homosexual imagery, or the incorporation of homosexual iconography, as a tool for the generation of iconoclastic images that offer a broader social, moral, or political critique of a given subject. The "queer idiom" is thus a tool for the criticism of further subjects (and, importantly, not of "queerness" itself), whose strategic deployment offers a certain shock value that all but guarantees that attention will be paid to the image. The benefit of the "queer idiom" is twofold: while the iconoclastic image becomes more noticeable through its deployment of queer iconography, the exclusive use of queer as a purely negative trait is subtly undermined; and while this use of the "queer idiom" is not necessarily resoundingly positive and rosy, the engagement of queer in the socio-political ("street art") dialogue as part of the critical iconoclastic apparatus sets the stage for a rehabilitation of "queer" as a concept. This is part of the manner in which visual metaphor and the introduction of parallelism allow the symbolic value of a depiction to influence the structure of the compound image. As we have seen, the symbolic value of the base or source domain is problematized – queered even – by the homosexuality introduced as part of the target domain. Indeed, at the very least, the use of queer iconography is indicative of more permissive attitudes – a public evolution in attitudes toward the portrayal of what was previously considered a deviant sexual and social practice. Taken together, these iconoclastic images point to an opportunity for a greater and more critical engagement with "street art" as a centre of (post)modern iconic production that reveals important aspects of the socio-political climate – where the manner in which the question of authority and the decadence (or perceived decadence) of authority is expressed becomes a point of iconoclastic discussion. Furthermore, the use of queerness, which previously was largely limited to the slur or to the demarcation of space (i.e. the declaration of an area as queer through the graffiti expressed in the space), now becomes part of the apparatus of socio-political critique, offering perhaps an alternative to the binary of insult or praise. That is, while Queen Victoria and the policemen are sexualized, the ultimate critique is the questioning of the validity of the authority in British society, and the use that is made of this authority.

The Iconoclastic Continuum: Banksy qua Banksy

In conclusion, and as if to underline the concept of the "queer critical idiom," two subsequent works inspired by Banksy's graffiti, drawing particularly on the works here under discussion, illustrate the manner in which even an iconoclastic image can become iconic, and thus open to iconoclasm in its own right. It is the very recognition and attention paid to the highly countercultural, satiric, and iconoclastic images produced by Banksy, and their subsequent mediation and diffusion, that ultimately render them iconic. These images, then, sold on canvases and printed on t-shirts, carry with them not only the iconoclastic semiotics as detailed in this consideration, but also a compressed, iconic semiotic that points to Banksy, to his work, and to his socio-political attitude. This compressed iconic status is precisely what becomes reused in the effective "recycling" of the iconoclastic image, carrying the former iconoclastic semiotic as subtext, indicative of the subcultural penetration of the "queer critical idiom." The movement from icon to an iconoclastic interpretation that, in turn, becomes iconic echoes Michael Taussig's consideration of the manner in which icons are reinvigorated by their defacement: "This would explain why icons suddenly burst into consciousness and seem to come alive only with their defacement. You smash them and – lo and behold! – they have become icons. This back-to-front logic is of a piece with the rhythm of taboo and transgression, attraction and repulsion that runs through all societies and all of social life."[11]

The initial transgression, which transforms these icons of traditional British cultural life through defacement, transposition, and, most importantly, queering, is once again at stake in two further artworks, which make new icons of these iconoclastic images, breathing fresh life into transgressive movements, pushing them once again to the fore of the public consciousness.

To this end, Hilary White, in a piece titled *Politics as Usual*, depicts Sarah Palin, in lieu of Queen Victoria, seated in the self-same manner on the self-same highly sexualized female figure, holding a gun instead of a sceptre. Transposing the imagery of the queen, White uses the underlying iconoclastic image initially produced by Banksy as an icon; her iconoclastic rendering undercuts both Banksy's original image (moving the locus of critique away from British authoritarianism) and the image of Sarah Palin. The critique here operates on the political ideals that are ascribed to Palin, including conservatism and questions on the right to possess arms. Similar to Banksy's image, the question is not clearly accusatory; rather, White uses the queerness of the iconoclastic image to suggest political deviance as opposed to actual lesbianism.[12]

Another work, which Luke Harding of the *Guardian* reports as produced by the Russian art collective Blue Noses and titled *Kissing Policemen (An Epoch of Clemency)*, evokes the now iconic image of Banksy's kissing policemen, reworking the image in terms of the confines of their socio-political framework. The image depicts two Russian policemen locked in a passionate embrace, mirroring that of Banksy's policemen in a snowy field of birch trees. The photograph, banned by Russia's minister for culture from a Paris exhibition of contemporary Russian artwork, is described by a member of the collective in these terms:

> Mr Shaburov said that he and fellow artist Viacheslav Mizin had created Kissing Policemen as a homage to the celebrated British graffiti artist Banksy. "We were inspired by Banksy's

> iconic image of two constables kissing. We wanted to do the same but in Russia," Mr Shaburov said.
>
> The image had nothing to do with gay people, he added. Instead, it was an absurdist fantasy about what might happen if everyone showed mercy and tenderness to each other. "Given the fact the state has banned it, we haven't quite reached this point yet," he noted.[13]

The iconoclasm of the photograph, together with the statement that "the image had nothing to do with gay people," underlines the manner in which the queer critical idiom can be deployed as part of the iconicity inherent in this reuse of Banksy's iconic image. That the artwork was banned by the state – due, no doubt, to the homosexual content of the image – reinforces nevertheless the degree of antiauthoritarian critique implicit in the image, but does not invalidate the deployment of the "queer critical idiom" evidenced by this work.

NOTES

1 Dickens, "Placing Post-graffiti," 472.
2 Cafe, "Banksy v Bristol Museum."
3 Lefebvre, *The Urban Revolution*, 19.
4 Peirce, *The Collected* Papers, sec. 2.277.
5 Lakoff and Johnson, *Metaphors We Live By*, 265.
6 Ibid.
7 Note that Banksy does not title his works; the "titles" I am using here are thus provisional, included for the sake of identifying the works.
8 Banksy, *Wall and Piece*, 30.
9 Ibid., 171.
10 Gary Slapper, "Weird Cases: Lesbian Litigants," *The Times* (UK), 2 May 2008, https://www.thetimes.co.uk/article/weird-cases-lesbian-litigants-pjg3knvvm75 (accessed 16 January 2019).
11 Taussig, "Iconoclasm Dictionary," pages 21–32 in this volume.
12 While the artist's portfolio is available at http://hillarywhite.daportfolio.com/about/, the image in particular seems no longer to be available.
13 Luke Harding, "No Paris Trip for Russia's Kissing Policemen," *Guardian*, 12 October 2007, http://www.guardian.co.uk/world/2007/oct/12/artnews.russia (accessed 16 January 2019).

BIBLIOGRAPHY

Banksy. *Wall and Piece*. London: Century, 2005.

Cafe, Rebecca. "Banksy v Bristol Museum." BBC News. 12 June 2009. http://news.bbc.co.uk/local/bristol/hi/people_and_places/arts_and_culture/newsid_8097000/8097022.stm (accessed 16 January 2019).

Dickens, Luke. "Placing Post-graffiti: The Journey of the Peckham Rock." *Cultural Geographies* 15, no. 4 (2008): 471–96.

Lakoff, George, and Marc Johnson. *Metaphors We Live By*. London: University of Chicago Press, 2003.

Lefebvre, Henri. *The Urban Revolution*. Translated by Robert Bononno. Minneapolis: University of Minnesota Press, 2003.

Peirce, Charles Sanders. *The Collected Papers of Charles Sanders Peirce*. Edited by Charles Hartshorne and Paul Weiss. Cambridge, MA: Harvard University Press, 1932.

Taussig, Michael. "Iconoclasm Dictionary." This volume, pages 21–32.

KEYWORD

NATION, *n. 1*[1]

Brit. /ˈneɪʃn/, US /ˈneɪʃ(ə)n/
Origin: A borrowing from French.
Etymon: French *nacion.*

I. A people or group of peoples; a political state.

There is an obvious difference between a crowd and a political state; nonetheless, crowds, gangs, and the masses and individuals can all desire sovereignty, a state of political independence. What is the relationship then between the "people" and the political state? Is it harmonious, as the utopian understanding of "democracy" would have us believe, or is there an embedded antagonism we have yet to discern?

The play of nation, the historical movement toward modern "nation" and nationalism is often imbricated with language and religion as ideological constructs. A people, a group of people, a political state, can only unite by communicating through a shared language; at a fundamental level, the conception of "us" and "them" relies on the ability to communicate with the rest of "us" that we are not like "them." Religion, of course, grows out of, into, and alongside these positions of "us" and "them," of people who believe and worship as we do, in the same language as we do. A dictionary is thus, of course, the encoding and embodiment of a shared understanding of a specific language, and a project that is inalienable from the project of Nation.

Nation is…

1.a. A large aggregate of communities and individuals united by factors such as common descent, language, culture, history, or occupation of the same territory, so as to form a distinct people. Now also: such a people forming a political state; a political state. (In early use also in *pl.*: a country.)

There exist the notions of a civic nation and an ethnic nation. While, on the one hand, the "large aggregate" shares common descent – read nation as a birthright, as the past participle of *nāscī* would suggest – and other cultural elements, mores that include a shared language, the stories such a language recounts, and the territorial roots from which they spawn.

Nation in the twenty-first century, rising from Western roots, is a multidimensional construct, simultaneously as much a geopolitical "fact" as an ideological state of mind, one of varied contradictions and dissonances. In the evolution of European states from the Middle Ages, through the Renaissance and early modern era, the Enlightenment, and into the "modern" period is contemporaneous with a move from Latin to vernaculars, not only as the languages of everyday, but, importantly, as the language of government, of laws, of religion, of *nation*. The language of rule, of history, of literature becomes tied to the people who live; yet, at the same time, the nation as an institution becomes involved in unifying and codifying that language that stands for the people, for the nation: English for the English, French for the French, German for the Germans.[2] The nations of Europe are called for the names of their people, the names of their languages.

1.c. A group of people having a single ethnic, tribal, or religious affiliation, but without a separate or politically independent territory.

Yet nation as political state, as cultural group, as occupiers of the same territory, is deeply contradictory. In Canada in 2019, the term "First Nations" is frequently preferred to talk about Indigenous groups who might previously have been referred to as "Indian" or "Native"; yet this term, which seems to respect the aspects of nation – common descent, language, culture, history, or occupation of the same territory – is a term with no official legal or political standing. It is also a term that does not include the entirety of the Indigenous and Aboriginal inhabitants – the Inuit and Métis are not covered by "First Nations" – of the modern geopolitical entity, the *nation* of Canada.[3] This contraction in the placement of "nation" between a "first" nation and the nation of Canada is one that is echoed repeatedly on a global scale, between aboriginal and indigenous inhabitants of a territory faced with the historical and ongoing forces of conquest, colonialism, and empire.

The British populist vote to leave the European Union – Brexit – offers a propitious backdrop to our discussion of nation and empire. Historians, cultural theorists, and economists are all sketching potential scenarios for the shape and path that the geopolitics of Britain and the EU might take, as well as trying to understand how Brexit became a reality in the first place. Brexit exists, researchers Sally Tomlinson and Danny Dorling suggest, as a result of the ideological remnants of the British Empire and a nostalgic desire to retrieve a past identity combined with a lack of education in schools and a general ignorance of history: precisely the history of the British Empire and the Commonwealth.[4]

The former colonies of Britain are certainly shaping notions of nation in diverse ways. The United States is reaching a boiling point in its melting pot, following the election of Donald Trump, whose politics of containment and protectionism advocate for physical barriers and immigration bans on several nations in order to protect its sovereignty. Such nationalistic policies come, in part, from the fear of a refugee system that could act as a Trojan horse for an Islamic state. However, where precisely is the boundary between "state" and "nation," and can religion transcend the boundaries of a geopolitical map where a nation without land thus becomes a nation in all lands?[5]

Typically, while the United States has viewed its policy on welcoming newcomers with the metaphor of the melting pot,[6] an ideal republic where all are welcome and, through cultural assimilation, can be equal, Canada has, in contrast, attempted to build its metaphorical "cultural mosaic," where the diversity of cultures is celebrated (although a certain, hidden level of assimilation is nevertheless necessary). New Zealand, a third example of a former British colony, instead celebrates biculturalism. Following the Treaty of Waitangi in 1840, which declared British sovereignty over New Zealand, Māori were expected to adopt Pākehā (European) culture as the Europeans quickly outnumbered the locals. In the 1970s, thanks to a Māori renaissance, the notion of biculturalism, as it now exists in government institutions, slowly came into being. The duality at play in biculturalism is not simply Māori culture, on the one hand, and European colonial culture – Pākehā – on the other; there is an understanding of multiculturalism on both sides of the bicultural spectrum. In other words, the multiple *iwi* (tribes) in both the North and South Islands make up the multicultural Māori. The second half of biculturalism celebrates not only the British colonists, but also the French colonists, as well as all immigrants to New Zealand after the Treaty of Waitangi, who live in harmony with Māori cultures. Thanks to historical and legal fictions, biculturalism also retroactively includes any settlers who came prior to the signing of the Treaty of Waitangi. Such a conception is not without flaws or criticism, as there are inevitable hierarchies within both sides of the bicultural spectrum that need to be addressed, not to mention that many individuals within particular *iwi* do not identify with the term Māori at all; they identify solely with their tribe. In Māori, the term *iwi* can mean both "tribe" and "nation." How do we reconcile these terms? When does the tribe become the nation?

Within the modern nation-state of Canada, the French-speaking province of Quebec stands apart: it stands apart on the grounds of language, of religion, of common law, of culture and history: it stands apart, perhaps, as a nation. The movement toward Quebec nationalism reached a political peak during the build-up to the 1995 referendum, which asked inhabitants – also *les habitants*, descendants of the original French colonists – on whether Quebec should leave Canada and establish itself as an independent state.[7] The language of the referendum question was one of sovereignty:

> Do you agree that Quebec should become sovereign after having made a formal offer to Canada for a new economic and political partnership within the scope of the bill respecting the future of Quebec and of the agreement signed on June 12, 1995?
>
> *Acceptez-vous que le Québec devienne souverain, après avoir offert formellement au Canada un nouveau partenariat économique et politique, dans le cadre du projet de loi sur l'avenir du Québec et de l'entente signée le 12 juin 1995?*

The slim failure of the referendum to pass was attributed in part to the First Nations and Inuit of Quebec, who had no nation-to-nation treaties (however exploitative) in place with that province.[8]

1.d. With the whole population of a country, freq. in contrast to a smaller or narrower body within it.

The case of Quebec's nationhood is tied in part to French president Charles de Gaulle's famous declaration during a state visit in 1967: "Vive le Québec libre!" (Long live a free Quebec!). In 2006, the Canadian House of Commons passed a non-binding motion that recognized the Québécois as a nation within a united Canada: here there is a clear shift between the people-as-nation and the state-as-nation, one that parliamentarian Stéphane Dion unpacks in a bilingual statement for the House. Dion, in French, restates the motion that the "House recognize that the Québécois form a nation within a united Canada," and begins to define "nation," first in French, then in English. "Before voting on a text that some of our fellow citizens believe will be of great significance," he says, "we have a duty to tell them clearly what that text means." He begins speaking in French, in which he lists three meanings of "nation" according to *Le Petit Robert*, namely the ethnic, state, and sociological definitions: common origin, a political unit under a "sovereign authority," and a group "characterized by awareness of its unity and a desire to live together," before reinforcing this sociological sense as also found in *Webster's Dictionary*. Having provided his definitions, he continues in French:

> In the first sense, the ethnic sense, Quebec and Canada are not nations, but French-Canadians are a nation, one that is concentrated primarily in Quebec but is present everywhere in Canada.
>
> There are several other groups of people in our country that can also be considered to be nations in ethnic terms. I would therefore vote in favour of a motion that said: In Canada, including in the province of Quebec, there are several nations in the ethnic sense of the word.
>
> In the second sense of the word "nation," the state sense, the only sense that confers legal existence in international law, Canada and Canada alone is a nation. I would therefore vote for a motion that said: Canada forms a single nation which holds a seat at the United Nations.
>
> In the third sense of the word "nation," the sociological

sense, we, the Québécois, are a nation, because we form a large group within Canada – nearly a quarter of the population – and we have an awareness of our unity and a desire to live together. In that sense, it is correct to say that the Québécois form a nation within a united Canada. I will therefore vote for the motion that is before us.

[In English:]
However, I add that the entire Canadian population is also a nation in the sociological sense of the term. As Canadians, we have the sense of our unity and the will to live together, and there is nothing that prevents the same individual to be part of different nations in the sociological sense of the term.

[In French:]
So I say, in this House, that I am a proud member of the Quebec nation and a proud member of the Canadian nation. I say that these identities are cumulative and indivisible, and that I will fight with every resource that democracy gives me against anyone who wants to make me choose between these two wonderful identities: Québécois and Canadian.

I know all too well the game that the independentist leaders want to play. They want to persuade us that we cannot be part of the Canadian nation because we, the Québécois, form a nation. In other words, they want to shift from the sociological to the state sense of the word "nation": from the "community" sense to the "country" sense. As usual, they want to conflate the meaning of words in order to sow confusion in people's minds.[9]

Thus Stéphane Dion, eloquently and bilingually, highlights the problems of the modern meanings of a nation, further complicating the distinction between country and community, and the question of whether diverse nations can live both within and alongside each other, a contiguity of nations either synonymous with symbiosis, commensalism, or parasitism.

NOTES

1 *Oxford English Dictionary Online*, s.v. "nation, n. 1," http://www.oed.com/ (accessed 14 December 2016).

2 French and German, among many other languages outside of English, reflect this: *français(e)/Français(e)* and *deutsch/Deutsch(e)* are simultaneously the name of the language, the name of the people, and the adjective that pertains to both. Yet in the case of former colonies, the name of the language is of the original colonial power.

3 In 2015, the Truth and Reconciliation Commission (TRC) issued ninety-four "calls to action" to address the legacy of colonial violence and oppression against First Nations, Métis, and Inuit peoples, and to attempt reconciliation between these peoples and the federal and provincial governments of Canada. On 15 December 2015, Prime Minister Justin Trudeau affirmed his government's commitment to the TRC's recommendations; other governments have been slower to act, or have rolled back commitments made by predecessors. Critiques of both the TRC and institutional responses to the "calls to action" are ongoing. See: "Delivering on Truth and Reconciliation Commission Calls to Action," Government of Canada, 25 October 2018, https://www.aadnc-aandc.gc.ca/eng/1524494530110/1524494579700 (accessed 21 January 2019); Crawley, "Ontario Cancels Curriculum Rewrite"; Coulthard, *Red Skin, White Masks.*

4 Tomlinson and Dorling, "Brexit Has Its Roots in the British Empire."

5 Since the election of Donald Trump in 2016, more and more populist governments have been elected around the world. Brazil's new president, Jair Bolsonaro, used his first day in office in January 2019 to drastically undermine the rights of indigenous peoples with regard to their traditional territories, among the dismantling of other human rights protections. Londoño, "Jair Bolsonaro." Human Rights Watch executive director Kenneth Roth notes the particular dangers that populist governments pose to universal human rights. Roth, "The Dangerous Rise of Populism."

6 David A. Hollinger discusses the semantic spaces between "melting pot" and "miscegenation," which former he dates to the late eighteenth century, but in the early twentieth century highlights the influx of racially white immigrants from eastern and southern Europe, where

> miscegenation would become an ostensibly neutral word, but one that flourished in a Jim Crow discourse alongside another term that came into use for the mixing of white Americans with each other. This was the notion of the "melting pot" … What made the term problematic was an ambiguity analyzed by Philip Gleason and others. Was the idea to melt down the immigrants and to then pour the resulting, formless liquid into pre-existing cultural and social moulds modeled on Anglo-Protestants like Henry Ford and Woodrow Wilson, or was the idea instead that everyone, Mayflower descendants and Sicilians and Irish and Ashkenazi and Slovaks, would act chemically upon each other so that all would be changed, and a new compound would emerge? (1366)

Hollinger, "Amalgamation and Hypodescent," 1363–90.

7 Of course, we cannot ignore the culmination of the nationalist movement in the October Crisis of 1970, with the kidnapping of Quebec cabinet minister Pierre Laporte and British (colonial) diplomat James Cross by

the Front de libération du Québec (FLQ); Laporte was killed by his captors. Prime Minister Pierre Elliott Trudeau invoked the *War Measures Act*, which temporarily limited civil liberties. The popular reaction against the FLQ's violent attempt to achieve nationalism accelerated the movement toward seeking greater autonomy or independence through electoral means. See: Fournier, *FLQ: Anatomy of an Underground Movement*, 256.

8 See: Grand Council of the Crees, *Sovereign Injustice*; and Wherrett, "Aboriginal Peoples."

9 Canada, Parliament of Canada, House of Commons Debates, vol. 141, issue 087, session 1, 5351–2 (The Hon. Stéphane Dion, MP).

BIBLIOGRAPHY

Canada. Government of Canada. "Delivering on Truth and Reconciliation Commission Calls to Action." 25 October 2018. aandc.gc.ca/eng/1524494530110/1524494579700 (accessed 21 January 2019).

Canada. Parliament of Canada. House of Commons Debates. 27 November 2006. Vol. 141, issue 087, session 1, 5351–2 (The Hon. Stéphane Dion, MP).

Coulthard, Glen Sean. *Red Skin, White Masks: Rejecting the Colonial Politics of Recognition*. Minneapolis: University of Minnesota Press, 2014.

Crawley, Mike. "Ontario Cancels Curriculum Rewrite That Would Boost Indigenous Content." CBC News, 9 July 2018. https://www.cbc.ca/news/canada/toronto/ontario-education-truth-and-reconciliation-commission-trc-1.4739297 (accessed 21 January 2019).

Fournier, Louis. *FLQ: Anatomy of an Underground Movement*. Translated by Edward Baxter. Toronto: NC Press, 1984.

Grand Council of the Crees. *Sovereign Injustice: Forcible Inclusion of the James Bay Crees and the Cree Territory Into a Sovereign Quebec*. Nemaska, QC: Grand Council of the Crees, 1995.

Hollinger, David A. "Amalgamation and Hypodescent: The Question of Ethnoracial Mixture in the History of the United States." *American Historical Review* 108, no. 5 (1 December 2003): 1363–90.

Londoño, Ernest. "Jair Bolsonaro, on Day 1, Undermines Indigenous Brazilians' Rights." *New York Times*, 2 January 2019. https://www.nytimes.com/2019/01/02/world/americas/brazil-bolsonaro-president-indigenous-lands.html (accessed 21 January 2019).

Roth, Kenneth. "The Dangerous Rise of Populism." Human Rights Watch, 2017. https://www.hrw.org/world-report/2017/country-chapters/dangerous-rise-of-populism#1e9c34 (accessed 21 January 2019).

Tomlinson, Sally, and Danny Dorling. "Brexit Has Its Roots in the British Empire – So How Do We Explain It to the Young?" *New Statesman*. 9 May 2016. https://www.newstatesman.com/politics/staggers/2016/05/brexit-has-its-roots-british-empire-so-how-do-we-explain-it-young (accessed 19 February 2017).

Wherrett, Jill. "Aboriginal Peoples and the 1995 Quebec Referendum: A Survey of the Issues." Background Paper BP-412E. Ottawa: Library of Parliament Research Branch, 1996. http://publications.gc.ca/collections/Collection-R/LoPBdP/BP-e/bp412-e.pdf.

T. Nikki Cesare Schotzko

6

What the Disaster Writes: Contemplations of the Fall

Preface: The Event[1]

For Martin Heidegger, the conflation between the event and its perception is the condition of modernity; it is only through representation that the world, or at least our understanding of it, and therefore of ourselves, exists. Therefore, it is only in its representational state, in relation to our own perception of it, that the event exists as something within our world.[2] For Alain Badiou, "there is no event save relative to a historical situation, even if a historical situation does not necessarily produce events." The event extends beyond its own occurrence or happening to encompass the discursive reality into which it enters as history. For Gilles Deleuze, an ideal event – which is every event because "events are ideal"; they are "the only idealities" – is a set of singularities that are at once both inclusive of but external to the discourse by which they are expressed as individual, subjective experience.[3] "Novalis sometimes says," Deleuze writes in *The Logic of Sense*, "that there are two courses of events, one of them ideal, the other real and imperfect. The distinction however is not between two sorts of events; rather, it is between the event, which is ideal by nature, and its spatio-temporal realization in a state of affairs. The distinction is between event and accident."[4] "Because I never understood the possible until you or an accident showed me," Matthew Goulish writes in memoriam to performance artist Bob Flanagan.[5] I am interested in this distinction between, or what I think might be better imagined as a space between, the event and the accident, and what that accident might show me about the event. Accident, as in "something that is present but not necessarily so"; as in, "a philosophical term denoting a contingent attribute, or an attribute necessarily resulting from the notion of something"; accident as the "noun of present participle of accidere to fall, to happen."[6] I am interested in the possible, which I expect also exists in the space between; I am interested in what happened then and how it might still be happening now; I am interested in the fall.

The Fall

> But heterogenous time, which he also calls the "time of the now," is a sudden rupture in time when something in the present leapfrogs unexpectedly so as to constellate with something in the forgotten past. There is a cessation of movement, a strange nothingness out of time, and here it is when the Messiah may return – in other words a revolutionary chance in the fight for the oppressed past.
> – Michael Taussig, "Iconoclasm Dictionary" (2012)

> He will soon be traveling at upwards of 150 miles per hour, and he is upside down. In the picture, he is frozen; in his life outside the frame, he drops and keeps dropping until he disappears.
> – Tom Junod, "Falling Man" (2003)

On 11 September 2001, Richard Drew took a photograph of a man falling from the North Tower of the World Trade Center. Over the next ten years, this photograph was reproduced, reiterated, and reframed through both documentary and aesthetic media, including other photographs and photo collages, documentary films and Hollywood movies, and several novels. It is a photograph that documents a moment and an act. It is a photograph that not only provides the evidentiary proof of the event, a capability intrinsic to the technology of photography and the complicated ethics of photojournalism, but it also creates an impetus to deny such proof.

What we know of the Falling Man in Drew's photograph is little, and much of this information is pieced together from supposition, imbricated within personal accounts of that day, and muddled by emotional response to the photograph itself. "The events of 9/11," writes Jill Bennett, "led writers of many kinds to abandon the constraints of disciplinary method in favour of forms of commentary that were often raw and impressionistic, grounded in emotion rather than clarity of vision."[7] This response, throughout critical analysis and public consciousness, emerges in relation to most if not all the art that takes as its aesthetic subject the remains of that day. These "raw and impressionistic" descriptions of what happened – from writers, photographers, filmmakers, and artists of all kinds – fill in information from experience, from emotion, and from an affect and affective investment that permeates both the literal space where the Towers once stood and the conceptual gap in our memory of what we did or did not witness.[8]

We still do not, and probably never will, know the Falling Man's name. Tom Junod's 2003 article "Falling Man," in which he, ultimately unsuccessfully, traces the identity of the man Drew captured in his image, is still one of the most comprehensive and compassionate sources of information we have, yet we are left at its end with only a philosophical return that brings us inevitably back to the beginning. "The only certainty we have is the certainty we had at the start: at fifteen seconds after 9:41 a.m., on 11 September 2001, a photographer named Richard Drew took a picture of a man falling through the sky – falling through time as well as through space … Richard Drew's photograph is all we know of [the Falling Man], and yet all we know of him becomes a measure of what we know of ourselves."[9] We do not know many things about the Falling Man, but we do know something about his fall. We know that it would have taken him approximately ten seconds to reach the ground. We know that as he fell, his body moving ever closer to terminal velocity (also the title of Carolee Schneemann's photo-collage of bodies falling on 11 September, including Drew's iconic image), time would have seemed to decelerate around him. It was not time slowing, however, but his memory expanding to take in everything around him.

When functioning under normal conditions, memory acts as a "sieve," self-editing the trivialities of daily experience. When mortally stressed, however, memory opens wide: it collects and compiles all available sensory

Figure 6.1 | Poster for season 5 of *Mad Men*. Photograph by Michael Surtees.

information. Time during the Falling Man's descent would have seemed to have lasted a duration that measures at least one third greater than the duration of the fall.[10] Even as a clock might tick "steadily, predictably forward," our experience of time differs: time "stretches and compresses, skips a beat and doubles back."[11] Or, as Jon Erickson suggests, "what our bodies experience and what our conscious minds experience in terms of the passing of time may not be exactly the same thing."[12] There is, with the choreography of the falling body, a concordant choreography, and chronometry, of falling time.

Fast-forward to winter 2012: the popular AMC serial drama *Mad Men* announces the premiere of its much delayed and desperately awaited fifth season with a "minimalistic 'falling man' poster," evoking both structurally and metaphorically Drew's photograph.[13] The opening credits sequence – with its dissolving ground through which the silhouetted Mad Man falls, accompanied by the perversely appropriate descending sequence of the theme song – was already evocative of Drew's photograph; this 2012 advertisement, however, prompted a rush of criticism from, primarily, the online community for its unequivocal reference to that "other" Falling Man, and, therefore, to September 11 (see figure 6.1).[14]

Junod, in the January 2012 issue of *Esquire*, responded to such criticism by framing *Mad Men*'s leading man, Don Draper (Jon Hamm), as a metaphor for the Falling Man, and, as such, for a Fallen America. As

Junod argues, *Mad Men* had already "exist[ed] within a peculiar set of quotation marks that 9/11 furnished, and travel[led] back fifty years in order to reckon obliquely with the last ten. The show doesn't merely begin with a sequence portraying a man's fall. The show begins with a man's fall to tell us that it's *about* a man's fall – to tell us that as it begins, it will also end."[15] *Mad Men* marks, through its historical context and aesthetic (self-)referentiality, a particular historical period that begins with the Second World War and ends with September 11. It is a period that coincides with the shift of the geographic and artistic centre of the historical avant-garde from Europe to the US, with the fast-paced process of globalization marked by the move from hefty analog to slick DIY digital technologies, and with the emergence of postmodernity – the "attempt to think the present historically," as Fredric Jameson describes it, "in an age that has forgotten how to think historically in the first place."[16]

This is also a period marked by the hero-making and -unmaking of men who stand in for a certain American masculinity even as the aesthetic and aestheticizing modes of said "making" challenge the stability of such iconography: Hans Namuth's artist-as-Marlboro-Man characterization of Jackson Pollock in his 1950 photographs and documentary of Pollock's painting; David Tudor's deanimated figure in the premiere of John Cage's *4'33"* at Black Mountain College in 1952; Herbert Blau's production of Samuel Beckett's *Waiting for Godot* at the San Quentin prison in 1957 – a production that Martin Esslin refers to in the opening lines of the introduction to the first edition of *Theatre of the Absurd*.[17] Esslin cites, in that introduction, an article from the *San Quentin News*, the prison newspaper, about the performance: "It was an expression, symbolic in order to avoid all personal error, by an author who expected each member of his audience to draw his own conclusions, make his own errors. It asked nothing in point, it forced no dramatized moral on the viewer, it held no specific hope.... We're still waiting for Godot, and shall continue to wait. When the scenery gets too drab and the action too slow, we'll call each other names and swear to part forever – but then, there's no place to go!"[18] I am not attempting to reiterate a particular moment of transition in the history of the shift from the historical avant-garde into the contemporary avant-garde, nor between modernism and postmodernism. What I am pointing toward here, instead, is a distinct moment in American history when the aesthetic and social – the "social" including here both the political and economic motivations that underlie such a broad categorization – coalesce into at least an attempted formulation of a coherent American psyche. Or, as Amelia Jones writes in "The 'Pollockian Performativity' and the Revision of the Modernist Subject," the curation and circulation of these images of the artist "exemplify the speaking of a new mode of thinking not only about 'art' as an expression of individual subjects, but about subjectivity itself."[19] This specific subjectivity was intended to stand in as an understanding of "America" at a moment when its cultural identity was in flux, predicated not only upon a particularly male construction of subjective self-realization but also upon one that was already a *construction of a construction*: each figure – Pollock, Tudor, Godot – is already in the process of performing some notion of self, whether implicitly or explicitly.[20] Such forced construction of a unified identity was always going to be a failed endeavour – but what a spectacular failure it was.

This is a trajectory of failing, told through the metaphor of the fall.

Drew's photograph signifies the pervasive cultural sense of what Junod refers to as "moral unease – an almost vertiginous sensation of the ground giving way beneath our feet, along with just about everything else."[21] It forces a confrontation of what we want or even what we need from the image with what we want or need from our memories of September 11. The *Mad Men* ad similarly confronts us with memory; however, whether that memory is of our own making or is generated from other mediatized and aestheticized renderings of that day becomes increasingly difficult to discern. Within the slippery reflection of the Plexiglas bus shelters on which the *Mad Men* posters hung during the winter and spring of 2012, we see not only the impression of the New York street behind us, but a ghostly reflection of ourselves, today, incorporated within the image that takes us back to ourselves, on that day.[22]

Twenty-something film and theatre director Vojin Vasović's 2011 animated short *5 Minutes Each* plays with such tricks of identity and time, interrogating the relationship between time and memory, technology and anachronism, and, in a manner not unlike Drew's 2001 photograph, between the aesthetic and, while not quite the "real," something like it. Maybe it is something like the human.[23]

Jon Erickson writes, "we have no objective sense of what a 'real' five minutes by clock time means," in "Tension/Release and the Production of Time in Performance."[24] *5 Minutes Each*, comprising not five, but just under ten minutes, exists outside of such objective realities. It is a "tale about upswing and downfall" and offers a climax that is simultaneous to the protagonist's literal falling-out of the cinematic frame. Vasović's protagonist, like the film's other characters, is not quite a man, but rather an anthropomorphized amalgamation of human figure and anachronistic media technology: a "newspaper-man" whose head is the rumpled pages of yesterday's paper; his irises show the stunned faces of witnesses framed in the lens of the photojournalist's camera.

Vasović was not intentionally referencing Drew's photograph in *5 Minutes Each* – it was not a photograph he was any more than tangentially familiar with. (Vasović told me, in our correspondence about his film, that the inspiration came from a delightful animated film of a wee kiwi bird experimenting with flight.)[25] Yet, the resonance between these falling men lingers, indicative of a certain cross-cultural sense of vertigo collected in a recognizable, if accidental, pop-cultural archive of falling. Drew's photograph, *Mad Men's* opening sequence, and Vasović's film challenge the relationship between technology and perception, history and memory, making evident not only the perceptual effects and chronometric affect of falling, but also, and more significantly, the *human imperative to fall.*

In *5 Minutes Each*, falling becomes a metaphor for and a process simultaneous to art. Its tagline reads, "highest [that] art can fall," and this conceit is manifest in the objects – a vintage radio microphone, a paintbrush and small canvas, a single LP, lengths of unspooled film, cassette tapes, a shovel – that fall from the waiting-room vending machine in the opening sequence and land in the dusty pile of detritus in the last scene, the pile onto which, it seems, all art not only can but eventually must fall.

5 Minutes Each was accepted to and shown at more than 120 festivals around the world, and has earned more than thirty awards, including Best Foreign Animation at the AniMazing Spotlight animation shorts festival, Burbank, California; Best International Animation at the Urban Mediamakers Film Festival, Georgia (US); and the Diamond Award at the 2011 California Film Awards, San Diego. In the official description of the film, available on various festival sites as well as IMDb, Vasović emphasizes the "constant struggle of the artist to reach those five minutes of limelight." Artists "are enclosed into their own world of ideas, striving to create the epochal masterpiece," which, inevitably, will only ever be "a reflection of themselves" – a process they are doomed to repeat endlessly.[26] "The basic idea of the movie looks into the relation between art and the artist, art as ever prevailing and the artist as the expendable … The aim of this movie is to portray a hyperbolical picture of an everyday artist, the vanities and rapture of creation of the work. They all have to flounder in order to ascend. In that sense their need of creating art is detrimental to their equilibrium, and the lure of fame a path towards their doom."[27] Foreshortened from Warhol's fifteen, this newspaper-man's five minutes of fame happen in relative isolation – attended only by rudimentary mechanisms of media and celebrity that, cast as they are in slightly smudged caricature, paradoxically still charm (see figures 6.2–6.4). He sits in a waiting room full of outmoded or at least unwanted technologies: oversized monitors, a parking meter, a computer keyboard, each perched unsteadily atop a lanky cartoon body. The techno-headed characters convey a sense of cultural nostalgia for the nascent days of virtual imbroglio. When it is his turn, our protagonist steps up to the vending machine, inserts his coin (because one must pay for such an experience), pulls the lever: a small canvas and paintbrush drop down. He opens the door and walks through to find himself standing on a precarious cliff ledge, complete with a windy sound track and armed only with the small canvas and brush. He drops the canvas over the edge, leaving him with only the brush. He furrows his brow and, in wondrous slow motion, takes a running leap.

Time, literally, moves with our newspaper-man in *5 Minutes Each*, and so it also moves with us. At first, falling through the clouds, all we see is his falling figure. He dives, he tumbles, he yells, accompanied by a descending carnivalesque melody. As a spooky-sweet theremin refrain enters above the oompah-oompah tune, the newspaper-man catches up to his canvas, and, leaning back into a more comfortable position (and still falling), he begins to paint.

The newspaper-man is falling through what seems to be a crevice within a mountain, framed on either side by rocky surfaces that at times take on an oddly spine-like look. The camera rushes ahead of him for just a moment, and we see a red cord strung between the surfaces; the newspaper-man twangs off it, still mid-fall, and it triggers an electric current that runs through a wire down one side of the crevice and sets off a series of techno-events. A vintage flashbulb camera, barely attached to the sides of the crevice by accordion-arm mounts, snaps a photograph; suddenly

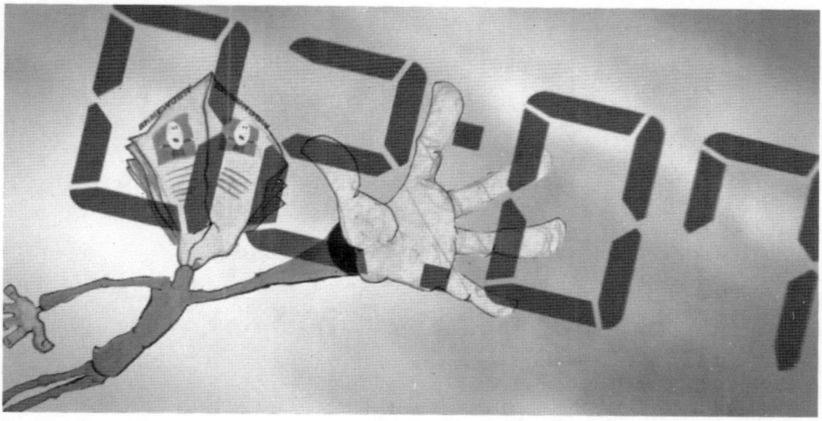

Figures 6.2–6.4 | Film stills, *5 Minutes Each*, dir. Vojin Vasović, 2011.

there are dozens of cameras jutting out on their accordion arms, flashing as the newspaper-man begins to preen and pose for them.

There is a brief pause, with the music slowing to a luxurious bridge, and we are brought back to the waiting room where a short tabletop-radio-headed man (or child?) lingers by the vending machine for his turn. Then back to our falling newspaper-man, floating on his back with his eyes closed and a warm grin on his face. I can only imagine he is basking.

With the original melody calmed down into an easy waltz, the newspaper-man continues to fall, more slowly and calmly now as well, passing mechanical cuckoo birds, which drift out of their houses on the same accordion arms that held the earlier cameras. And now he brushes against two similarly suspended, white-gloved hands that spring back from his touch to clap, joined by other armless pairs. The clapping, however, is less celebratory than the cameras' flashing, and, with a quiet "hmmph?" and a concerned look on his face, the newspaper-man clips a lever further along on his way down that releases a flowing red carpet and gives way to more clapping hands.

Time reappears occasionally during the fall, in the form of an early 1990s LED clock face with familiar, red-lit, stencil-like numbers. The clock itself hangs in the waiting room, just above the door to the cliff, and its seconds descend from 5:00 to 4:09 to 2:42. The newspaper-man, still surrounded by the disembodied hands and the red carpet, and falling like floating like flying slowed down, finishes his painting. As he adds a final flourish to his signature, though, the hands and carpet jerk back out of sight with a *whoosh*, and suddenly he drops back from his float – and drops his canvas and brush – into the fall. The carnivalesque music returns and, at 2:16, time doubles as the numbers on the old-school LED screen slip away from the waiting-room clock and into the frame with the newspaper-man. Time, in the form of the ghosted clock face, hovers, still counting down, just in front of him, and when he reaches to grab the lower crossbar of the "2" it breaks off in his hand, leaving him a minute less to fall. The break accelerates time, and the numbers speed by until, at 00:31, he lands upon a dusty heap of the detritus from previous falls.

In the waiting room, a CRT-television-man meanders up to the vending machine, while, at precisely 00:00, the newspaper-man's canvas lands on the rubbish heap. As the camera pulls back from the newspaper-man's signature, we see that he has drawn a self-portrait mid-fall with eyes and mouth wide; it lies among other renderings of the fall: a music score titled "The Fall"; an LP with *Fall* scripted over a red-brick label; a pirouetting sculpture on a pedestal on which is inscribed "FEAR"; a book titled *FALL*. The CRT-TV-man in the waiting room above pulls a shovel from the vending machine, and the fall begins anew.

What else is memory but the perception of passing, even of falling, time? In *5 Minutes Each*, outdated technology falls and creates art, and in the end the artist's body presumably lands somewhere in the background, while the remainders of all artworks pile up in the foreground, in a heap. As it moves through the fall, and as we watch, the artist's body creates art. For Maurice Merleau-Ponty, "it is by lending his body to the world that the artist changes the world into paintings. To understand these transubstantiations we must go back to the working, actual body – not the body as a chunk of space or a bundle of functions but that body which is an intertwining of vision and movement."[28] The artist here, a blurring of vision and movement, changes the world he sees into painting, scribbling happily away at the canvas the vending machine belched out at him; he changes the fall into, and I mean no pun here, suspended animation. But all he sees is himself. It is only when he illegibly signs his name – a certain Derridean move, no doubt – that the fall begins again. And we learn that time, when grasped too tightly, might be broken and might be lost.

What is lost in the advertisement for *Mad Men*'s fifth season is the sense of context. It is the empty white ground that makes the poster so jarring – just as it is the lack of immediate context for Richard Drew's photograph that makes it, as well, jarring. Yet it is not just the falling Mad Man that brings me back to Drew's Falling Man; I see that photograph as well in Vasović's animated falling newspaper-man, and in the rendering-of-his-rendering of his own fall.

Drew's image, an (or *the*) image of September 11, unexpectedly, and jarringly, creates a context for my viewing of Vasović's film. No single photograph can stand for an event of the immensity of September 11 when it is proffered as evidence; it is only when it is construed as symbolic that such a photograph does any meaningful work. However, it may be that any and every other image, still or moving, that bears some even symbolic relation to *that image* collectively stands in for Drew's photograph, and stands in, too, for September 11.

In the shadow of that photograph, we are always already, and always ever, falling.

André Lepecki begins his reflection, "Limitless," on the relationship between dramaturgy and the catastrophic event *in medias res*: "So, as bodies kept falling from the sky, some in flames, some in suits, some as poised and still as if riding translucent elevators, those witnessing the fall without mediation, without media noise, found themselves pulled into the question of the limit."[29] For Lepecki, the question of the limit puts the capacity of what one might witness into question – and puts as well into question the ability to articulate, and therefore to acknowledge, the actuality of the disaster that one has witnessed: "Witnessing seemed far removed from any possibility of articulating, of reaching; very far from dramaturgy. As if the disaster had no place in it."[30]

Question #1: What, then, is the place of the disaster?

Lepecki's epigraph to his article, from Maurice Blanchot's *The Writing of the Disaster*, reads: "The disaster: not thought gone mad; not even perhaps, thought considered as the steady bearer of its madness."[31] Slightly further down the page – of Blanchot's book, not Lepecki's article – we learn that the "disaster is related to forgetfulness – forgetfulness without memory, the motionless retreat of what has not been treated – the immemorial, perhaps. To remember forgetfully: again, the outside."[32]

But then, back to the beginning, the beginning of the English translation of Blanchot's book: Ann Smock, in her translator's remarks, relates the difficulties of translating Blanchot's work. It encompasses the complexity of translation "when the expression in question is a proper name, or has a cognate in English, or is a perfectly ordinary expression whose equally ordinary equivalent in English comes to mind automatically … For though you can write down 'the multiple,' 'the disaster,' and so on, with some assurance, you have to learn from the whole book what these words could possibly mean, or what it could possibly mean that they be written."[33] It may be only at the end that we know what the beginning meant.

There are those expressions that might suggest an inherent reversibility but, according to Blanchot, "cannot be turned around." Smock continues: "'The writing of the disaster' means not simply the process whereby something called the disaster is written – communicated, attested to, or prophesied. It also means the writing done by the disaster – by the disaster that ruins books and wrecks language. 'The writing of the disaster' means the writing that the disaster – which liquidates writing – is."[34] The writing of the disaster means the writing that the disaster is.

Question #2: What, then, does the disaster write?
Question #3: And who writes this disaster that writing is?

To return to Lepecki, by way of some sort of translation: "Standing within the force field of the catastrophe, withstanding its blatant intrusion, it becomes obvious that the disaster is never something that 'can be shown.' The disaster takes place while refusing to make an appearance ... Its falling into narrative requires the instantiation of a temporal lag, and *a remembering that is already Writing*."[35] Not dissimilar from Peggy Phelan's "writing toward" (but never at the point of) "disappearance":[36] "To remember forgetfully," through a "remembering that is already Writing," is to suggest that the necessary condition of Writing is forgetting – or, to follow through with Blanchot's rule, *the Writing that forgetting is* means that forgetting *is* Writing; and that this is, and both are, necessary to the condition of the disaster. Both are necessary to the condition of experience – the condition of experience, which is what the disaster is.

Question #4: Why do I keep writing this disaster that I can't forget?

Perhaps, too, this forgetting that writing is, is in itself a process of falling; or, more specifically, a process of *falling-through*. Falling-through writing in citation (which is something like remembering); falling-through remembering toward forgetting; falling-through forgetting and back, and perhaps back into, experience. Back into the disaster.

For Lepecki, the process of dramaturgy after September 11 becomes a process-in-motion, a process of trying to capture an image not by stilling it but rather by acknowledging and sustaining the movement within it. The collaborative project with Rachael Swain that he began the week of September 11, initially titled *Fall – a visual essay on mourning* (and which eventually became a video installation entitled *proXy*),[37] was based on photographs of missing persons that appeared all over surfaces throughout New York City in the days immediately following the terrorist attacks. It was a performative means "of trying to bring meaning to the catastrophe": "Every single image asked Rachael to find in her body a specific condition to move – a specific unchoreographed response to what each face, each set of eyes asked Rachael to perform for them … Rachael had to make sure not to Write, so she would not be turned back. Rather, she trembled with the image."[38] This is dramaturgy at the limit: at the limit of choreography, of representation, and of meaning. These limits resonate with a warning Lepecki takes with him from Blanchot: "the danger that the disaster acquire meaning instead of body."[39] It is a warning that the disaster might be written over, and thus, forgotten.

Richard Drew's photograph stops time. The man caught in it, his graceful posture offering a different kind of suspended animation, exists perpetually and perceptually at the point of the disaster, the disaster that never appears. Rachael Swain "trembled with the image[s]" she could not avoid. As she continued walking (falling?) down the streets after September 11, she found a corresponding movement to each face that confronted her; hers became the body "which is an intertwining of vision and movement."

Question #5: What, then, does the disaster write?

Or, if forgetting is writing, what might the writing that the disaster writes *remember?*

Walter Benjamin begins thesis 6 of *On the Concept of History* in disagreement with German historian Leopold von Ranke. "Articulating the past historically does not mean recognizing it 'the way it really was,'" Benjamin writes. "It means appropriating a memory as it flashes up in a moment of danger."[40] David Couzens Hoy, in *The Time of Our Lives: A Critical History of Temporality*, takes up Benjamin's thesis, describing memory as "like a shooting star. It must be seized hold of, or memorialized, the instant it flashes by."[41] It is a concept of history as an ongoing process that, as Hoy indicates, might not change the past but "changes … our understanding of the past."[42]

Going back into the past, going back at all, is a dangerous endeavour. But holding on to the time of the present, too, has its dangers. We might hold on too tightly; time might break in our hands.

Erickson writes that, in performance, "every moment of spectator attention to the present seems to represent the nature of the whole in microcosm, in its repetitive endlessness, even if coupled with the most gradual degradation. *The source of dread isn't death but endlessness.*"[43] History is an attempt to mark the endlessness of time, to fix it. Performance as an aesthetic process – as Jill Bennett imagines it, a process of practical aesthetics – opens up such fixedness to the possibility of interpretation, to re-enact the real again so as to create a new re*act*ion to it. Both history and the real, though, keep changing. Perhaps it is only me, changing with it, and so changing the past, and the present, through these new ways of perceiving it. Perhaps it is that time is the most changeable of all. Perhaps I should stop writing so that I can go back to remembering.

Coda: The Chronometry of Falling

Upon realizing that the diurnal orbits of stars were not adequately described as circular phenomena, as previously believed, but rather seem to travel in slightly flattened ovals as a result of the perceptible effects of refraction, nineteenth-century astronomer J.F.W. Herschel wrote to future students of astronomy: "This new law once established, it became necessary to modify the expression of that anciently received, by inserting in it a *salvo* for the effect of refraction, or by making a distinction between the *apparent* diurnal orbits, as affected by refraction, and the *true* ones cleared of that effect. This distinction between the *apparent* and the *true* – between the *uncorrected* and *corrected* – between the *rough* and *obvious*, and the *refined* and *ultimate* – is of perpetual occurrence in every part of astronomy."[44] Based on these new findings, Herschel established that a day spent on a star – that is, a *sidereal* day – was slightly shorter than a *solar* day spent on the sun: only 23 hours, 56 minutes, and 4.09 seconds, rather than 24 hours; and frolicking on the moon during a *lunar* day would last that much longer: 24 hours and 54 minutes.[45] However, because *all stars* travel in orbits lasting the same durational limit – 23 hours, 56 minutes, and 4.09 seconds – it is our day, the *solar* day (along with the moon's), that is the exception. It is our time that is, universally, out of time.

Herschel coined the term *chronometry* in *The Outlines of Astronomy*, first published in 1833. Its designation derived from the ancient Greek χρόνος (time) and μέτρον (to measure), chronometry "enables us to fix the moments in which phenomena occur, with the last degree of precision."[46] Astronomers used the *transits* of the brightest stars "to ascertain their exact time, or, which comes to the same thing, to determine the exact amount of error of their clocks."[47]

Time is predicated on movement, and movement remains perpetually and beautifully inexact. It corresponds to other movements, and therefore to other times and to other bodies; it allows us to read these movements, these fallings and *fallings-through*, through all the others. And each corresponding fall might remember the other.

What, then, does the disaster write? What does the writing that the disaster writes *remember?*

The disaster is written onto and through memory; the disaster writes this.

NOTES

1 This chapter is adapted from my book *Learning How to Fall: Art and Culture after September 11*.

2 Heidegger, "The Age of the World Picture."

3 Deleuze, *The Logic of Sense*, 52.

4 Ibid., 53.

5 Goulish, "Why Devise, Why Now?," 130.

6 *Oxford English Dictionary Online*, s.v. "accident, n.," http://www.oed.com/ (accessed 19 January 2019).

7 Bennett, *Practical Aesthetics*, 16.

8 While "affect-at-large finds expression in an image," Jill Bennett locates affect not in any one particular image or object, but rather in a space or in relation to an event: "We are confronted … not only with the life and wants of imagery but with the question of *what affect wants*, what it does, and how it transforms objects and perceptions." Ibid., 25.

9 Junod, "The Falling Man," 199.

10 Eagleman, "Brain Time," 155–69. See also: David M. Eagleman, "Why a Brush with Death Triggers the Slow-Mo Effect."

11 Bilger, "Profiles: The Possibilian."

12 Erickson, "Tension/Release," 83.

13 Blazenhoff, "Mad Men Promotes Fifth Season."

14 *Forbes* writer Doug Hill reads the public discomfort created by the ad for *Mad Men*'s fifth season as located not in the series but rather, specifically, in Drew's image. It is no longer (only) a general fear of terrorism that permeates a general underlying anxiety in mainstream American culture, but rather a "loss of psychic footing in a world of overwhelming change." To have our destabilized worldview (re)emerge in commercial television is jolting in its almost casual juxtaposition.

Hill, "Decoding Mad Men's Falling Man." See also: Zutter, "*Mad Men*'s Season 5 Poster"; Copyranter, "The 'Mad Men' Season 5 Teaser Poster"; and Dooley, "'Mad Men's' Long-Standing 9/11 Connection."

15 Junod, "Falling (Mad) Men."

16 Jameson, *Postmodernism*, ix.

17 Esslin, *The Theatre of the Absurd*, 19ff.

18 Ibid., 20.

19 Jones, *Body Art/Performing the Subject*, 55.

20 Referring both to Hans Namuth's photographs and documentary and Harold Rosenberg's 1952 treatise "American Action Painting" – two works foundational to the creation of Jackson Pollock as a celebrity icon – Amelia Jones writes: "This performing Pollock ... was, from early on, constructed largely in relation to the photographs and, to a lesser extent, the film of Hans Namuth. Even Rosenberg's construction of Pollock as laboring existentialist hero was taking off from the photographs; as Barbara Rose has written: "In retrospect, I realize Rosenberg was not talking about painting at all; he was describing Namuth's photographs."' Ibid., 55.

21 Junod, "Falling (Mad) Men."

22 Michael Dooley notes this evocative facet of the *Mad Men* advertisements: "It's undeniably deliberate, and most dramatic when seen on Manhattan's bus shelters, where the Plexiglas superimposes the city's surrounding buildings over the falling mad man. But of course, he's been falling ever since the show's very first episode." Dooley, "'Mad Men's' Long-Standing 9/11 Connection."

23 To view the trailer for *5 Minutes Each*, visit: http://5minuteseach.blogspot.ca/.

24 Erickson, "Tension/Release," 83.

25 The animated film is *Kiwi!*, directed by Dony Permedi (2006). Permedi submitted it as his MFA animation thesis project. It is available on his website: http://www.donysanimation.com/#portfolio=461.

26 "5 Minutes Each (2011)," Internet Movie Database, 2011, https://www.imdb.com/title/tt1817080/ (accessed 21 January 2019).

27 From the website for the film: Vasović, *5 Minutes Each*.

28 Merleau-Ponty, *The Visible and the Invisible*, 2.

29 Lepecki, "Limitless," 17.

30 Ibid.

31 Quoted in ibid.

32 Blanchot, *The Writing of the Disaster*, 3.

33 Smock, Translator's Remarks to *The Writing of the Disaster*, viii–ix.

34 Ibid., ix.

35 Lepecki, "Limitless," 18. Emphasis added.

36 Phelan, *Unmarked*, 148ff.

37 For more information about and images from *proXy*, visit: http://scanlines.net/event/proxy. The video installation was exhibited at Performance Space, in Sydney, Australia, in December 2002. About the project, Lepecki and Swain write: "The onset of the peculiar overlaying of coincidences, accidents, unforeseen plannings, geo-political strategies, devastation, personal dramas, historical forces, hauntings, media noise, reproduction technologies at full throttle, violent acts and traumatic shocks on the edge of hallucination is the reason why we feel *proXy* must be seen both as a response as well as a calling." Lepecki and Swain, "proxy."

38 Lepecki, "Limitless," 23.

39 Ibid., 22.

40 Benjamin, *Walter Benjamin*, 391.

41 Hoy, *The Time of Our Lives*, 156.

42 Ibid.

43 Erickson, "Tension/Release," 98–99. Emphasis added.

44 Herschel, *Outlines of Astronomy*, 84.

45 Ibid., 85.

46 Ibid., 88.

47 Ibid.

BIBLIOGRAPHY

"5 Minutes Each (2011)." Internet Movie Database, 2011. https://www.imdb.com/title/tt1817080/ (accessed 21 January 2019).

Badiou, Alain. *Being and Event.* Translated by Oliver Feltham. London: Continuum, 2005.

Benjamin, Walter. *Walter Benjamin: Selected Writings, Volume 4: 1938–1940*. Edited by Howard Eiland and Michael W. Jennings. 1940. London: Belknap Press, 2003.

Bennett, Jill. *Practical Aesthetics: Events, Affects, and Art after September 11.* London: I.B. Taurus, 2012.

Bilger, Burkhard. "Profiles: The Possibilian." *New Yorker*, 25 April 2011. http://www.newyorker.com/reporting/2011/04/25/110425fa_fact_bilger?currentPage=all (accessed 19 January 2019).

Blanchot, Maurice. *The Writing of the Disaster.* Translated by Ann Smock. Lincoln: Nebraska University Press, 1995.

Blazenhoff, Rusty. "Mad Men Promotes Fifth Season with Minimalistic Teaser Poster." *Laughing Squid*, 17 January 2012. http://laughingsquid.com/mad-men-

promotes-fifth-season-with-minimalistic-teaser-poster/ (accessed 19 January 2019).
Cesare Schotzko, T. Nikki. *Learning How to Fall: Art and Culture after September 11*. London: Routledge, 2015.
Copyranter, Mark. "The 'Mad Men' season 5 teaser poster is macabre." *copyranter* blog, 17 January 2012. https://copyranter.blogspot.com/2012/01/mad-men-season-5-teaser-poster-is.html (accessed 21 January 2019).
Deleuze, Gilles. *The Logic of Sense*. Translated by Mark Lester with Charles Stivale. Edited by Constantin V. Boundas. New York: Columbia University Press, 1990.
Dooley, Michael. "'Mad Men's' Long-Standing 9/11 Connection." *Salon*, 24 January 2012. https://www.salon.com/2012/01/24/mad_mens_long_standing_911_connection/ (accessed 21 January 2019).
Eagleman, David M. "Brain Time." In *What's Next: Dispatches from the Future of Science: Original Essays from a New Generation of Scientists*, edited by Max Brockman, 155–69. New York: Vintage, 2009.
– "Why A Brush With Death Triggers The Slow-Mo Effect." Narrated by Jad Abumrad and Robert Krulwich. *Radiolab*. WNYC. 17 August 2010. http://www.npr.org/templates/story/story.php?storyId=129112147.
Erickson, Jon. "Tension/Release: The Production of Time in Performance." In *Archaeologies of Presence: Acting, Performing, Being*, edited by Nick Kaye, Gabriella Giannachi, and Michael Shanks, 82–100. London: Routledge, 2012.
Esslin, Martin. *The Theatre of the Absurd*. 1961. Garden City, NY: Doubleday, 1969.
Goulish, Matthew. "Why Devise, Why Now? In Memory of Bob Flanagan." *Theatre Topics* 15, no. 1 (2005): 129–30.
Heidegger, Martin. "The Age of the World Picture." In *Off the Beaten Track*, edited and translated by Julian Young and Kenneth Haynes, 57–72. 1938. Cambridge: Cambridge University Press, 2002.
Herschel, Sir John Frederick William. *Outlines of Astronomy, Fourth Edition, with Numerous Plates and Wood-cuts*. 1833. New York: Sheldon and Company, 1869.
Hill, Doug. "Decoding Mad Men's Falling Man." *Forbes*, 23 February, 2012. https://www.forbes.com/sites/oreillymedia/2012/02/23/decoding-mad-mens-falling-man/#5b56156521f8 (accessed 21 January 2019).
Hoy, David Couzens. *The Time of Our Lives: A Critical History of Temporality*. Cambridge, MA: MIT Press, 2009.
Jameson, Fredric. *Postmodernism, or, The cultural logic of late capitalism*. Durham: Duke University Press, 1991.

Jones, Amelia. *Body Art/Performing the Subject*. Minneapolis: University of Minnesota Press, 1998.
Junod, Tom. "Falling (Mad) Men." *Esquire*, 30 January 2012. https://www.esquire.com/entertainment/a12565/falling-mad-man-6648672/ (accessed 21 January 2019).
– "The Falling Man." *Esquire*, September 2003, 176–99.
Lepecki, André. "Limitless." *Women & Performance* 13, no. 2 (2003): 17–28.
Lepecki, André, and Rachael Swain. "proXy." scanlines.net, December 2002. http://scanlines.net/event/proxy (accessed 21 January 2019).
Merleau-Ponty, Maurice. *The Visible and the Invisible*. Translated by Alphonso Lingis. 1964. Evanston: Northwestern University Press, 1969.
Phelan, Peggy. *Unmarked: The Politics of Performance.* London: Routledge, 1993.
Schneider, Rebecca. *Performing Remains: Art and War in a Time of Theatrical Reenactment.* London: Routledge, 2011.
Smock, Ann. Translator's Remarks to *The Writing of the Disaster*, by Maurice Blanchot. Translated by Ann Smock. Lincoln: Nebraska University Press, 1995.
Vasović, Vojin, dir. *5 Minutes Each*. Serbia and Montenegro, 2011. https://www.toblinkanimation.com/5minmain (accessed 21 January 2019).
Zutter, Natalie. "*Mad Men*'s Season 5 Poster Criticized for Looking Like Tragic 9/11 Photograph." *Crushable*, 25 March 2012. http://www.crushable.com/2012/01/17/entertainment/mad-men-season-5-poster-march-25/ (accessed 21 January 2019).

Adam Swann

7

Twilight of the Idle, or How to Historicize with a Hammer: Milton, Nietzsche, and the Iconoclasm of English Identity

The *Pict* and Painted *Britain*, Treach'rous *Scot*,
By Hunger, Theft, and Rapine, hither brought.
Norwegian Pirates, Buccaneering *Danes*,
Whose Red-hair'd Offspring ev'ry where remains.
Who join'd with *Norman-French*, compound the Breed
From whence your *True-Born Englishmen* proceed.
– Daniel Defoe, *The True-Born Englishman*[1]

In his essay in this volume, Michael Taussig considers one of the paradoxes of iconoclasm: its intertwining of creation and destruction. To illustrate this, Taussig draws a parallel between two nineteenth-century iconoclasts, Mikhail Bakunin and Friedrich Nietzsche. For Taussig, Bakunin's declaration that destruction was a "creative passion" and Nietzsche's assertion that "we destroy only as creators" are but two sides "of the same coin."[2] Destruction was an equally creative act two centuries earlier, when the iconoclasts of the English Civil War sought to create a new religious and political order through the purgation of idolatry.

On 28 April 1643, the Royalist newspaper *Mercurius Aulicus* reported that Oliver Cromwell had "bestowed a visit" on Peterborough, where he "did most miserably deface the *Cathedrall* Church, breake downe the *Organs*, and destroy the glasse windows," and later had his troops quarter their horses in the cathedral.[3] The report describes Peterborough as providing Cromwell with "entertainment," but it also concedes that the destruction in the cathedral was carried out "in pursuance of the thorow *Reformation*."[4] Church defenestration and horse defecation were thereby transformed into religious acts, which purified as they defiled; they purified *because* they defiled.

Destruction thus becomes a necessary condition of renewal, and nowhere is this more evident than in the work of one of the great seventeenth-century iconoclasts, John Milton. Milton's *History of Britain* (1670) charts a thousand years of British history, from the Roman conquest to the Norman. Successive invasions of Romans, Saxons, Danes, and Normans scar the national narrative, but the destruction wrought by each band of invaders brings with it the opportunity for self-governance. However, the Britons repeatedly fail to shrug off foreign yokes and instead regress into indolent subservience, for which the punishment is another invasion.

The *History* charts a national trajectory which is not linear but cyclical, and the text's fascination with the cyclical nature of history is a remarkable precursor to Nietzsche's idea of eternal recurrence. Like Nietzsche, Milton believes that seizing agency is the only way to escape the eternal recurrence of history, and he also shares Nietzsche's skepticism regarding the idea of national purity. Through a Nietzschean reading of the *History*, this essay will demonstrate that Milton's text represents destruction as a creative process, and thereby resonates with Taussig's reading of Nietzschean iconoclasm.

It might be argued that a Nietzschean reading of Milton is anachronistic, but William Shullenberger asserts that "we limit the possibilities of critical insight if we restrict the direction of Milton's ethical and aesthetic discourse … only towards those who precede and surround him in time."[5] Even if Milton can tenably be read via Nietzsche, it is initially unclear on what grounds the two iconoclasts could be compared, considering that one was a "Protestant humanist deeply instructed by the dualisms of monotheistic ethics," while "Nietzsche's thought is set within the framework of a rejection of God and Christian morality."[6] But both thinkers' writings on history share a common didactic purpose. Milton's *History* narrated England's calamitous past to his countrymen to prevent "the Revolution of like Calamities," while in *On the Uses and Disadvantages of History for Life* (1874), Nietzsche hoped that he and his readers would be "instructed and put right about the character of our own time."[7]

Milton and Nietzsche deny a teleological view of history, and reject the idea that nations are progressing toward any ultimate goal, or even progressing at all. Rather, history moves in cycles. In each cycle, nations are intermingled by both force and choice, problematizing any appeals to the notion of fixed national character. Both Nietzsche's and Milton's surveys of history reveal that nostalgia for nobler cultures and peoples of the past is misplaced. Great men do occasionally emerge from the apathy that characterizes much of the populace, but their momentary brilliance is soon swallowed by an atavistic regression to vice and sloth. If there is any constant feature of national character, it is not nobility, bravery, and genius, as many nationalist thinkers of both the seventeenth and nineteenth centuries had it, but torpidity and turpitude. Milton and Nietzsche, then, raise their iconoclastic hammers against the idols of nationalism, demonstrating that the notion of fixed national identity is a fallacy and that most people of the past are "progenitors not to be glori'd in."[8]

Arthur Danto has identified Nietzsche's goal as a metaphysician as being "to provide a picture of the world as it actually is – a blank picture, as it happens, since the world has neither structure nor order – so that men might have no illusions either about it or about themselves, and, unimpeded by mistaken views, might set about their proper task, which was to make of humankind something more than it had been."[9] Nietzsche's rejection of objectivism is clear in his claim, in *Twilight of the Idols*, that "*there are no moral facts whatever.*"[10] The denial of the existence of objective facts also underpins Nietzsche's opposition to the notion of racial purity, as he claims that "the concept of 'pure blood' is the opposite of a harmless concept."[11] Objective morality and the concept of immutable collective identity are errors that impede the realization of the Overman.[12] Nietzsche is a "well-known denouncer of the state," and he emphasizes that monolithic national apparatuses and the Overman are fundamentally incompatible: "there, where the state *ends* – look there, my brothers! Do you not see it, the rainbow and the bridges of the Overman?"[13]

In the *History*, Milton, like Nietzsche, attacks the idea of the continuity and purity of national identity. The *History* can be read as a response to the contemporary tendency to look back to Saxon England as a golden age tarnished by the Norman conquest. Many Englishmen justified the overthrow of Charles I as a return to the status quo ante, when the "Anglo-Saxon inhabitants of this country lived as free and equal citizens, governing themselves through representative institutions."[14] In 1649, Gerrard Winstanley's communistic Christian sect, the Diggers, appropriated lands for common cultivation. Winstanley defended their actions in a December 1649 letter to Thomas Fairfax, Lord General of the Parliamentary army: "seeing the common people of England by joynt consent of person & purse, have cast our Charles our Norman oppressour wee have by this victory recovered ourselves from under this Norman yoake, & the land now is to returne into the joynt hands of those who have conquered, that is the commonours."[15]

The *History* rejects the notion of a lost sense of Englishness by demonstrating that a thousand years of national turmoil leave British national identity diluted and hybridized. It becomes clear that the English national character of the Saxon age was far from being as noble, pure, and free as Milton's contemporaries remembered it. Moreover, the trajectory of the *History* is shaped by successive periods of invasion, assimilation, and atavism, which construct a cyclical view of history that embodies Nietzschean eternal recurrence.[16] Zarathustra, "the teacher of the doctrine of eternal recurrence," describes eternal recurrence as follows: "from this gateway Moment a long eternal lane stretches *backward*: behind us lies an eternity … must not whatever *can* happen, already have happened, been done, passed by before? And if everything has already been here before … must this gateway too not already – have been here? And are not all things firmly knotted together in such a way that this moment draws after it *all* things to come?"[17] In "facing the question" of the eternal recurrence, Bernard Williams maintains, "one is supposed to have a real and live consciousness of everything that has led to this moment, in particular to what we value."[18] This combination of the awareness of historical circularity and the questioning of fundamental values is crucial to the *History*.

Milton begins the *History* by emphasizing the congruence between historiography and civility, as the absence of reliable pre-Roman historical sources reduces him to mere "conjectur[e] … that this Iland also had her dwellers, her affairs, and perhaps her stories, eev'n in that old World … [before] the Flood."[19] Nietzsche also recognized this overlap, claiming that, "when it attains a certain degree of excess, life crumbles and degenerates, and through this degeneration history itself finally degenerates too."[20] The movement from excess to disintegration is evident in the ancient Britons, who are "under many princes and states, not confederate or consulting in common, but mistrustfull, and oft-times warring one with the other, which gave them up one by one an easie Conquest to the *Romans*."[21]

The *History* lacks native British historiographical sources for centuries, as Milton notes that "the only Authors wee have of *Brittish* matters, while the power of *Rome* reach'd hither … [are] *Roman*."[22] It falls to Roman historians to teach the British about their shared history, which demonstrates the didactic role played by the Romans for both Milton and Nietzsche. Milton looked back to classical Rome for his civic, intellectual, and political ideals, and so, too, Nietzsche believes the Romans were "a people by whom we can and should be inspired," even placing them above the Greeks: "I received absolutely no … strong impressions from the Greeks; and, not to mince words, they *cannot* be to us what the Romans are. One does not *learn* from the Greeks – their manner is too strange, it is also too fluid to produce an imperative, a 'classical' effect. Who would ever have learned to write from a Greek! Who would ever have learned it *without* the Romans!"[23]

However, Milton challenges the notion, common among his republican-minded contemporaries, that classical Rome provided an invariably positive model to be followed. Cracks begin to appear in the icon of Roman didacticism during the very first battle between the Romans and Britons, when a "*Roman Souldier*," Scæva, broke ranks and "press'd too farr among the *Britans*, and besett round, after incredible valour shewn, single against a multitude, swom back safe to his General."[24] But Scæva was not chastised for his indiscipline, and "such a deed wherin valour, and ingenuity so much out-weigh'd transgression, easily made amends and preferr'd him to be a Centurion."[25] Milton demonstrates the value of breaking away from fixed notions or expectations of national character. While Milton later suggests that "of the *Romans* we have cause not to say much worse, then that they beate us into some civilitie," even the notion of "civilitie" is problematic, as he notes how "then were the *Roman* fashions imitated, and the Gown; after a while the incitements also and materials of Vice, and voluptuous life, proud Buildings, Baths, and the elegance of Banqueting; which the foolisher sort call'd civilitie, but was indeed a secret Art to prepare them for bondage."[26]

We might also expect the *History*'s account of the Britons' rebellion against perceived tyranny to be reported with approbation, but this is not the case. The key word here is *perceived*; for all his lifelong fulmination against tyranny, Milton had no time for rebels who didn't know what was good for them. In *Observations upon the Articles of Peace* (1649), Milton was perplexed by the Irish rebels, who "preferre[d] their own absurd and savage customes before the most convincing evidence of reason and demonstration," and he reminded them that they were "justly made our vassalls."[27] Analogously, the ancient Britons' decision to follow a woman, Boudicca, into rebellion against the Romans, was an act that "brands us with the rankest note of Barbarism."[28] Milton claims that there is "nothing more awry from the Law of God and Nature, then that a Woman should give Laws to Men," and Willy Maley has rightly observed that "Milton's depiction of Boadicea captures the anxiety around female rule."[29]

The rebels' perversion of the natural order is evident in the account of their sack of a Roman town, where Tacitus says, "nor did the angry victors deny themselves any form of savage cruelty."[30] The *History* provides more gruesome details: "no crueltie that either outrage or the insolence of success putt into thir heads, was left unacted. The *Roman* Wives and Virgins hang'd up all naked, had thir Breasts cut off, and sow'd to thir mouthes; that in the grimness of death they might seem to eat thir own flesh."[31] Milton laments that "in this Battel, and whole business, the *Britans* never more plainly manifested themselves to be right *Barbarians*; no rule, no foresight, no forecast, experience or estimation, either of themselves or of thir Enemies; such confusion, such impotence, as seem'd likest not to a Warr, but to the wild hurrey of a distracted Woeman, with as mad a Crew at her heeles."[32] The unnaturalness of this "distracted Woeman" having a "Crew at her heeles" anticipates Nietzsche's dictum: "if a woman possesses manly virtues one should run away from her; and if she does not possess them she runs away herself."[33]

Eventually the British rebels' wish was granted and the Roman yoke was removed. The departure of the Romans left the Britons, for the first time in generations, with the burden of civil autonomy. Proponents of the

Norman Yoke held that a British golden age began after the withdrawal of the Romans and ended with the Norman conquest, and indeed, the Britons "seem'd awhile to bestir them with a shew of diligence in thir new affairs, som secretly aspiring to rule, others adoring the name of liberty."[34] But the truth of Zarathustra's warning that "commanding is harder than obeying … the commander bears the burden of all obeyers, and … this burden easily crushes him" becomes apparent, because, "so soon as [the Britons] felt by proof the weight of what it was to govern well themselves, and what was wanting within them, not stomach or the love of licence, but the wisdom, the virtue, the labour, to use and maintain true libertie, they soon remitted thir heat, and shrunk more wretchedly under the burden of thir own libertie, than before under a foren yoke."[35]

For Nietzsche, it is not enough merely to escape a yoke. One must grasp the consequent opportunity to gain power. Without doing this, freedom is undeserved: "you call yourself free? Your dominating thought I want to hear, and not that you escaped from a yoke. Are you the kind of person who had the *right* to escape from a yoke? There are some who threw away their last value when they threw away their servitude. Free from what? What does Zarathustra care! But brightly your eyes should signal to me: free *for what*?"[36] The question of what the sub-Roman Britons were free *for* is answered by a regression into their pre-Roman state, the first instance of the eternal recurrence in the *History*.[37] Each kingdom engaged in petty disputes with its neighbours, and soon after a famine led to "discord and civil commotions among the *Britans*: each man living by what he rob'd or took violently from his Neighbour. When all stores were consum'd and spent where men inhabited, they betook them to the Woods, and liv'd by hunting, which was thir only sustainment."[38]

Despite this regression, one aspect of Roman rule the British retained was the meritocratic election of leaders. However, they appear to have drawn their Roman example in this respect from the last legions stationed in Britain, who were far from the greatest embodiments of Roman virtue. These soldiers feared invasion by the Vandals, and, "in tumultuous manner set up *Marcus* … but him not found agreeable to thir heady courses, they as hastily kill: for the giddy favour of a mutining rout is as dangerous as thir furie. The like they do by *Gratian* a *British Roman*, in four Months advanc't, ador'd, and destroy'd."[39] This is similar to the sub-Roman Britons, according to whose wishes "kings were anointed … not of Gods anointing, but such as were cruellest, and soon after as inconsiderately, without examining the truth, put to death by thir anointers, to set up others more fierce and proud."[40]

This cycle of accession and usurpation still revolved in Nietzsche's time, as he mockingly observed: "watch them scramble, these swift monkeys! They scramble all over each other and thus drag one another down into the mud and depths. They all want to get to the throne, it is their madness – as if happiness sat on the throne! Often mud sits on the throne – and often too the throne on mud."[41] The potential flaw in any meritocratic system of election thus becomes apparent: it hinges upon what is considered meritorious by the electorate. As Don Wolfe points out, "to Milton it was axiomatic that wicked men, slaves to their passions, would elect to office men of their own unbridled desires."[42] Vortigern, a sub-Roman king of Kent, certainly supports Wolfe's reading of the Miltonic axiom of meritocracy, as he is "decipher'd by truer stories a proud unfortunate Tyrant, and yet of the people much belov'd, because his vices sorted so well with theirs. For neither was he skill'd in Warr, nor wise in Counsel, but covetous, lustful, luxurious, and prone to all vice."[43]

Milton suggests that the Britons were divinely punished for their atavism by being set upon by "swarms" of Picts and Scots "unanimous to rob and spoile."[44] But the "dominating thought" – which is the Nietzschean hallmark of deserved freedom – is wholly absent, as the Britons, like "frightened chicks huddling under the wings of their faithful parents," entreated the Romans to return, without success.[45] Just as anxieties about a Vandal invasion caused the last Romans to look to their tyrannical leaders, so too the Britons ran "to the Palace of thir King Vortigern with complaints and cries of what they suddenly fear'd, from the *Pictish* invasion," leading Vortigern to call a council to decide a course of action.[46]

While Nietzsche exhorted, "if you want to climb high and beyond, then use your own legs! Do not let yourselves be *carried* up, do not seat yourselves on strangers' backs and heads!," the sub-Roman Britons were incapable of such self-sufficiency.[47] They resolved to invite the Saxons, despite their reputation as a "barbarous and heathen Nation, famous for nothing else but robberies and cruelties done to all thir Neighbours."[48] This evokes *The Readie and Easie Way to Establish a Commonwealth* (1660), in which Milton deplores the "ignominy" of a newly emancipated nation that "should be so heartless and unwise in their counsels as not to know how to use [freedom] … butt basely and besottedly to run their necks again into the yoke which they have broken."[49] The Saxons promised to defend the Britons, yet soon claimed "that thir pay is too small for the danger they undergo, threatning op'n Warr unless it be augmented."[50] The Britons could not offer enough to satisfy the Saxons, so the latter overthrew their hosts, and "wasted without resistance almost the whole Land eev'n to the Western Sea, with such a horrid devastation, that Towns and Colonies overturn'd, Preists and people slain, Temples, and Palaces, what with fire and Sword lay alltogether heap'd in one mixt ruin."[51] Then followed a succession of Saxon kings whose reigns were characterized more by "giving scope to [their] own cruel nature, rather then proceeding by mildness or civility."[52]

Soon after, Milton records with approbation the reign of Ethelbert, a Saxon king who was so "convinc't by [the] good life and miracles" of visiting Christian missionaries that he converted to Christianity.[53] After Ethelbert's death, his son Eadbald "took the course as fast to extinguish" this progress, "not only falling back to Heathenism, but that which Heathenism was wont to abhor, marrying his father's second wife. Then soon was perceiv'd what multitudes for fear or countenance of the King had profess't Christianity, returning now as eagerly to thir old Religion. Nor staid the Apostacy within one Province, but quickly spread."[54]

The regression was not limited to religion but was also civically manifested, as we hear of kings being "murder'd in the night by [their] own guard" and being "without just cause … slain by [their] own Servants."[55] These events are accompanied by apocalyptic portents, such as "wondrous Serpents then seen in *Sussex*" and "many strange thunders and fiery Dragons, with other impressions in the air."[56] Analogously, in 1647 John Booker, a republican licenser of almanacs, connected "'strange wonders in the Ayre' with the downfall of monarchy, the defeat of Antichrist and the spread of Christ's kingdom."[57] A further parallel may be drawn here between Christian apocalypticism and Nietzsche's belief that "the purpose of destroying and clearing is … to allow a future already alive in anticipation to raise its house on the ground thus liberated."[58]

The scale of the destruction in the *History* is apocalyptic, and it has a particularly eschatological tenor in that it gives the Britons the opportunity to resist their oppressors and start afresh. But they repeatedly fail to deliver themselves from the vale of tears, and it becomes clear as the

History progresses that the nation will lurch from one period of savagery to another. At this point, Milton explicitly recognizes the cyclical nature of the *History*'s narrative, as he anticipates a "new and fatal *revolution* of calamity," that is, "the Danes landing."[59]

In his description of the Danish invasion, Milton emphasizes the parity between different historical periods: "God had purpos'd to punish our instrumental punishers, though now Christians, by other Heathens, according to his Divine retaliation; invasion for invasion, spoil for spoil, destruction for destruction."[60] The Danes were "as barbarous as the *Saxons* themselves were at first reputed," and the distinction between invader and invaded is further destabilized by the fact that the Saxon Britons were "now full as wicked as the [sub-Roman] *Britans* were at their arrival, brok'n with luxurie and sloth."[61] Milton details their specific failings as being that they, "laying aside the exercise of Arms, and the study of all vertuous knowledge, some betook them to over-worldly or vitious practice, others to religious Idleness and Solitude, which brought forth nothing but vain and delusive visions … [of] Ceremonies, Reliques, Monasteries, Masses, [and] Idols."[62] This evokes Zarathustra, whose exultations at having achieved his goal of "teach[ing] … the Overman" are cut short when

> the cave which up till now had been full of noise and laughter became deathly still all at once – but his nose sensed an aromatic smoke and incense, as of burning pine cones.
>
> "What is happening? What are they doing?" he asked himself and crept closer to the entrance, in order to watch his guests surreptitiously. But, wonder of wonders! What did he have to behold with his own eyes?
>
> "They've all gone *pious* again, they're *praying*, they're mad!"[63]

The distinction between invader and invaded, already unstable, is now entirely elided, as "in [the Danish] invasion, *Danes* drove out *Danes*, thir own posterity. And *Normans* afterwards, none but antienter [ancienter] *Normans*."[64] As Martin Dzelzainis has noted, this "darkly comic" observation "makes a mockery of conquest theory as such, and with it the myth of the Norman Yoke."[65] We see here the doctrine of eternal recurrence manifest itself exactly in the *History*. One of the defining tenets of eternal recurrence is that "it has all happened before, and will happen again, exactly in the same way each time, forever. Nothing happens that has not happened an infinite number of times and which will not happen again, for all eternity, in exact iterations of itself," and this is precisely what occurs at this point in the *History*.[66] The Danish invasion is not simply *like* the Saxon, nor will it be *like* the Norman; they are identical, and each band of invaders conquers a previous iteration of themselves.

The Danish invasion brought "Spoil, Desolation, slaughter of the many, [and] slavery of the rest," which is, Milton argues, a just punishment for a people so depraved.[67] But from the quagmire of British wickedness emerges the figure who towers over the *History*: Alfred the Great. Alfred is an archetypal example of the Nietzschean "great man," those rare few who oppose, and arise out of the apathetic spirit of their age: "Great men, like great epochs, are explosive material in whom tremendous energy has been accumulated; their prerequisite has always been, historically and physiologically, that a protracted assembling, accumulating, economizing, and preserving has preceded them – that there has been no explosion for a long time. If the tension in the mass has grown too great the merest accidental stimulus suffices to call the 'genius,' the 'deed,' the great destiny, into the world."[68] This echoes *Samson Agonistes*, which describes

> Vertue givn for lost,
> Depr est, and overthrown, as seem'd,
> Like that self-begott'n bird
> In the Arabian woods embost,
> That no second knows nor third,
> And lay e're while a Holocaust,
> From out her ashie womb now teem'd
> Revives, reflourishes, then vigorous most
> When most unactive deem'd.
> Virtue, given for lost.[69]

Alfred embodies the "strong executive presence [which] is a legitimate part of the ideal state," no less for Nietzsche than for Milton.[70] Nietzsche's "great men" must willingly place themselves above the common herd, and in this he draws on Schopenhauer: "One giant calls to another through the weary space of centuries, without the world of dwarfs which crawls below hearing more than sound, and perceiving more than that something is going on. Besides, these dwarfs carry on endless buffoonery and make a great noise, adorn themselves with what the giants have dropped, proclaim heroes who are dwarfs themselves, and such like, while the giant spirits do not let themselves be disturbed, but continue their lofty converse"[71]

Nietzsche rejects a teleological approach to history because the doctrine of the eternal recurrence denies finality. Rather, the meaning of history, if any, is found in these "great men" who sporadically appear, as in them "we find examples of those whom we should emulate; we obtain a clear picture of what we ought to make ourselves."[72] The archetypal example of the hero cited by Nietzsche is Napoleon, and the philosopher notes that "the France of the Revolution, and even more pre-Revolution France, would have brought forth the type antithetical to Napoleon: it *did* bring it forth."[73] So for Nietzsche, the "great men" of history are those antithetical to their age; Gildas wrote because he was disgusted by the dissoluteness of his countrymen and Alfred battled the apathy of his English contemporaries. Nietzsche draws a distinction between "great men" and "last men," who are slaves to their passions and defined by their lethargy: "this is the herd-man of contemporary life, and Nietzsche-Zarathustra holds him in contempt ... he has in mind men, no matter where or whom, who are complacent or resigned and prepared to let well enough alone, taking the world as they find it."[74] It is this tendency toward idleness and apathy which Milton also attacks.

Alfred's success was rooted in the vigour with which he combated English complacency. A representative example is his expansion of English naval forces, for which he is "traditionally described as the founder of the British Navy."[75] Alfred "found that the want of Shipping and neglect of Navigation, had expos'd the Land to these Piracies."[76] The following year, the Danish fleet "met with such a tempest ... as wrack'd 120 of thir Ships, and left the rest easie to be maisterd by those Gallies which *Alfred* had set there to guard the Seas ... the loss of thir Navy ... distressed them so, as that they gave [Alfred] as many hostages as he requir'd, and as many Oaths, to keep thir covenanted peace, and kept it."[77]

But the peace did not last long, and Alfred spent most of his reign alternately fighting and negotiating with the Danes. The Danish forces in Britain eventually dwindled to a few isolated groups, and Alfred "caus[ed] to be built other [ships] twice as long as usually were built, and some of 60 or 70 Oars higher, swifter, and steddier than such as were in use either with *Danes* or *Frisons* [Frisians], his own invention, some of these he sent out against six *Danish* Pirats, who had done much harm in the Ile of *Wight* and parts adjoining … the Pirats at length were either slain or tak'n."[78] Shortly after, we see the conquerors being resisted, as "*Rollo* the *Dane* or *Norman* landing heer … after an unsuccessful fight against those [British] forces which first oppos'd him, sail'd into *France* and conquerd the Country, since that time called *Normandy*."[79]

But Alfred did not, as might be expected, lapse into customary British idleness, but "three years of peace [was] spent, as his manner was, not idlely or voluptuously, but in all vertuous emploiments both of mind and body."[80] The praise of Alfred's polymathic virtues is remarkably similar to Milton's treatment of Oliver Cromwell in the *Second Defence*. Cromwell was "sprung from renowned and illustrious stock," just as Alfred is "of noble descent," but while the representation of Alfred in the *History* comes close to panegyric, Milton is not, like Nietzsche, an "inveterate worshipper of heroes."[81] Milton recounts with admiration that Alfred possessed a "great desire of learning" and was "exact in doing justice," but we are also reminded that despite Alfred's "noble minde, which renderd him the miror of Princes; his body was diseas'd in his youth with a great soreness in the Seige."[82] There are few heroes with haemorrhoids.[83]

The progress made during Alfred's reign, however, was soon squandered after his death. This regression accords with Nietzsche's belief that "the great human being is a terminus … the genius – in his works, in his deeds – is necessarily a prodigal: his greatness lies in the fact that *he expends himself*."[84] And so, if Alfred is the "great man" that signifies the end of one cycle, his death must surely be followed by a regression into the Nietzschean "last man," a ruler ruled by idleness. Ethelred was indeed a king "with many sluggish and ignoble vices," and shortly after his accession, "one midnight, a Cloud sometimes bloody, sometimes fiery, was seen over all *England*; and within three years the *Danish* Tempest, which had long surceast, revolv'd again upon this Iland."[85]

The renewed Danish raids could not be resisted by the dilapidated English armies and navy, and so Ethelred "thought best for the present to buy that with Silver which [the English] could not gain with thir iron; and Ten Thousand pound was paid to the *Danes* for peace."[86] However, Ethelred's strategy merely taught the Danes "the ready way how easiest to come by more."[87] The Danes soon demanded more money and Ethelred paid 16,000 pounds, before being subjected to further Danish incursions. The armies raised by the English were "either betray'd by the falsehood, or discourag'd by the weakness of thir Leaders, [and] put to rout, or disbanded themselves. For Souldiers most commonly are as thir Commanders, without much odds of valour in one Nation or other, only as they are more or less wisely disciplin'd and conducted" – a far cry indeed from the Caesars and Napoleons whom Nietzsche lauded.[88] With his ineffective armies soon crushed, Ethelred paid 24,000 pounds, and soon 36,000, which, "out of the people all over *England*, already half beggerd, was extorted and paid."[89]

Ethelred's inability to resist foreign invaders is reflected in the Britons falling into a state of apathetic weakness, no longer judiciously assimilating foreign practices to create a composite national character, but instead returning to the fallacy of monolithic national identity as they adopt another culture in its entirety: "then began the English to lay aside thir own antient Customes, and in many things to imitate French manners … asham'd of thir own."[90] Nietzsche uses the same example to criticize "we Germans of the present day who are more afflicted than other nations by [a] weakness of personality … we dwell even today in a careless inaccurate copy of French convention: a fact to which all our comings and goings, conversations, clothing and habitations bear witness. We thought we were retreating into naturalness, but what we were really doing was letting ourselves go and electing for ease and comfort and the smallest possible degree of self-discipline."[91] Milton suggests that the English aping of French customs was "a presage of thir subjection shortly after to that people, whose fashions and language they affected so slavishly."[92] This final regression paves the way for the Norman Conquest, the invasion that begins the next iteration of the eternal recurrence in which the Britons are trapped.

In the *History*, successive invasions gradually hybridize national identity, leaving any appeal to the notion of Englishness on very uncertain ground. If anyone in the *History* could be considered culturally and racially pure, it is the pre-Roman Britons, but they are evidently "progenitors not to be glori'd in." The Saxon Britons are shown to be no less dissolute, and the purported Saxon golden age, where an enlightened populace embraced justice and self-governance, is shown to be a falsehood. Milton's historicizing hammer shatters the icon of a British golden age. He shares Nietzsche's contempt for modern man, who "stands high and proud upon the pyramid of the world-process," by showing that history is not linear, but cyclical, and no real progress is made.[93] Certainly we find the occasional Nietzschean "great man" in the *History*, but they are soon expended, their legacies squandered by the morass of self-interested dwarves whose appetites are for apathy, not action.

In his survey of a millennium of British history, then, Milton saw not hope but despair. Nietzsche asserts that eternal recurrence is a nightmarish proposition to all but the Overman: "What, if some day or night a demon were to steal after you into your loneliest loneliness and say to you: 'This life as you now live it and have lived it, you will have to live once more and innumerable times more; and there will be nothing new in it, but every pain and every joy and every thought and every sigh and everything unutterably small or great in your life will have to return to you, all in the same succession and sequence … Would you not throw yourself down and gnash your teeth and curse the demon who spoke thus? Or have you once experienced a tremendous moment when you would have answered him: 'You are a god and never have I heard anything more divine.'"[94] Nietzsche claims that the Overman had not yet been attained, even in his own time, and we certainly do not find it in Milton.[95] While the *History* is shaped by eternal recurrence, the text closes not with an exultant affirmation of the desire to continue the cycle, but a desperate plea to escape "the Revolution of like Calamities."[96]

NOTES

1 Defoe, *The True-Born* Englishman *a Satyr*, 15.
2 Taussig, "Iconoclasm Dictionary," pages 21–32 in this volume.
3 Royle, *Civil War*, 259.
4 *Mercurius Aulicus*.
5 Shullenberger, "Nietzsche for Girls," 118.
6 McBride, "Tragic Philosophy," 25.
7 Milton, *Complete Prose Works*, 5.1.403. All Milton's prose works are quoted from the Yale edition, hereafter cited as "CPW" by volume and page number.
8 Ibid., 5.1:61.
9 Danto, *Nietzsche as Philosopher*, 198.

10 Nietzsche, "Twilight of the Idols," 66. Note that the italics here and in quotations throughout this essay are from the original text; no emphases have been added.
11 Ibid., 69.
12 Exactly what Nietzsche meant by the Overman is frustratingly unclear. In *Ecce Homo*, he claims the word Overman "designate[s] a type that has turned out supremely well, in antithesis to 'modern' men, to 'good' men, to Christians and other nihilists." Nietzsche, *Ecce Homo*, 41. From scattered references elsewhere in Nietzsche's corpus, it may be surmised that the Overman is one who rejects the otherworldliness of Christianity and engages in the "revaluation of all values." Nietzsche, "Twilight of the Idols," 31. While Nietzsche cites with approbation numerous great men throughout history – such as Julius Caesar, Cesare Borgia, and Napoleon – we are told that "never yet has there been an Overman." Nietzsche, *Thus Spoke Zarathustra*, 71.
13 Sedgwick, *Nietzsche*, 146; Nietzsche, *Thus Spoke Zarathustra*, 36.
14 Hill, *Puritanism and Revolution*, 52.
15 Winstanley, *Complete Works*.
16 The notion of cyclical time goes back to the Ancient Greeks, but it proved to be an enduring source of fascination in Milton's time. In 1657, Thomas Browne wrote to a friend about the astrological significance of the "ouroboros," a common symbol for the circularity of time, saying that it was "remarkable … that the Tail of the Snake should return into its mouth." Browne, *A Letter to a Friend*, 5. Nietzsche's descriptions of eternal recurrence often allude to the ouroboros; see: Yelle, "The Rebirth of Myth?," 175–202.
17 Pletsch, "History and Friedrich Nietzsche's Philosophy," 126.
18 Williams, "Nietzsche: *The Gay Science*," 145.
19 CPW, 5.1:4.
20 Nietzsche, "On the Uses and Disadvantages of History," 67.
21 CPW, 5.1:60.
22 Ibid., 5.1:40
23 Bett, "Nietzsche and the Romans," 8; Nietzsche, "Twilight of the Idols," 117.
24 CPW, 5.1:45.
25 Ibid., 5.1:46.
26 Ibid., 5.1:61; 85.
27 Ibid., 3:304, 302. For a recent discussion of Milton's attitude to the Irish rebels in the *Observations*, see my essay, co-authored with Maley, "'Is This the Region,'" 139–52.
28 CPW, 5.1:79.
29 Ibid., 5.1:32; Maley, "That Fatal Boadicea," 307.
30 Tacitus, *Tacitus on Britain and* Germany, 66.

31 CPW, 5.1:78.
32 Ibid., 5.1:80
33 Nietzsche, "Twilight of the Idols," 35.
34 CPW, 5.1:131.
35 Nietzsche, *Thus Spoke Zarathustra*, 89; CPW, 5.1:131.
36 Nietzsche, *Thus Spoke Zarathustra*, 46.
37 "Sub-Roman" refers to the period following the Roman withdrawal from Britain in the early fifth century CE.
38 CPW, 5.1:135.
39 Ibid., 5.1:124.
40 Ibid., 5.1:140.
41 Nietzsche, *Thus Spoke Zarathustra*, 36.
42 CPW 4:264.
43 Ibid., 5.1:124.
44 Ibid., 5.1:134. Milton is drawing here on Henry of Huntingdon, who took a similar view in his *Historia Anglorum* (1129). Seeing the Britons' "drunkenness, enmity, dispute, strife, envy, and other similar acts of wickedness … God determined to put an end to that people. And he immediately commanded the tools of his wrath, the Scots and Picts, who … rushed in on the Britons like wolves on lambs." Henry of Huntingdon, *Historia Anglorum*, 75–77.
45 Gildas, *The Ruin of Britain and Other Works*, 22.
46 CPW, 5.1:141.
47 Nietzsche, *Thus Spoke Zarathustra*, 236.
48 CPW, 5.1:142.
49 Ibid., 7:428.
50 Ibid., 5.1:148.
51 Ibid.
52 Ibid., 5.1:157.
53 Ibid., 5.1:189.
54 Ibid., 5.1:196.
55 Ibid., 5.1:236.
56 Ibid., 5.1:238, 244.
57 Booker, *Mercurius Coelicus*, quoted in Simpson, "The Apocalypse in *Paradise Regained*," 214.
58 Nietzsche, "On the Uses," 95.
59 CPW, 5.1:242 (italics added), 244.
60 Ibid., 5.1:259.
61 Ibid., 5.1:258, 259. This recalls Sallust's observation that "most armies are tempted by the removal of immediate danger to relax their standards of care and discipline." Sallust, *The Jugurthine War*, 123.

62 CPW, 5.1:259.

63 Nietzsche, *Thus Spoke Zarathustra*, 5; CPW, 5.1:253–4. Of course, Milton and Nietzsche had rather different opinions of the type of religious display that demonstrates debasement. For Milton, the Saxons' degeneracy is evidenced by their idolatry, "when Religion it self grew so void of sincerity, and the greatest shews of purity were impur'd." CPW, 5.1:259. For Nietzsche, any religious feeling whatsoever is evidence of debasement.

64 Ibid., 5.1:258.

65 Dzelzainis, "History and Ideology," 287.

66 Danto, *Nietzsche as Philosopher*, 201.

67 CPW, 5.1:257.

68 Nietzsche, "Twilight of the Idols," 108. The young Milton evidently viewed Alfred as heroic material, as he noted that "a heroic poem may be founded somewhere in Alfred's reign, especially at his issuing out of Edelingsey on the Danes; whose actions are well like those of Ulysses." Milton, *Works*, 18:243.

69 Milton, *Complete Shorter Poems*, 11.1699, 1704–5.

70 Riebling, "Milton on Machiavelli," 584.

71 Nietzsche, "On the Uses," 111; Zimmern, *Arthur* Schopenhauer, 151.

72 McBride, "Tragic Philosophy," 31.

73 Nietzsche, "Twilight of the Idols," 108.

74 Danto, *Nietzsche as Philosopher*, 197.

75 Rodger, *The Safeguard of the Sea*, 1:12.

76 CPW, 5.1:277.

77 Ibid., 5.1:278–9.

78 Ibid., 5.1:288.

79 Ibid. This movement of Danes into Normandy prefigures the Norman Conquest, which involved Normans conquering "none but antienter *Normans*."

80 CPW, 5.1:289.

81 Ibid., 4:666, 5.1:289; Danto, *Nietzsche as Philosopher*, 198.

82 CPW, 5.1:290.

83 While the mention of Alfred's haemorrhoids sits somewhat uneasily with the panegyric tone of the account of his life in the *History*, his "soreness in the Seige" is reported by authors far earlier than Milton. Asser, a ninth-century Welsh bishop who was asked by Alfred to write a biography of the king, mentions "piles, which kind of most troublesome affliction he had, even from early childhood." Asser, *The Medieval* Life of King Alfred the Great, 32.

84 Nietzsche, "Twilight of the Idols," 109.

85 CPW, 5.1:331, 332.

86 Ibid., 5.1:332.

87 Ibid., 5.1:335.
88 Ibid., 5.1:337.
89 Ibid., 5.1:339, 342.
90 Ibid., 5.1:377.
91 Nietzsche, "On the Uses," 80.
92 CPW, 5.1:377.
93 Nietzsche, "On the Uses," 80.
94 Nietzsche, *The Gay Science*, 273–4.
95 Nietzsche, *Thus Spoke Zarathustra*, 71.
96 CPW, 5.1:403.

BIBLIOGRAPHY

Asser. *The Medieval* Life of King Alfred the Great*: A Translation and Commentary on the Text Attributed to Asser*. Translated by Alfred P. Smyth. New York: Palgrave Macmillan, 2002.

Bett, Richard. "Nietzsche and the Romans." *Journal of Nietzsche Studies* 42 (2011): 7–31.

Booker, John. *Mercurius Coelicus, Sive, Almanack*. London, 1647.

Browne, Thomas. *A Letter to a Friend, upon Occasion of the Death of His Intimate Friend by the Learned Sir Thomas Brown, Knight*. London, 1690.

Danto, Arthur C. *Nietzsche as Philosopher*. New York: Columbia University Press, 1980.

Defoe, Daniel. *The True-Born* Englishman *a Satyr*. London, 1700.

Dzelzainis, Martin. "History and Ideology: Milton, the Levellers, and the Council of State in 1649." *Huntington Library Quarterly* 68 (2005): 269–87.

Gildas. *The Ruin of Britain and Other Works*. Edited and translated by Michael Winterbottom. Chichester: Phillimore, 2002.

Henry of Huntingdon. *Historia Anglorum: The History of the English People*. Translated by Diana Greenaway. Oxford: Clarendon Press, 1996.

Hill, Christopher. *Puritanism and Revolution: Studies in Interpretation of the English Revolution of the 17th Century*. London: Martin Secker and Warburg, 1995.

Maley, Willy. "That Fatal Boadicea: Depicting Women in Milton's *History of Britain*, 1670." In *Early Modern Nationalism and Milton's England*, edited by David Loewenstein and Paul Stevens, 305–30. Toronto: University of Toronto Press, 2008.

Maley, Willy, and Adam Swann. "'Is This the Region … That We Must Change for Heav'n?': Milton on the Margins." In *Region, Religion and English*

Renaissance Literature, edited by David Coleman, 139–52. Farnham, UK: Ashgate, 2013.

McBride, Joseph. "Tragic Philosophy and History in the Thought of Friedrich Nietzsche." *Maynooth Review* 5, no. 2 (1979): 25–33.

Mercurius Aulicus, Communicating the Intelligence and Affaires of the Court to the Rest of the Kingdome. The Seventeenthe Weeke. Oxford: Henry Hall, 1643.

Milton, John. *Complete Prose Works*. Edited by Don M. Wolfe. 8 vols. New Haven: Yale University Press, 1953.

– *Complete Shorter Poems*. Edited by Stella P. Revard. Translated by Lawrence Revard. London: Wiley-Blackwell, 2009.

– *Works*. Edited by Frank Allen Patterson. 18 vols. New York: Columbia University Press, 1931.

Nietzsche, Friedrich. *Ecce Homo: How One Becomes What One Is*. Translated by R.J. Hollingdale. London: Penguin, 2004.

– *The Gay Science, with a Prelude in Rhymes and an Appendix of Songs*. Translated by Walter Kaufmann. New York: Random House, 1991.

– "On the Uses and Disadvantages of History for Life." In *Untimely Meditations*, edited by Daniel Breazeale, translated by R.J. Hollingdale, 57–123. Cambridge, UK: Cambridge University Press, 1997.

– *Thus Spoke Zarathustra*. Edited by Robert Pippin. Translated by Adrian Del Caro. Cambridge, UK: Cambridge University Press, 2006.

– "Twilight of the Idols, or, How to Philosophise with a Hammer." In *Twilight of the Idols and Anti-Christ*, edited by Michael Tanner, translated by R.J. Hollingdale. London: Penguin, 2003.

Pletsch, Carl E. "History and Friedrich Nietzsche's Philosophy of Time." *History and Theory* 16, no. 1 (1977): 30–9.

Riebling, Barbara. "Milton on Machiavelli: Representations of the State in *Paradise Lost*." *Renaissance Quarterly* 49, no. 3 (1996): 573–97.

Rodger, N.A.M. *The Safeguard of the Sea: A Naval History of Britain, Vol 1: 660–1649*. London: Harper Collins, 1997.

Royle, Trevor. *Civil War: The Wars of the Three Kingdoms, 1638-1660*. London: Abacus, 2010.

Sallust. *The Jugurthine War and the Conspiracy of Catiline*. Translated by S.A. Handford. London: Penguin, 1963.

Sedgwick, Peter R. *Nietzsche: The Key Concepts*. London: Routledge, 2009.

Shullenberger, William. "Nietzsche for Girls." In *Milton's Legacy*, edited by Kristin A. Pruitt and Charles W. Durham, 116–35. Susquehanna, PA: Susquehanna University Press, 2005.

Simpson, Ken. "The Apocalypse in *Paradise Regained*." In *Milton and the Ends of Time*, edited by Juliet Cummins, 202–23. Cambridge, UK: Cambridge University Press, 2003.

Tacitus. *Tacitus on Britain and Germany: A New Translation of the* Agricola *and the* Germania. Translated by H. Mattingly. London: Penguin, 1948.

Taussig, Michael. "Iconoclasm Dictionary." This volume, pages 21–32.

Williams, Bernard. "Nietzsche: *The Gay Science*." In *Introductions to Nietzsche*, edited by Robert Pippin, 137–51. Cambridge, UK: Cambridge University Press, 2012.

Winstanley, Gerrard. *Complete Works*. Edited by Thomas N. Corns, Ann Hughes, and David Loewenstein. 2 vols. Oxford: Oxford University Press, 2009.

Yelle, Robert A. "The Rebirth of Myth? Nietzsche's Eternal Recurrence and Its Romantic Antecedents." *Numen* 47, no. 2 (2000): 175–202.

Zimmern, Helen. *Arthur Schopenhauer: His Life and Philosophy*. London: Longmans and Green, 1876.

KEYWORD

sexy, adj.[1]

Brit. /ˈsɛksi/, US /ˈsɛksi/
Origin: Formed within English, by derivation.
Etymons: sex *n.1*, -y *suffix1*.
Etymology: < sex *n.1* + -y *suffix1*. Compare slightly earlier sexful *adj.* orig. *US*

Whether something or someone is *sexy* is entirely subjective, and the equations for what constitutes sexiness are nearly endless. If magazines and television often portray what ought to be sexy on their front covers and in commercials, several Internet memes and hashtags – such as "porn for women," with a picture of a man vacuuming or doing the dishes, or #menwhodochores – demonstrate that "sexy" is as much an action imbued with symbolic value – here, of men's appreciation of or participation in domestic tasks, as well as a (potentially parodic) underlying feminist discourse – as an image of arousal. What then are the boundaries that separate "sexy" from "desire," "kink" from the (fifty) shades of "fetish," the socially acceptable from the transgressive forms of attraction and arousal? Similarly, the shift from "Sexy Ryan Gosling" to "Feminist Ryan Gosling" sees photos of the Canadian actor, often shirtless, staring into the camera, paired with "Hey Girl" comments, which, in the original meme, encourage the (female) viewer to empower herself by demanding respect and comfort. The shift to *feminist* Ryan Gosling, however, breaks down assumptions around what women might find sexy – in this case, more than an attractive image: here, the "Hollywood" image of (white, heterosexual) sexiness is conjoined with the clichéd "Hey Girl" pickup line, yet constantly undoes it by pairing it with quotations from literary theorists, critics, and philosophers, from bell hooks to Michel Foucault. And yet, this coopting of the normative "Hey Girl" meme became monetized when the founder of the Feminist Ryan Gosling Tumblr,[2] Danielle Henderson, signed a book deal for *Feminist Ryan Gosling: Feminist*

Theory (as Imagined) from Your Favorite Sensitive Movie Dude (Running Press, 2012).

"Sexy" is therefore an adjective that describes or modifies something else, and its etymons demonstrate that the suffix "y" is an appendage to the noun "sex," added to it as a derivative; and yet, "sexy" is, more often than not, the very instigator, a hope for gratification, the beginning of sex, and anything but an appendage (excluding, of course, the context of sex toys and fetishes!). In paronomastic terms, embedded within "sexy" is the very question: why ("y") sex? The answers are multiple, and they may not include pleasure, arousal, consent, or anything considered necessarily erotic or sensual. In fact, the adjectival form of "sex" can detach itself entirely from the sexual act – for example, exclusively as a means of procreation, or worse, rape.

Sexy is…

I. Containing or characterized by explicit sexual content; erotic, risqué; bawdy, saucy.

Sexy or dirty magazines, movies, and texting/sexting contain "explicit sexual content," but is it truly meant to be "contained," as this definition might suggest? An implicit need to not let "sexy" out, as though it were one of the evils in Pandora's box, alongside hope, is counterproductive to sexy's very essence, whether sexy means showing too much ankle or performing music videos in the nude. Those liable for the content produced often state that "viewer discretion is advised"; however, to exercise discretion originally meant *to discern* – that is, *to separate* – so perhaps we ought to discern, or separate, "sexy" from the dictionary's supposed synonyms above.[3] What is sexy may be erotic, but "bawdy" can displace sexiness through humour, and although Eric Barker's piece in *Time* magazine, "Science of Sexy: 5 Things That Can Make You Irresistible," states that "humour" is number one on their list – "funny people are smart, and smart is sexy"[4] – desire and arousal may be far removed from bawdy. Then there's "risqué" – the need to revert to French in order to denote shock and potential transgression. What is the *je ne sais quoi* in French that automatically makes risk sexy?

In your search for sexy, whatever your poison, you can certainly find it online, a space in which much of contemporary dating also takes place. Dating sites are therefore both sexy and a search for sex(y). The Tinderization of dating, as well as other social media and dating engines, have placed the iconic profile picture front-and-centre in this quest. One glance at the picture – and perhaps a brief look at your common interests – and you decide whether or not this person befits you, choosing to swipe right ("yes") or left (the sinister "no"). That picture, often a selfie, frequently contains many features of sexy: from vestimentary choices to the cosmetic adornment of the skin: piercings, tattoos, or the lack thereof. Dating profile pictures that appeal to an iconic form of "sexy" – plastered with makeup or Photoshopped to the point of severing any plausible ties to the referent – can, in a world where the real and virtual occasionally clash, lead to one failure after another – or, as A.R. Ammons writes in his short poem "Their Sex Life," to "One failure on / Top of another."[5] The selfie, with or without duck-face, has gained in popularity: it is the posted proof someone was somewhere, in front of a particular monument, with someone, or wearing something. It marks an event, or the banal, in a new form of representation of the world and how we engage with and document it. According to Jacques Rancière, this is a logic of "metamorphic images" inscribed into the quotidian, which can be used and remixed, thus becoming an "emblem of aesthetic modernity," and one in which modern subjectivity is fabricated and performed.[6] Similar to gender, we constantly perform and transform sexy; it is the mirror of our desires, the secretion of our fantasies.

1.a. Of a person (esp. a woman): sexually attractive or alluring; (also) sexually charged, highly sexed.

The archetype of sexually charged varies from culture to culture, and especially from epoch to epoch: from the creations of the Venus de Milo or Botticelli's Venus to Venus Williams and Priyanka Chopra; and from Greek *ephebes* and Byronic Don Juans to Paul Newman and Ryan Gosling and Ryan Reynolds. Alluring and tempting can quickly become synonymous with downfall, as Mr Deasy clumsily remarks in James Joyce's *Ulysses*, echoing the male gaze present in the very definition above: "A woman brought sin into the world. For a woman who was no better than she should be, Helen, the runaway wife of Menelaus, ten years the Greeks made war on Troy. A faithless wife first brought the strangers to our shore here, MacMurrough's wife and her leman, O'Rourke, prince of Breffni. A woman too brought Parnell low."[7] The siren call of patriarchy and late capitalism is certainly more deceiving and dooming than the chronology above, unsexy – as in "not sexually attractive" – as capitalism and patriarchy may be.

1.b. Of a personal attribute, thing, etc.: characterized by sexuality or sexual appeal; sexually attractive, stimulating, or suggestive.

When dealing with a particular "thing" "characterized by … sexual appeal," an implicit incantation is present, as the etymology for "fetish" calls forth "sorcery" and "charm."[8] Wallace Stevens, in "Peter Quince at the Clavier," narrates the attraction and repulsion of the voyeuristic observers (and in a garden!), who shudder and are pinched (*pizzicati*) by the joy they experience:

> Of a green evening, clear and
> warm,
> She bathed in her still
> garden, while
> The red-eyed elders, watch-
> ing, felt
>
> The basses of their beings throb
> In witching chords, and
> their thin blood
> Pulse pizzicati of
> Hosanna.[9]

Taboos participate in multifarious ways in the complexities of attraction, stimulation, and suggestion. The following list offers an incomplete record of some fetishes, normal or bewitching as they may seem: acrotomophilia: the arousal to amputees; actirasty: the arousal to the sun's rays; agalmatophilia: the arousal to statues; apotemnophilia: the arousal to oneself as an amputee; chasmophilia: the arousal to caverns, crevices, and valleys; cimacophilia: the arousal to falling down stairs; coprophilia: the arousal to feces; ephebophilia: the arousal to adolescents; katoptronophilia: the arousal to sex in front of mirrors; psellismophilia: the arousal to stuttering; savantophilia: the arousal to the cognitively impaired or developmentally delayed; urophilia: the arousal to urine or urinating on others; vorarephilia: the arousal to eating another person's body parts; zoophilia: the arousal to nonhuman animals.[10]

1.c. *colloq.* In extended use: appealing, stimulating; liable to excite interest.

This is the unsexy definition of "sexy." It excites "interest," and is therefore fashionable, en vogue, popular. What is it about fashion that hides or reveals sexiness or rubs sexy off onto everything it touches?

NOTES

1 *Oxford English Dictionary Online*, s.v. "sexy, adj.," http://www.oed.com/ (accessed 14 December 2016).

2 See: http://feministryangosling.tumblr.com.

3 *Oxford English Dictionary Online*, s.v. "discretion, n.," http://www.oed.com/ (accessed 4 March 2017).

4 Barker, "Science of Sexy."

5 Ammons, *The Really Short Poems*, 136.

6 Rancière, *Le Destin des images*, 1.

7 Joyce, *Ulysses*, 43.

8 *Oxford English Dictionary Online*, s.v. "fetish, n.," http://www.oed.com/ (accessed 4 March 2017).

9 Quoted in Ruth Miller and Robert A. Greenberg, eds., *Poetry: An Introduction* (London: Macmillan, 1981), 494.

10 These more iconoclastic fetishes are drawn from a list published in the *Huffington Post*: "46 Sexual Fetishes You've Never Heard Of."

BIBLIOGRAPHY

"46 Sexual Fetishes You've Never Heard Of." *Huffington Post*. US edition. 23 October 2013. http://www.huffingtonpost.com/2013/10/23/sexual-fetish_n_4144418.html (accessed 14 January 2017).

Ammons, A.R. *The Really Short Poems of A.R. Ammons*. New York: Norton, 1990.

Barker, Eric. "Science of Sexy: 5 Things That Can Make You Irresistible." *Time.com*. 12 June 2014. http://time.com/2859728/science-of-sexy-5-things-that-can-make-you-irresistible/ (accessed 15 February 2017).

Joyce, James. *Ulysses*. Edited by Declan Kiberd. London: Penguin Books, 2000.

Rancière, Jacques. *Le Destin des images*. Paris: La Fabrique éditions, 2003.

Stevens, Wallace. "Peter Quince at the Clavier." In *Poetry: An Introduction*, edited by Ruth Miller and Robert A. Greenberg. London: Macmillan, 1981.

Angela Toscano

8

The Idolatry of the Real: Form, Formula, and Happy Endings in Romance Literature

1. A Short History and a Definition of Popular Romance

Printed on pulp paperback, sold in supermarkets and airport gift shops, popular romance is immediately recognizable by its clinch covers: burly, half-naked men with long-flowing hair, clutching to their chests scantily clad women whose breasts burst from ripped bodices. This is the ubiquitous image of the romance novel; it is an iconic image – a symbol for low tastes, bored housewives, and the pornographic, all barely obscured by purple prose and the compulsory heterosexuality of the marriage plot. It is no surprise then that when scholars first began to examine romance novels, they did so with a suspicious and condemning eye. Early and seminal critical works by Janice Radway and Tania Modleski shared a concern about the effect romance novels have on their female readers.[1] These scholars affirmed what popular interpretation had already determined – that romance novels were "mass-produced fantasies,"accomplices to patriarchy, and purveyors of petty and petit bourgeois ideology.[2]

In the intervening thirty years since Radway first published *Reading the Romance*, the criticisms levelled against the genre – while varied – have essentially maintained two primary and reductive critiques. The first is that romances are mere fantasies; the second is that romances are formulaic. For detractors of the genre, the problem with romance is that it presents to women a false perception of the world, an illusion that incites in them a desire for relationships and love that cannot, does not, and will not exist. In short, romance is unrealistic. It presents and represents an impossible vision of the world. There are many problems with this conventional critique, but as my title would suggest, I am primarily interested in the specific criticism of popular romance that focuses on it as unrealistic and formulaic. This criticism asserts that what is literary – that is, what is idealized and idolized – are those texts that adequately convey reality to the reader. This idolatry of realism confines the purpose of literature to the depiction and representation of a "true," authentic vision of the external world, the world of objects. It is empirical. Setting aside the epistemological problem of the real, the fact that a work of literature can still be criticized for its lack of reality, its lack of accuracy, suggests that despite the problems of representation, reality or realism is considered a desirable, even a fundamental characteristic of "good" literature.

But popular romance is not only criticized for being unrealistic; it is also consistently criticized for its lack of originality, both in prose and plot – for being, in a word, formulaic. The phrase "purple prose," which often gets attached to descriptions of romance texts, conveys a gluttonous, decadent, overwrought, and campy language intended to create a sentimental response. The formulaic nature of romance, so the criticism goes, is emotional propaganda, engineered to force not only a reaction, but also a predetermined ideological conclusion in the reader. The accusation that these novels are mass-produced implies that authorship equates with manufacturing – as if all that a romance novelist need do is pick and choose from an assembly line the various tropes, clichés, and generic conventions required to build yet one more paperback product as fungible as any other mass-produced good. This derogatory view reifies the belief that what is literary must be original, both in language and plot.

What these criticisms of popular romance reveal is that Platonic and Aristotelian concepts of art still pulse beneath the surface of critical rhetoric, and seep through sophisticated discourses to affect how scholars define, categorize, and attribute value to a genre. As such, the Platonic problem of mimesis functions in literary criticism much like Freud's primal scene. For Plato, the ideal is the real. Art can only be an imitation of that reality. Representation is viewed with suspicion because it is at one or more removes from the real; consequently, it must either be repressed or incorporated into an understanding of poetics. This notion of representation has had a profound influence on how critics engage literature generally, but becomes most obvious when they encounter "trash" genres they do not value. As such, the demand for realism, whether it is in what is depicted (objects in the world) or how it is depicted (language on the page), is an idolatry of perspective. In *Meditations on Quixote*,[3] Ortega y Gasset says of realism that "we do not consider real what actually happens, but a certain manner of happening that is familiar to us,"[4] and that what is most familiar is not the "seen, but the foreseen."[5] Therefore, what is real is not just what can be predicted by natural laws, but how the story conforms to our expectations, whether experiential or ideological. Realism, then, is the representation of the accustomed, not the actual. Subsequently, "adventures are impossible in this new order of things."[6] What has become idolized or idolatrized is not gods or golden calves, but the empirical – matter made quantifiable, event made probable.

This is an idolatry that sees the happy ending – the happily-ever-after that concludes the romance and defines its form – as a symptom of a delusional worldview, as a failure to recognize the material world as it appears, as well as a failure to see beyond the discourse that shapes that appearance. This delusion is purportedly supported by clichés, pandering truisms, and narrative formulas. Romance, by definition, is a comic genre. Its form relies on the fulfillment of an adventure and the climatic marriage of the hero and heroine. In its oldest form, it is the genre of quests. Although love has always played a central role in this form, the lovers' courtship did not become the focus of the plot until the eighteenth century. However, despite this evolution, the genre remains structurally coherent, conforming to comic rather than tragic representations. It is this structure that is at odds with realism and originality. The romance novel, according to much of this criticism, is bad literature because it employs clichéd language to depict a world that, untrue to the facts of history, biology, and psychology, does not, will not, and cannot exist. It is a criticism as old as the genre itself, aimed at all of its variations from its earliest expressions as adventures to its current incarnation as a love story.

By the end of the eighteenth century, the novel had become the dominant prose form, defining itself against the romance through the use of parody. Voltaire satirized the classical romance's impossible adventures in *Candide*,[7] while *Don Quixote*[8] parodies not only the act of reading romance but also its plot and structure. Each of these criticisms is presented in these novels in narrative form. Cervantes's novel pivots on the romance's ability to corrupt the reader, making him unable to distinguish between fantasy and reality, while Voltaire mocks romance's unrealistic depiction of time and space. The joke is that time passes according to natural law for Candide and Cunégonde, who, unlike Leucippe and Clithophon, age and decay as would anyone who has journeyed so far and who has been through so much.[9] As for the eighteenth-century critics, they often demonstrated a hand-wringing concern over young women's reading habits, convinced that such activity would result in immodesty, disobedience, and ruin.[10]

Two hundred years later, the conversation has changed very little. Discussions about the potential of the *Twilight* series to normalize abusive and harmful romantic relationships illustrate that critics still see female readers as particularly susceptible to suggestion via the act of reading. British self-help author Susan Quilliam proclaims that "sometimes the kindest and wisest thing we can do for our clients is to encourage them to put down the books – and pick up reality."[11] As for romance's uniformity, this too has been a complaint trod again and again. In a telling review in *The New Republic* of Eva Illouz's new book *Hard-Core Romance*, William Giraldi says, "romance novels, like racists, tend to be the same wherever you turn."[12] Thus, these accusations assert that readers will be equally corrupted by the clichés regurgitated ad nauseam as they have been by the false consciousness of the world prevalent in romance's fantasy. Academic scholarship, too, has repeated these critiques, albeit with more nuance and care than its mainstream counterparts.

In their introduction to *New Approaches to Popular Romance*, Sarah S.G. Frantz and Eric Murphy Selinger outline the history of popular romance's contemporary criticism.[13] Beginning in the 1970s and continuing into the 1980s, the "first wave" of scholars viewed popular romance through the lens of second-wave feminism.[14] "The ideological focus of that first generation of scholars," argue Frantz and Selinger, "had its uses – but it also implicitly framed their work as an updated, feminist version of a very old, patently moralizing question: 'Are these books good or bad for their readers?'"[15] Literary scholars have abandoned this question when looking at other kinds of popular texts. Yet, it is "only with popular romance fiction" that "otherwise sophisticated academics continue to treat this question seriously."[16] Like any interpretive framework, these critical examinations have attended deeply to some aspects while disregarding other angles and attitudes. Romance, for this first wave, was understood as a collective genre. Individual texts were subsumed into the larger generic body, viewed less as unique instances of the form than as ideological artefacts – artefacts that, when unpacked, reveal how female readers navigate their desires within a patriarchal culture. So, though *Reading the Romance* offers a structural interpretation, it is in service to an argument about these texts as effects of culture. Radway is occupied with the way readers read romance, and the way that this reading shapes their understanding of themselves as women in late-twentieth-century America. Similarly, Modleski analyzed the formal aspects of the romance because, as she clarified in the introduction to the second edition of *Loving with a Vengeance*, she "felt it necessary to dig beneath the surface of supposedly escapist fare, to go beyond mere content analysis to the formal properties of the texts" in order to demonstrate "how romances' happy endings function to guide women's interpretation of enigmatic male behaviour and to alleviate female anxieties about men."[17] Here, too, structural analysis is subordinate to Modleski's concern with female readers working out ideological contradictions through their reading. In response to this first body of criticism, contemporary romance writers produced a 1992 book of essays entitled *Dangerous Men and Adventurous Women*, a collection that sought to counter the assumptions and interpretations made by Radway et al.[18] This endeavour's significance was twofold: first, it showcased romance writers' awareness of how the genre was censured within the critical discourse. Second, it actively attempted to contradict that censure by demonstrating how romance writers engaged consciously in shaping and crafting their own novels. Since then, there have been sporadic interventions into this conversation; but, until recently, there has been no sustained renewal of the popular romance field.

The recent renewal began with the publication in 2003 of Pamela Regis's *A Natural History of the Romance.*[19] This monograph represented a distinct break with previous critical interpretations. Unlike most of its predecessors, it took the position that genre romance was a cluster of individual texts with a shared narrative structure, rather than an aggregate, ideological object. That is, it focused on the texts themselves rather than their cultural and psychological effects. Since the publication of Regis's book, there has been a revival of critical interest in the romance genre. Scholarly articles and monographs published in the last ten years demonstrate a varied and rich set of methodologies and approaches to which my own thinking and scholarship is greatly indebted.[20] This paper attempts to intervene in this conversation by teasing out the implications of those original and persistent criticisms: romance fiction as unrealistic and formulaic.

2. Thesis Question

In Michael Taussig's "Iconoclasm Dictionary," he says: "Yet what is disturbing about the phallus is that it is the very model of the icon and of iconicity. What does it mean, then, to make an icon out of an icon, of the mother of all icons?"[21] Something similar could be said of the real; that it is the very model of the icon and iconicity. In its literary expression, it functions as the sacrosanct measure of "good" taste. As for romance, is it merely a corrupting and unrealistic cliché, or is it an iconoclastic rejection of the idol of realism? I contend that it is the latter and that the happily-ever-after conclusion that defines contemporary popular romance is emblematic of this alternative vision.

The happily-ever-after collapses into a single cliché both condemnations of the genre, namely that it is unrealistic and formulaic. It does this via the fantastic event that ends the action of the plot; and it does this through an expression of the genre's form, the phrase that literally ends fairy tales and metaphorically ends romance novels. The question then becomes: If the idol is realism, whether empirical or discursive, does the happily-ever-after function as an iconoclastic act? How does it shatter or break the icon of reality?

Furthermore, if romance is based upon two separate but connected ideas of the real – the material and the discursive, the abstract and the empirical – then what is the relationship between the two? Or, to be more precise, how does the representation of form become formulaic through the apparatus of conventional language?

3. Form and the Formulaic

There are two ways that realism is iconized as the ideal mode of representation: through the plot and through the prose. The first occurs at the level of the plot. It occurs in the story's claim to depict the material world as it is. This mode is concerned with the image, the carnal, and the empirical. It is about properly conveying the truth – the truth of nature, the truth of matter, the truth of human experience, and the truth of a transcendent real. Here, representation is highly Platonic. What is real and what realists wish to represent is the ideal form, and they do so by utilizing detail, accuracy, and verisimilitude. While Platonism's concept of the real has been diluted since the advent of *The Republic*, its continuing influence is testified to by the perpetual rebuke of romance as unreal.

In Jan Patočka's *Heretical Essays*, he says that "Platonic rationalism, the Platonic effort to subject even responsibility itself to the objectivity of knowledge, continues to affect the nether regions of Christianity."[22] Here, Patočka is delineating a fine point between what he sees as the transcendence at work in Plato versus the transcendence that he believes Christianity offers but has not yet achieved. However, I am interested in neither Patočka's treatment of religion nor of responsibility. Rather, I am interested in extrapolating upon his identification of Platonism as a defining paradigm for Western thought. His assertion is one that could equally be made about literary criticism. Platonism affects the nether regions of critical theory just as much as it does metaphysics, and literature, as a means to represent the real, still struggles in the shadow of this ideal.

According to Plato, poetry must be as authentic or as simple a representation as possible. The more it mimics, the more likely it is to represent an imitation, and the more it imitates an imitation, the more dangerous it is – dangerous precisely because, in this further imitation, the more it distances the readers from the real and, consequently, from virtue itself. When a genre is accused of being unrealistic, this accusation reasserts that the purpose of art is to assist in the moulding of character, the formation of virtue, and the transcendence of the soul. In order to be considered "good" literature, narrative must move in this direction, and it only has value insofar as it assists in this objective. As such, poetry must ascend out of the orgiastic, the pleasure of escapism, and into illumination.

This characterization of literature as a means through which to achieve virtue is most likely to resurface in those moments when poesy and prose undergo a categorical shift – that is, when the genre is being redefined. For example, in the *Biographia Literaria*, part of Coleridge's justification of his own poetic project is to make a clear distinction between the Imagination and the Fancy. Imagination works for Coleridge as a synthesizing force. It bridges the gap between the ideal form and its representation. As a poetic faculty, it works on language in a way that will get closer to that truth, whereas the Fancy works on language only as "its drapery."[23] Fancy is a mode of memory, one that works by the "law of association" – which is to say that it is metonymic.[24] Fancy is associated with fantasy and thus is at a greater distance from the real than other poetic modes. It is delightful, but insubstantial. The Imagination occupies the privileged position for Coleridge because he sees it as being closer to the real. The Fancy, and romance as its narrative expression, remains the lesser variant of the *ars poetica*. It becomes the Other against which the solidness of the real – i.e., the Imagination – is defined.

So, too, does the novel, literary fiction, etc., require an Other to be defined against in order to attain value. Even as all literature is an imitation of the real, some imitations are better than others, and the best imitations are those which can come closest to that real. In contrast, those novels, genres, and texts that depart from this end can only be regarded as decadent, debased, and demonic. By this measure of literature, romance can never achieve literary significance for it represents a far less real vision of the world. It repeats mere fancy. It creates fantasy – worlds that are not now, cannot be, nor ever were possible. As such, it is too far removed from the expected, the everyday, and the familiar to be considered a right representation. After all, if literature must represent, then it ought to represent the truth – i.e., the real; otherwise, one might conclude, it has no other purpose but pleasure.

This is not to suggest that romance is, in fact, either a realistic or a transcendent genre. Rather, it is to point out that the merit we ascribe to certain literary endeavours is still determined by a Platonic notion of mimesis that is itself intensely concerned with virtue. This is true whether we consider virtue to be transcendence writ large or merely the assumption that literature must educate as well as delight. For we don't actually think "to teach *and* delight,"but rather to delight in order to teach.[25] So rarely is delight seen as education's equal. Delight is secondary to education, just as fancy is secondary to imagination, and representation secondary to the real. This denigration of delight constitutes a suspicion of pleasure – more specifically, a suspicion of pleasure without a higher purpose. It favours the pleasure of certain kinds of literary interactions, those where pleasure aids the cultivation of the intellect and the enlightenment of the self. The pleasure romance provides, in contrast, is suspected of being pleasurable for the sake of pleasure itself, an unmediated enjoyment fecund with unbridled emotion. To paraphrase Northrop Frye, there is a dark suspicion that romance is mere entertainment[26] – a suspicion that this body of texts exists solely to incite solipsistic delight in the reader.

If romance's pleasure lies in its escapism – in its movement away from so-called illumination, away from the ordinary, the everyday reality, and into the mythic and the impossible – then this can only be a move away from truth, an escape from truth. As such, realistic depiction must not only virtuously attempt to render the real correctly, it must render it with the right language. So where the first critique is that romance is a fantasy and that fantasy imitates the world in a duplicitous and untrue way, the second critique is that romance's conventional language is insensible to the problem of signification. Romance's purple prose suggests that as a genre, it has no apprehension that any attempt at depicting the real is impeded by language. Prior to Modernism, realism in literature referred primarily to the content of the novel, the believable depiction of human action and reaction. After Modernism, the ability to depict the real was questioned with the increasing awareness of the mediated nature of language itself. As such, the second critique is suspicious of romance's use of language because convention and cliché behave as if it were possible to represent the real unmediated by the tangle of meaning. The real that is idealized is language. It is an iconizing of the word, the discourse, and the latent referent. Clichéd language in romance, then, is just as much of a fantasy as its plot. Or, as a friend of mine recently said of Trollope's *Framley Parsonage*, "his language is transparent. He wants me to fall into the story." The comment was intended to be pejorative. Clichés, tropes, and generic conventions all serve to make language transparent. They ask the reader to fall into the story and to ignore the problem of representing the world through the word. What is real is that language is a barrier between the subjective and the objective, the signifier and the signified. And what romance fails to do is to represent the problem of representation.

The "purple prose" of romance is as unrealistic in its transparency as it is in its disavowal of a mediated system of signs. Moreover, its transparency is an effect of its sentimental intentions. Here romance's impossibility is not the events that it depicts but how it depicts them. Clichés are unoriginal. Thus, a reader does not need to linger, to think, or to unpack a cliché in order for it to mean. Rather, the cliché insinuates its sense and its sensibility automatically. It is a language that is consumed. As such, clichés appear to be symptomatic of the very quality of mass production that Modleski accused romance novels of having. They perform as if meaning were clear, as if connotation were obvious, and as if the reader's visceral reaction alone were the object of the story. Thus, the formulaic language of the romance seems to the post-modern eye to be disingenuous, for to make language formulaic is to make it transparent, and thus obscure that it is a representation mediated by other representations. Furthermore, clichés are themselves a sign of romance's lack of originality. To be original, according to Derek Attridge, "is to create something that marks a significant departure from the norms of the culture matrix within which it is produced and received."[27] Cliché, on the other hand, is banal, tedious, and void of substance; it does not seek to depart from the culture matrix, but to regurgitate it. It is a worn-out, second-hand language. It reproduces rather than creates.[28] In this way, cliché is an imitation of metaphor.

Thus originality of language is to prose what verisimilitude is to plot. It functions as the aesthetic sign of the text's accuracy. By these terms, romance can only fail. It fails to be realistic because it does not depict the world as it is, nor does it describe the word as it cannot be. Rather, romance insistently and perpetually escapes from the real and the referent. It attempts, like Don Quixote, to access a world that no longer is nor ever was through the invocation of cliché. How, then, do we represent something that never existed and what is the effect of this on the narration and on the reader? More specifically, how and what does romance represent?

Ortega y Gasset calls the romance the epic diluted by history.[29] The epic occurs outside of historical time. It deals with events said to have happened, but not events that have happened in history. That is, epic deals in myth. The events of myth occur in our same world, but occur in a time before time. Where the historical past once was the present, the epic past never was; like a mirage in the desert, it is always receding into the horizon. As such, "the epic past is not our past,"[30] for "the men of Homer belong to the same world as their desires," while we do not.[31] Like Eden, the epic past is a world in which there is no distance between desire and actuality. It is "an ideal past"[32] in which desire can be fulfilled. History is the actual past and is marked by a longing that can never be satisfied. Thus, for Ortega, realism is no closer to the truth than the epic. Reality, the world of matter and material, is as equally inaccessible as the epic past. And romance is the narrative form that swings between epic and realism.

The mythic and the real collide in *Don Quixote*, when Don Quixote tries to enter Master Pedro's puppet show. In this episode, Don Quixote's madness makes him unable to recognize the fiction of theatre. He breaks the fourth wall, pushing his way on stage and crossing into the imaginary as if it were the actual. Thus, Ortega writes, "Don Quixote stands at the intersection where both worlds meet forming a bevelled edge."[33] Don Quixote is heroic because he is the figure that crosses over this threshold between the world of the romance and the world of realism. Yet, his attempt to cross the boundary between the mythic and the real fails, both in this episode and in the denouement of the novel. It is this attempt and its failure that make him a tragic figure. This is why we laugh at Don Quixote, even as we cheer for him. We, the readers, like the other characters in the novel, understand what Don Quixote refuses to acknowledge: that the mythic can never enter the real. Romance, though, awakens a desire for the mythic in the reader, a desire for a world other than this. Yet reality, and realism as its literary mode, consistently yanks the reader back from myth into the world of matter. Thus, Don Quixote becomes not just a model for the reader, but a tragic hero – tragic because he cannot exist in a world where his desires and his reality are one. His heroism, though, in Ortega's summation, is because "his life is a perpetual resistance to what is habitual and customary."[34] Don Quixote, in the final reckoning, is as noble as the heroes of Troy because he refuses to accept that what is now, always was and always will be.

5. Adventure Time

Where Ortega sees romance as the hinge between epic and realism, and its narration as a form of resistance to the reductive nature of reality, Bakhtin deals with romance's impossibility through the concept of adventure-time. Both Bakhtin and Ortega see romance as outside temporal time. While Ortega understands romance as a bridge between two different kinds of pasts, Bakhtin sees romance as a suspension of ordinary, linear time. He defines adventure-time as the period that occurs between the "flareup of [the hero's and heroine's] passion for each other" and "their successful union into marriage."[35] As such, adventure-time is no more part of historical time than the epic past. Since adventure-time is not temporal, the hero and heroine are subject neither to change and decay, nor to death and distance. In realism, their journey would be shaped by pragmatic elements: the miles between one city and another, the passage of time, old age, hunger, and sickness. Yet, through the suspension of linear time, their romance – i.e., their adventures – is conducted by chance and circumstance. Like an aria in an opera, adventure-time stops the clock for as long as it takes to say – or sing – all that is necessary. And just as time suspends for the duration of the romance, distance shrinks and expands as the adventure requires. Bakhtin is exclusively discussing romance in terms of the ancient Greek romances. In these, the cliché functions as the device which breaks the narrative out of reality into an "alien world,"[36] a world where time and space contract and dilate to allow for adventure. Thus, the real must be suspended in order for romance to take place.

6. The Actuary and the Gambler

High romance copes with the intrusion of the real, either by colliding realist and mythic narratives, as in *Don Quixote*, or by suspending linear time, allowing the mythic to take place, as in the ancient Greek romances. These accounts of romance's structure, though, focus on the genre before its shift to a more domestic variation where courtship, not adventure, is primary. However, this shift does not abandon the older structures. Rather, it reshapes them into a new, more commonplace setting. As such, contemporary romance must deal with depicting scenarios as equally unreal as a knight's quest – such as a satisfying sexual and romantic relationship for women. Yet, like its older form, it conveys this fantasy through the use of tropes – particularly the cliché. Why does this genre insist on depicting a mythic world using conventional language, particularly when its plot is focused not on gods or quests, but on domesticity? The answer is in its domestic setting. By shifting the focus to the quotidian, the older methods for incorporating myth no longer work precisely because adventure itself has become mythic. As such, contemporary popular romance must grapple with the real in a different way than prior instantiations. It can neither fully suspend linear time nor can it cross the boundary between the mythic and the real. This is due to it now being the genre in which love is the impossible elsewhere, not the mythic past. As such, it must find a third way to resist the disenchantment of the real.[37] Thus, popular romance seeks to *summon* myth, rather than represent it. It invokes the mythic into the material.

Exemplary of this is Jennifer Crusie's novel *Bet Me*.[38] This text consciously engages both with the unrealistic nature of the romantic love story and with the cliché language typically associated with that story. She adroitly employs not only the expected plot conventions, but cliché language. Unlike most romance novels, Crusie explicitly uses the phrase "happily ever after" to end her text. In so doing, she turns a phrase that both romance readers and critics use to describe the genre's conventional optimistic ending into the actual language of the text. In this novel, the fairy tale stands in for the mythic past, and therefore it is the fairy tale that must invade the contemporary world in which the novel is set. Crusie enacts this invasion through the use of allusions and the adaptation of clichéd expressions. We see this integration occurring at the novel's outset. The opening sentence is: "Once upon a time" – but, unlike a fairy tale, the text does not maintain an ahistorical temporality. It immediately positions the story in history – i.e., in the real world.

Set in a specific time (2004) and a specific place (Ohio), the opening scene is one that most any modern reader would already be familiar with: a yuppie bar and a breakup. "*Once upon a time*, Minerva Dobbs thought as she stood in the middle of a loud yuppie bar, *the world was full of good men.*

She looked into the handsome face of the man she'd planned on taking to her sister's wedding and thought, *those days are gone*."[39] This scene meets the realists' expectations in every way but one – the "Once upon a time." The gap between that traditional opening phrase and the actual events being depicted is discordant. It draws our attention to the very problem of realism. So in this short paragraph, Crusie abbreviates what Ortega relates in *Meditations on Quixote*: the epic past of myths and heroes, where desire and actuality meet and are manifest, is now inaccessible. The fairy tale cannot take place in the real world. For Minerva, it is as un-get-at-able a past as it was, according to Ortega, for the ancient Greeks – and as much as it is for any realist who can track back through history and never find either giants or true love.

The gap between once-upon-a-time and right now cannot be bridged. As such, there is no way for the narrative to get from the present to the happily-ever-after. Minerva cannot even get her boyfriend to stick around long enough to take her to her sister's wedding, and this is a sign to her, as well as to the reader, that the fairy tale is impossible. Even in fiction, it only exists in fiction. For Minerva, as much as for the reader, the happily-ever-after is impossible – no matter how many times it is uttered. Crusie plays with the modern sensibility that the fairy tale is not only impossible, but dangerous to an ordinary and everyday lived experience. Throughout the text, she has several characters theorize about what love is and how it functions in the real world.[40] These characters support their ideas with psychology, physics, grim realism, and practicality. Yet, their explanations always seem to fall short of what is actually happening in the plot, nor are they adequate answers for the reader.

Tellingly, Minerva works as an actuary. It is her job to compile and analyze statistics on mortality and accidents. She is a keeper of records, an accountant of the accounts of the real. She quantifies and measures what is possible in the world. So when she falls in love with Cal, the hero, Minerva's first move is to calculate the risk. There is no data to support that Cal is a good bet. He is too handsome, too charming, and has a reputation for being a heartbreaker. Unlike Minerva's ex-boyfriend, Cal does not seem like a "sensible choice."[41] Neither character nor history would suggest that Cal and Minerva could ever make it as a couple, could ever have a happily-ever-after, for Cal is not only a risk, but a risk-taker – a gambler. To be in love with him, to date him, and to have a relationship with him end well seems to Minerva as utterly improbable as the appearance of a fairy godmother, her desire to be with Cal as distant and unlikely as the return of Odysseus. The obstacle to the romance is structural. It is in the gap between what Minerva wants and what she believes is possible. And yet, despite acknowledging its improbability, she wants this love to be true.

The only character in Crusie's novel not proclaiming a theory of love based on the real is Minerva's friend Bonnie. She alone insists not just on the fairy tale's possibility but on its imminent manifestation, its actual presence in everyday life. "What do you want, Min? … If life were a fairy tale, if there truly was a happy ending, what would you want?"[42] she asks at one point. This question forces Minerva not only to confront her desire for the fairy tale but to allow that desire to exist without qualification – without recourse to a pragmatic vision of the real. "Stop it … God, you can't even dream without qualifiers."[43] The fairy tale for Bonnie is not a theory about love. It does not describe what happens or what is. Rather, it is immanent and impending. The risk, the gamble, is trusting in its eventual appearance. Much like conceptions of the divine, the myth is always in the process of invading the material.

7. Liturgical Time, or An Invocation

For Bonnie, as for the novel itself, realism is as much of a fiction as romance; it is a mode that is as much a cliché as the language of the fairy tale. This is because realism insists upon a true and accurate representation, whether through detailed depiction of the material world or via a meta-discourse that foregrounds language. But romance is attempting neither of these forms of narration. It has no interest in recounting the real, materially or discursively. Rather, romance ritualizes language through the use of the cliché in order to invoke, *not* to represent. The purpose of romance is neither to describe nor to depict, but to call forth. Cliché, then, is not a failure to understand the problem of representation or the reality of the material world. It is a liturgical act, a ritual speech. It is a-representational. In the repetition of the gestures, of the actions, of the words, romance attempts to summon into the present mythos – to manifest myth into reality. And in the retelling and re-performance of this form, the invocation alters the world of the real, infecting it and invading it with the impossible.

This is a liturgical language, a ritual narrative. Like liturgy, it suspends linear time, opening up a space for the divine to enter the realm of the human. In this, it combines both Ortega's and Bakhtin's sense of the romance. What's distinct, though, is that liturgical time does not simply allow for adventure to happen in the moment but intends for its continuance beyond the end of the story. As such, liturgical time is not merely an utterance; it is a rite. It demands a reciprocal encounter between the author and the reader, the hero and the heroine, the priest and the supplicant. So, as with the Catholic mass, the repetitive language may invoke the presence of God (or mythos) but the transfiguration is only complete with the ingestion by the supplicant of the material transformed by the intangible. Like the wafer, myth is reified in the real and consumed by the reader.

8. Happily Ever After: An Apology of the Real

The use of the cliché to transfigure the material world by invoking myth is an iconoclastic act. It is iconoclastic in its destruction of the hegemonic hold of realism. When the story ends in happily-ever-after, it acts as an apology for the real. It does so because it is a turn away from logic, from a rational logos toward a different paradigm – a paradigm of relation rather than description. Thus, the clichéd language and plot devices required by the generic conventions of popular romance, particularly the happy ending, tell a different story about literature than one that is preoccupied with the representational. Romance refuses the singular, linear perspective of realism and instead enacts encounters – encounters between logos and mythos, encounters between self and other, encounters between the material and the intangible. Encounters that are invoked through the liturgy of cliché and that demand a response, not a representation. After all, what is love except an encounter and a cliché?

NOTES

1 Radway, *Reading the Romance*; and Modleski, *Loving with a Vengeance*.
2 Modleski, *Loving with a Vengeance*, xxix.
3 Ortega y Gasset, "From *Meditations on Quixote*," 271–93.

4 Ibid., 280.

5 Ibid.

6 Ibid., 282.

7 Voltaire, *Candide.*

8 Cervantes, *Don Quixote.*

9 Tatius, *Leucippe and Clitophon.* This is just one example of many. Voltaire is parodying not only the ancient Greek romances *Daphnis and Chloë*, *Aethiopika*, etc., but the very popular French romances exemplified by the novels of Madeleine de Scudéry.

10 For more on this, see: Bray, *The Female Reader*; and Pearson, *Women's Reading in Britain.*

11 Alison Flood, "Mills & Boon blamed for sexual health problems," *Guardian*, 7 July 2011, http://www.theguardian.com/books/2011/jul/07/mills-and-boon-sexual-health-problems (accessed June 2014).

12 Giraldi, "Finally, an Academic Text."

13 Frantz and Selinger, *New Approaches.*

14 Regis, "What Do Critics Owe the Romance?"

15 Frantz and Selinger, *New Approaches*, 5.

16 Ibid.

17 Modleski, *Loving with a Vengeance*, xvi.

18 Krentz, *Dangerous Men.*

19 Regis, *A Natural History.*

20 In addition to the work of Eric Selinger, Sarah Frantz, and Pam Regis, I'm also indebted to the work of: Fletcher, *Historical Romance Fiction*; Teo, *Desert Passions*; Kamblé, *Making Meaning*; Vivanco, *For Love or Money*; as well as the *Journal of Popular Romance Studies*, An Goris, Jonathan Allan, Jodi McAlister, and many others.

21 Taussig, "Iconoclasm Dictionary," 31.

22 Patočka, *Heretical Essays*, 110.

23 Coleridge, *Biographia Literaria*, 174.

24 Ibid., 167.

25 Sir Philip Sydney, "Defence of Poesy," in *Sir Philip Sydney: The Major Works*, ed. Katherine Jones-Duncan (Oxford: Oxford University Press, 2002), 217.

26 The original quote is as follows: "Dickens fared rather better: he too was darkly suspected of being a mere entertainer." Frye, *The Secular Scripture*, 24.

27 Attridge, *The Singularity of Literature*, 35.

28 I have further developed this idea of cliché as invocation and performative utterance in *The Liturgy of Cliché: Ritual Speech and Genre Convention in Popular*

Romance, paper presented at the conference "Popular Romance in the New Millennium," McDaniel College, Westminster, MD, November 2011).

29 Ortega y Gasset, "From *Meditations on Quixote*," 274–82.

30 Ibid., 274.

31 Ibid., 286.

32 Ibid., 274.

33 Ibid., 282.

34 Ibid., 286.

35 Bakhtin, *The Dialogic Imagination*, 89.

36 Ibid., 101.

37 My use of the word "disenchantment" alludes to Charles Taylor's *A Secular Age*, where he says: "People lived in an 'enchanted' world. This is perhaps not the best expression; it seems to evoke light and fairies. But I am invoking here its negation, Weber's expression 'disenchantment' as a description of our modern condition." Taylor, *A Secular Age*, 25.

38 Crusie, *Bet Me*.

39 Ibid., 1. Emphasis in the original.

40 Eric Murphy Selinger discusses these theories of love in his paper "Nothing but Good Times Ahead." He says, "each of these [theories] turns out, on inspection, to account for the facts at hand, but only Beth's is offered to the reader as able to transform Min's future, precisely because it is based on Min allowing herself to articulate her actual desires for that future."

41 Crusie, *Bet Me*, 4.

42 Ibid., 276.

43 Ibid., 279.

BIBLIOGRAPHY

Attridge, Derek. *The Singularity of Literature*. New York: Routledge, 2004.

Bakhtin, M.M. *The Dialogic Imagination: Four Essays.* Edited by Michael Holquist. Translated by Caryl Emerson and Michael Holquist. Austin, TX: University of Texas Press, 1981.

Bray, Joe. *The Female Reader in the English Novel: From Burney to Austen*. New York: Routledge, 2009.

Cervantes, Miguel de. *Don Quixote*. Translated by Edith Grossman. New York: HarperCollins, 2003.

Coleridge, Samuel Taylor. *Biographia Literaria or Biographical Sketches of My Literary Life and Opinions*. Edited by George Watson. 1848. London: Dent, Everyman's Classics, 2018.

Crusie, Jennifer. *Bet Me*. New York: St Martin's Press, 2004.

Fletcher, Lisa. *Historical Romance Fiction: Heterosexuality and Performativity*. Hampshire, UK: Ashgate, 2008.

Frantz, Sarah S.G., and Eric Murphy Selinger, eds. *New Approaches to Popular Romance Fiction: Critical Essays*. Jefferson, NC: McFarland, 2012.

Frye, Northrop. *The Secular Scripture: A Study of the Structure of Romance*. Boston: Harvard University Press, 1978.

Giraldi, William. "Finally, an Academic Text Devoted to '50 Shades of Grey.'" *New Republic*, 19 May 2014. http://www.newrepublic.com/article/117814/50-shades-grey-academic-study-feminist-point-view (accessed June 2014).

Kamblé, Jayashree. *Making Meaning in Popular Romance Fiction: An Epistemology*. London: Palgrave Macmillan, 2014.

Krentz, Jayne Ann, ed. *Dangerous Men and Adventurous Women: Romance Writers on the Appeal of the Romance*. Philadelphia: University of Pennsylvania Press, 1992.

Modleski, Tania. *Loving with a Vengeance: Mass Produced Fantasies for Women*. 2nd edition. New York: Routledge, 2007.

Ortega y Gasset, José. "From *Meditations on Quixote*." In *Theory of the Novel: A Historical Approach*, edited by Michael McKeon, 271–93. Baltimore: Johns Hopkins University Press, 2000.

Patočka, Jan. *Heretical Essays in the Philosophy of History*. Translated by Erazin Kohak. Edited by James Dodd. Chicago: Open Court, 1999.

Pearson, Jacqueline. *Women's Reading in Britain, 1750–1835: A Dangerous Recreation*. Cambridge, UK: Cambridge University Press, 1999.

Radway, Janice A. *Reading the Romance: Women, Patriarchy, and Popular Literature*. Chapel Hill: University of North Carolina Press, 1984, 1991.

Regis, Pamela. *A Natural History of the Romance Novel*. Philadelphia: University of Pennsylvania Press, 2003.

– "What Do Critics Owe the Romance? Keynote Address at the Second Annual Conference of the International Association for the Study of Popular Romance." *Journal of Popular Romance Studies* 2, no. 1 (2011). http://jprstudies.org/wp-content/uploads/2011/10/JPRS2.1_Regis_Keynote.pdf (accessed July 2014).

Selinger, Eric Murphy. "Nothing But Good Times Ahead: Romance Fiction, Learned Optimism, and 'Authentic Happiness.'" Paper presented at the Popular Culture Association/American Culture Association national conference, San Francisco, March 2008.

Tatius, Achilles. *Leucippe and Clitophon*. Translated by Tim Whitmarsh. Oxford: Oxford University Press, 2009.

Taussig, Michael. "Iconoclasm Dictionary." This volume, pages 21–32.
Taylor, Charles. *A Secular Age*. Boston: Belknap Press of Harvard University Press, 2007.
Teo, Hsu-Ming. *Desert Passions: Orientalism and Romance Novels.* Austin, TX: University of Texas Press, 2013.
Toscano, Angela R. "The Liturgy of Cliché: Ritual Speech and Genre Convention in Popular Romance." Paper presented at the conference "Popular Romance in the New Millennium," McDaniel College, Westminster, MD, November 2011.
Vivanco, Laura. *For Love or Money: The Literary Art of the Harlequin Mills & Boon Romance*. Penrith, UK: Humanities-Ebooks, 2011.
Voltaire. *Candide*. Translated by Robert M. Adams. 2nd edition. Norton, 1991.

Helen Hester

9

Vampire, Cannibal, Iconoclast: Displacing Genitality and Desecrating Genre

Introduction: Pornography and Iconoclasm

This article aims to explore the centrality of iconoclasm to the concept of the pornographic and, in doing so, proffers a seemingly somewhat perverse argument. Drawing evidence from a number of examples from the world of adult entertainment, I will suggest that the desecration of popular cultural objects is as important to certain forms of pornography as the explicit representation of sexual acts. Pornography, I will argue, cannot simply be defined by an interest in the graphic depiction of sexual organs and sexual acts, but must rather be conceptualized as a genre with an investment in a far more diverse set of factors, including the iconoclastic (mis)use of other cultural forms. Indeed, it is my contention that an overt interest in the iconoclastic lies at the heart of the genre's identity and self-image, to the extent that (within certain marginal examples) we witness a preoccupation with iconoclasm that comes to surpass, displace, and undermine pornography's apparently definitional interest in sex.

Before I allow my argument to progress any further, I think it is important that I remark upon my understanding of some of the key terms that I will deploy here. My usage of the iconoclastic as a concept, in particular, warrants some initial clarification. Iconoclasm's links with visual imagery make it a particularly useful idea when it comes to critically interrogating the topic of pornography – especially when one considers the fact that pornography as a contemporary representational genre is currently more often associated with visual rather than literary cultures. As the critic Jennifer Wicke remarks, written pornographic texts have perhaps become "less visible as targets of critique or analysis because the prevailing figure for pornographic consumption lies so squarely in the arresting of the visual, in the enthralled spectatorship of the eye."[1] When discussing the violations enacted within pornography, then, the idea of an iconoclastic breaking of images may be particularly pertinent.

More importantly for our purposes, however, is the idea that much of the disruptive power of the iconoclastic stems from its links with the concept of transgression. After all, as the *Oxford English Dictionary* suggests, iconoclasm is a term that refers not merely to the destruction of images but also, and especially, to the "destruction of images and pictures set up as objects of veneration."[2] There is an element of violation at play in iconoclasm – an element of the deliberate and irreverent misuse of those representations which are considered to be particularly sacred or which are cherished in some way. This idea that desecration might be central to iconoclasm is of course reminiscent of the notion that prohibition lies at the heart of any act of transgression: as Georges Bataille puts it, a "prohibited act invites transgression, without which the act would not have the wicked glow which is so seductive."[3]

Iconoclasm, then, can largely be thought of as revolving around the defilement of precisely those representations which are widely respected or, at least, imbued with acknowledged cultural significance. It is for this reason that the idea of transgression pervades much of my argument here, and for this reason that much of my discussion is dedicated not to the *literal* destruction of cultural texts but to the transgressive appropriation or misuse of such texts. How does adult entertainment work to utilize the wider culture? What other cultural forms does it incorporate into its pornographic project, upon what other territories might it infringe, and in what ways does it transgress the conventional distinctions of genre? These are the questions that will concern me here.

A tendency toward cultural appropriation makes pornography – another key concept within this discussion, and already a notoriously elusive term to pin down – particularly difficult to characterize. Indeed, rather than attempting to offer an authoritative definition of the term, this article will in some ways be talking about various distinct (if related) understandings of the pornographic, and about the sometimes uncritical slippages that take place between them within contemporary discourse. On the one hand, pornography can viewed as something largely synonymous with the genre of adult entertainment; that is, as Bernard Arcand puts it, as "a commercial enterprise entirely dedicated to pleasure and enjoyment," and "a mass-market product based exclusively on sexual stimulation."[4] However, the idea of the pornographic can also be seen to function in a broader and less specific manner at times, attaching itself to somewhat less expected representations and ideas.

As we shall see, the word "pornographic" frequently operates as an adjectival label applicable to an increasingly wide range of cultural phenomena, including (perhaps surprisingly) material that might not be widely considered sexually explicit. This can be related to the genre's insistent iconoclastic tendencies. In this article, then, I will endeavour to demonstrate not only that pornography (in its photorealistic, moving image form) is currently somewhat fixated with drawing upon the content and conventions of other representational regimes, but also that it to some extent *transgresses itself*. Pornography can be seen as being perversely willing to sacrifice its own generic identity in order to be better able to indulge in iconoclasm.

Adult Entertainment as Cultural Vampire

There is much evidence to support the idea that pornography iconoclastically uses and abuses the culture of which it is a part, for it frequently displays a somewhat vampiric relationship with other (often seemingly incompatible) genres and forms. As Stephen Maddison notes, contemporary examples of the adult entertainment genre can be seen to "combine gonzo hand-held camera work and low-tech style with conventions derived from slasher movies, the reality TV genres of *Jackass* stunts and gross-out and fly-on-the-wall documentaries."[5] Pornography, Maddison is suggesting here, can be seen to utilize the representational conventions of other genres – genres which, although displaying a marked interest in the human form, do not typically prioritize the sexual body and its performances over other forms of corporeality.

Maddison's focus is largely upon those rare and marginalized examples of adult entertainment that can be seen to imitate certain facets of the slasher film genre. Another relevant example, however, is the *Cocktails* series, produced by the controversial adult entertainment company Extreme Associates.[6] This series, and others like it, recalls the gross-out style of programming that became so popular on youth and music television outlets during the first years of the new millennium. It depicts porn actresses drinking abject bodily substances, such as semen, saliva, and vomit, in a manner that recalls famous affecting moments from the *Jackass* franchise, such as cast member Ehren McGhehey eating urine-doused snow in 2002's *Jackass: The Movie* or Dave England consuming a regurgitated omelette during a scene from 2009's *Jackass: The Lost Tapes*. Interest in the body is, in the case of *Cocktails*, apparently displaced from the realm of the arousing to the realm of the repulsive, as reflected by elements of apparent generic slippage. There is a sense in which the featured actresses are there not to experience pleasure or to perform their arousal, but to be put through an endurance test of the kind so frequently signed up to by the performers in *Jackass*.

Indeed, the subterranean connections between the genres of adult entertainment and the stunts-and-pranks format of some reality television is made even more explicit by websites such as *Fear Factor Fuck* (which was renamed *Sicko Games* after the makers of the NBC reality show *Fear Factor* contacted the site regarding trademark infringement), and *Porn Jackass*, which, as the homepage declares, offers "CUNNING XXX STUNTS BY STUNNING XXX CUNTS."[7] As one critic from the adult entertainment reviews website *Rabbit's Reviews* states, the material here combines explicit depictions of sexual acts with scenes of less sexual bodily feats such as women inserting fireworks into bodily orifices or being shot at by paintball guns. The reviewer's verdict on this rather peculiar fusion of content is, tellingly, that it is "fun to browse through, but not all of it will get your dick hard."[8] It is porn, in other words, but it is not necessarily sexy.

In these examples, the conventions of a seemingly distinct genre are being appropriated by adult entertainment to the extent that some of porn's own typical conventions – namely "hotness" or the ability to provoke a state of genital sexual arousal – can be seen to be displaced, or to no longer apply.

From Pranks to Parody

A further example of porn's generic vampirism can be found in adult entertainment's famous interest in direct parody as a vehicle for representing hardcore sex acts. As a quick Google search will demonstrate, everything from *Curb Your Enthusiasm* to *The Big Lebowski* has received the porn treatment. As long as it is sufficiently recognizable and culturally visible, it seems, every genre and text is available for a pornographic reimagining. Emily Shelton refers to this pornographic sub-category as "the 'pornedy': a hybrid mode that pornographically lampoons a mainstream cultural product or media event."[9] While critics such as Nina K. Martin have questioned the extent to which such films really do hybridize differing representational conventions – she suggests that many "do not retain a connection to their parodied text beyond their title" and that "they do not undermine the conventions of porn but *solidify and reify* those conventions by highlighting their ubiquitous presence"[10] – I believe that this idea of the "pornedy" represents both a reimagining of mainstream cultural conventions and a playful recalibration of what constitutes the pornographic.

The porn parody is a particularly clear example of the transgression of generic boundaries, of course, because the pornographic films in question can be seen to intertextually appropriate the aesthetics and thematic content of pre-existing cultural objects in order to transform them into adult entertainment. As Christopher Rosen notes in his discussion of *The Big Lebowski – A XXX Parody* [*sic*], for example, the parody "looks exactly like the original. Save for a few line swaps (the John Goodman stand-in chides The Dude for using colloquialisms for semen and not Asian Americans), this version of *The Big Lebowski* plays it mostly straight."[11] In this instance, we see that the presence of hardcore sexual performance works to transform a mainstream film into something rather more ex-centric. To quote Shelton, "in the case of a movie or television show, the pornedy aims not only to contaminate the complacency of popular taste, but also intentionally to subvert any boundary that implicitly exists between 'legitimate' and 'illegitimate' culture."[12] Pornography, then, can be thought of as iconoclastically invading alternative generic territory through parody, and as thereby destabilizing conventional cultural categories.

Adult entertainment's investment in this kind of appropriation can even be seen to extend to forms seemingly irreconcilable with its own customary practices. The live-action porno versions of animated texts such as *Avatar* and *The Simpsons*, for example, represent some particularly intriguing examples of porn's generic vampirism.[13] A key convention of photorealistic moving-image adult entertainment is a preoccupation with seeming to be authentic – with seeming to provide the viewer with representations of real sexual acts and genuine sexual pleasure. As Linda Williams argues, the genre "attempts to solicit what it can never be sure of: the out-of-control confession of pleasure, a hard-core 'frenzy of the visible.'"[14] But in this kind of parodic example, a focus upon generating an authenticity effect co-exists with the use of characters best known as animated entities. The real and the fantastical are thrown into a strange kind of tension here, as the conventions of photorealistic pornographies are forced to jostle and co-exist with more cartoonish elements.[15] This is clearly represented by one of the taglines used on the *Simpsons: The XXX Parody* webpage: "Ever Wonder What The Simpsons Would Look Like In Real Life? Or Better Yet.. [*sic*] If They Were FUCKING???"[16]

These examples can certainly be thought of as being transgressive in some (albeit limited) ways. Transgression is, after all, about the violation of boundaries, and here the boundaries between distinct realms of representation are very obviously being compromised and temporarily broken down. The generic integrity of certain cultural categories is violated and undermined via the operations of hybridization, and certain culturally recognizable forms are appropriated and reimagined. The iconoclastic operations of breaking and remaking – or, rather, in this case, breaking *by* remaking – are, I would suggest, very much in evidence within these examples. But this mischievous appropriation of other genres is certainly not the most powerful or convincing example of porn's iconoclasm.

While *The Simpsons* is clearly a beloved Western cultural phenomenon, it could hardly be described as an object of veneration, and subversively appropriating it may warrant little more than a wry smile or a roll of the eyes. This example of generic transgression is, in other words, a relatively insignificant act of boundary crossing – one unlikely to provoke profound unease. There are, however, some far clearer examples of the operation of iconoclasm within adult entertainment. Indeed, one of the things that first prompted me to consider pornography as an iconoclastic genre was a certain linkage, traceable at least back to the First World War, between pornography and documentary accounts or images of war.[17] My thinking was particularly informed by several attempts to reimagine the events of the War on Terror, including the Abu Ghraib scandal, as pornographic scenarios.[18] I want to focus here upon the particular example of *Gag Factor 15* – the fifteenth instalment of a noughties heterosexual porn series centred upon rough deep-throat fellatio – which uses the infamous events of Abu Ghraib as material and as direct inspiration.

Cultural Violations and Generic Transgressions

Distributed by JM Productions in 2004, the year that the Abu Ghraib prisoner abuse scandal broke, the opening scene of *Gag Factor 15* not only makes explicit reference to the controversy but also attempts to co-opt it for the purposes of sexual arousal. The scene opens on a group of five actors, all apparently Caucasian yet all wearing the same version of an Arab terrorist costume: long, loose-fitting black garments with black head and face coverings that leave only the eyes exposed. The man positioned down stage right "rants angrily at the camera in gibberish intended to sound Arabic," while the man next to him translates this as: "Listen to us now, for you will be sorry, you Western devils. We will do to your women what you have done to our men. Look what you have done to my fellow brother."[19]

At this point, Polaroid pictures restaging some of the more iconic Abu Ghraib images are briefly shown to the camera. They depict the scene's female star, Ashley Blue, in the Private First Class Lynndie England role, dressed in a khaki t-shirt and camouflage-print combats, giving the camera the thumbs up and resting her booted foot on the back of a male prisoner, who is naked but for his black hood and white socks. Over one of the photos is scrawled the message "We conquered you." In another image, Blue is shown holding the end of a leash attached to the prisoner's neck, in an obvious imitation of one of the most infamous images to emerge from the prisoner camp.[20] The dialogue continues: "The Western scum will pay. You have degraded our people, and now we will degrade yours. The streets will spill over with spit, semen will flow from your pores, and you will know the true wrath of the Arab world." The ringleader and the translator then step aside to reveal Blue, dressed in the same military attire, seated on the floor behind them. One of the terrorist figures brandishes a sword, as if threatening Blue with decapitation, before the hardcore action of multiple rough blowjobs begins.

In this example, I would contend, the operations of iconoclasm are far more obvious. Not only are the boundaries between the cultural forms of adult entertainment and documentary or war reportage transgressed here, but images that are invested with huge cultural importance in the West are desecrated, and appropriated for the sake of generating an affective charge. Indeed, the sheer inappropriateness of using then-recent events of torture and murder as the inspiration for a pornographic scenario may have been part of the appeal for JM Productions. Certainly, it would appear that the concept of transgression is crucial to any attempt to understand how and why these culturally valued images are evidently so appealing for utilization and defacement within a pornographic context.

JM Productions has built its reputation on producing controversial content, and the idea of ostentatious vulgarity seems to be central to its brand identity. This is reflected not only in the content and the concept behind the series, but also in paratextual features such as the series' logo and DVD box covers. The brand tends to deploy garish colours and gross-out imagery, such as photographs that include details like spit bubbles or globules of mucus. The *Gag Factor* logo and branding, meanwhile, utilize a white, viscous-looking font, a cartoonish image of freshly ejaculated semen. In this way, a wilfully crude and tasteless aesthetic is foregrounded – one that seems designed to provoke reactions of bourgeois disgust. *Gag Factor 15* seems intent on continuing the brand's usual tastelessness, incorporating the still-raw events surrounding Abu Ghraib into its pornographic purview with politically incorrect glee.

The opening scene despoils the original images of torture by recontextualizing them, thereby violating those normative standards of decency which require that war, particularly its atrocities and its victims, be treated with an appropriate level of respect and reverence. The fact that this scene – and indeed the action of purchasing, watching, and enjoying this scene – contravenes our society's deeply felt need for respectful seriousness when it comes to discussing the ongoing events of war is, it would appear, precisely the point. A particular thrill of violation attaches itself to the act of transgressing standards to which one still wholeheartedly subscribes – to those moments when "the taboo still holds good and yet we are yielding to the impulsion it forbids."[21] In this instance, the relatively innocuous generic transgressions in operation in the act of bringing together distinct cultural forms are definitively surpassed and eclipsed by a more profound and discomfiting transgression in the form of the violation of strongly felt cultural taboos.

Pornography as Self-Devouring

This article has so far considered a number of ways in which adult entertainment (in its photorealistic moving-image form) can be seen to engage with representations that hold a firmly established cultural identity in order to reframe them iconoclastically. It is apparent that certain examples of the genre are invested in appropriating cultural objects of various kinds in order to (mis)use them transgressively as vehicles for sexual representation. However, I now want to argue that the issue is more complex than the mere appropriation of representations. For me, pornography's iconoclasm is not limited to the desecration of objects and forms external to itself, but is part of the elemental constitution of pornography's self-image. That is, transgression and iconoclasm can be seen as part of the genre's relationship to itself. Pornography is not only vampiric, I suggest, but also auto-cannibalistic.

Adult entertainment can readily be seen to transgress certain of its own definitional constraints. By plundering other genres as it does, porn can be seen to undermine that which is widely assumed to be its own, unique selling point – that is, its direct attempts to generate arousal in its viewers. What I am suggesting here is that, with certain porn texts now borrowing from other moving-image genres, such as body-shock documentaries, stunts-and-pranks reality television formats, and documentary images of war, the sexual body and its performances can at times be seen to be de-prioritized in favour of other, less directly corporeal pleasures. I would refer you back, at this point, to the review of *PornJackass.com*: "not all of it will get your dick hard." Porn's interest in absorbing other forms at times takes precedence over its traditional investment in depicting and eliciting sexual arousal. Certain marginal categories of adult entertainment can be seen to sacrifice hotness – the characteristic which supposedly gives them their market identity – in favour of transgressing their own boundaries and those of other pop-cultural texts. This can be demonstrated via one further example from the world of adult entertainment.

There has been a recent fad in the porn world – clearly related to the genre's pre-existing penchant for parody – for producing pornographic reimaginings of popular superhero texts. In 2010, the influential high-end porn production company Vivid Entertainment decided to rework the 1960s *Batman* television series as *Batman XXX: A Porn Parody*. The film featured a number of recognizable elements from the original show, including characters such as the Riddler and the Joker, and equipment such as the Batmobile. This endeavour inspired the company to go on to launch an entire specialist imprint, entitled Vivid-Superhero.[22] This may seem pretty mundane in and of itself, of course, particularly when one considers the similarities between the stereotypical images of a pornography consumer and a comic book aficionado. Both groups, it is popularly and pejoratively assumed, consist of men with few conventional social skills, an air of desperation, and little erotic contact with other flesh-and-blood human beings. As Martin remarks, "porn parodies, in their continued address to heterosexual male spectators, tend to parody male-identified genres, such as science fiction."[23] A franchise like Vivid-Superhero would (by this logic) appear wholly predictable.

What interests me about this imprint, however, is the manner in which its parodic output was received and interpreted by its audience. There was an enormous amount of interest in the films within both comic book and porno fan cultures; the popular comics blog site *Bleeding Cool* reported that its most popular post of 2010 consisted of a trailer for and screen captures of *Batman XXX: A Porn Parody*.[24] In fact, this post got two-and-a-half times the amount of traffic of any other article on the site, and was followed by a flood of appreciative comments about factors such as the faithfulness of the costumes, the accuracy of the props, and the general fidelity of the aesthetic. There was notably little comment addressing the topic of the sexual content or the hotness quotient. Borys Kit remarks upon this in his article about the film, stating that "part of the interest and appeal is what seems like high production values and eye to detail such as hiring the original TV show's costume designers to re-create outfits."[25] While we might be tempted to put this down to a kind of a disavowal –

the contemporary equivalent of claiming to read *Playboy* for the articles – there seems to be no denying that *Batman XXX: A Porn Parody* and the other offerings from Vivid-Superhero are deliberately courting and tapping into cultural interest in factors other than hardcore sex. In so doing, I would suggest, they challenge porn's widely perceived market identity as a genre that is solely interested in securing the maximum possible visibility for sex.[26]

With this example, then, we might argue that it is not the explicit erotic content that is being positioned at the centre of the viewing experience, but a range of other factors that would not immediately or typically be thought of as provoking a genitally sexual response. Sex is to some extent displaced here. Of course, this somewhat undermines the widespread assumption that, as Laurence O'Toole puts it, "the hard and softcore truth is that arousal is porn's main event" and adult entertainment "is a sex thing."[27] While these factors would certainly seem to be central to the genre's market identity, it would appear that porn is interested in iconoclastically subverting not only other genres, but itself as well. In engaging with reality television, mainstream Hollywood, war reportage, and so on, pornography begins to depict the body in ways that are not conventionally conceived of as pornographic, and thereby goes some way toward shaking its own foundations. As we have seen, the genre becomes interested in exploring the body as disgusting, or as enduring, or as suffering, or as a site of fan cultural signifiers, as well as exploring the body as a site of explicit sexual performance.

Corporeality, as it is represented within diverse popular cultural forms, is incorporated into contemporary adult entertainment, and hardcore action is to some extent temporarily de-centred by the heightened interest in and visibility of these other representational regimes. A pervasive preoccupation with iconoclasm – with using and abusing the representational conventions of other genres and forms – has, in certain instances, resulted in pornography defying even the generic imperative that it be "a sex thing." In light of this, we might argue that iconoclastic tendencies are as important to understandings of the genre as explicit representations of sex acts. Both vampire and cannibal, pornography can be viewed not only as appropriating and misusing the conventions of other genres, but as transgressing its own generic identity in the pursuit of an iconoclastic thrill.

Conclusion: Changing Understandings of "Porn" and "The Pornographic"

This article has touched upon the notion that certain forms of commercial pornography have recently called into question the centrality of sexual explicitness and hardcore action as definitional criteria. What, we might ask, does this mean for pornography? How does the displacement of sex impact upon the genre? I certainly do not wish to imply that this displacement of sex marks the end, or even the endangerment, of the genre as we know it. Adult entertainment is an incredibly flexible and resilient cultural phenomenon, infinitely capable of diversifying and perpetually identifying new cultural forms to exploit, utilize, and vampirize. What I would suggest, however, is that this iconoclastic reimagining of the representational conventions of other genres is bound up with shifts in contemporary understandings of the pornographic.

It is interesting to note, I think, that the way that we use the words "porn" and "pornographic" is evolving. The historian Sarah Leonard, for example, remarks upon the changing resonances of such terms, noting that "it is now not uncommon to use the word 'obscene' to describe images of the mass destruction of bodies in German concentration camps during the Second World War – or, perhaps better put, the use of 'pornographic' to describe the combination of horror and pleasure with which we view such images."[28] From this, we can establish that the word "pornographic" is no longer simply applied to an object or group of objects that explicitly depict sexual acts.[29] It can, in fact, be applied to graphic, but not explicitly sexual, representations of the body, and to the response of an enthralled yet conflicted observer. It would seem that reactions of shock or discomfort – those classic indicators of transgression – have become central to understandings of the pornographic. After all, if documentary images of suffering can be described in this way, then it would seem that we now use the adjective as much to designate material that produces reactions of shock and discomfort as we do to designate material that generates arousal.

Similar slippages have taken place around the word "porn" in recent years, with its popular usage being extended, most noticeably in its deployment as a kind of descriptive suffix. "Porn" has become attached to a surprisingly diverse set of texts and affects, few of which actually put the sexual body front-and-centre. The term "warporn" has emerged to describe "the hybridization of war documentation and pornography" within contemporary visual culture, for example.[30] This phrase covers a fairly diverse range of phenomena, and has been applied not only to texts like *Gag Factor 15*, but also to the "popular tabloids and government talk-shows [*sic*] fascination with super-sized weapons,"[31] and to the gory images of war casualties circulating online as gross-out entertainment.[32] A category of reality TV programming depicting the urban working classes, meanwhile, is "increasingly being referred to as the 'poverty porn' genre,"[33] and the term "torture porn" has emerged to designate a certain type of horror film revolving around the spectacle of corporeal violation.

There are, in fact, surprisingly numerous examples of this use of the "porn" suffix. The fact that these genres have been labelled in this manner suggests that they are all popularly understood as being at least partially related to porn, and yet none of them necessarily include graphic representations of hardcore sex. It seems as if porn's iconoclastic appropriation and transgressive misuse of other genres – its interest in conventions not its own – is to some extent being mirrored here, as non-sexual genres appropriate and misuse the once specifically sexual designation "porn."

Adult entertainment's iconoclastic reimagining of other genres is seemingly part of a series of more profound adjustments in understandings of the pornographic. The meaning of porn is becoming increasingly distorted, as certain forms of adult entertainment displace arousal in favour of engaging with other cultural forms, and as culture more broadly starts to use the word "porn" differently. There is, it would appear, something of a paradigm shift occurring in contemporary understandings of the pornographic – one that has yet to be fully acknowledged, let alone properly theorized,[34] but one in which the concepts of iconoclasm and transgression are thoroughly implicated.

NOTES

This article developed from a paper I presented as a PhD student at the twenty-second annual conference of the Centre for Comparative Literature at the University of Toronto in March 2011. Thanks are due to Benjamin Noys and Diarmuid Hester for the excellent guidance they offered me at that time, and (most particularly) to Rachel Stapleton, who has provided generous support in revising the manuscript whilst I have been on maternity leave.

1 Wicke, "Through a Gaze Darkly," 67.

2 *Oxford English Dictionary Online*, s.v. "iconoclasm, n.," http://www.oed.com/ (accessed 11 May 2011).

3 Bataille, *The Tears of Eros*, 67.

4 Arcand, *The Jaguar and the Anteater*, 18, 126.

5 Maddison, "'Choke on It Bitch!,'" 38.

6 This company was involved in an extended obscenity case known as *United States v. Extreme Associates*. In 2003, the company and its owners, Robert Zicari (a.k.a. Rob Black) and Janet Romano (a.k.a. Lizzie Borden), were indicted by a federal grand jury in Pittsburgh "on charges of violating federal obscenity laws." United States, Department of Justice, "News Release," 2. These charges concerned six Internet clips and three videos, including Borden's *Forced Entry*, which "depicts the brutal rapes and murders of several women" (4). The case ended with negotiations and a guilty plea in March 2009. Charlie Deitch, "Buchanan Wins Another Online Obscenity Case," *Pittsburgh City Paper*, 11 March 2009, http://www.pittsburghcitypaper.ws/gyrobase/Content?oid=oid%3A60259 (accessed 11 May 2011). In July of that year, over half a decade after their business premises were originally raided, the couple were sentenced to a year and a day in prison for violating federal obscenity laws. Paula Reed Ward, "Porn Producer, Wife Get 1-Year Jail Terms," *Pittsburgh Post-Gazette*, 2 July 2009, http://www.post-gazette.com/pg/09183/981250-53.stm (accessed 11 May 2011).

7 It is perhaps no coincidence that *Dirty Sanchez*, the British interpretation of the *Jackass* format, takes its name from a slang term for a sex act.

8 "Porn Jackass," par. 4.

9 Shelton, "A Star Is Porn," 125.

10 Martin, "Never Laugh at a Man," 196.

11 Rosen, "*The Big Lebowski* Porn," par. 1. The obsessive accuracy of the porn parody is a topic to which I shall return later, but for now suffice it to remark that this fastidiousness represents a somewhat peculiar (because seemingly extra-sexual) mode of engagement on the part of porn.

12 Shelton, "A Star Is Porn," 125–6.

13 Entitled *This Ain't Avatar XXX* (2010) and *Simpsons: The XXX Parody* (2011) respectively, both were produced and distributed by branches of Larry Flynt Publications.

14 Williams, *Hard Core*, 50.

15 Animated pornography drawing upon existing popular characters is a subgenre in and of itself, encompassing everything from Tijuana Bibles to x-rated versions of *Family Guy*. Susanna Paasonen's rich discussion of "toon porn" provides a particularly relevant discussion of the pornographic appropriation of Lara Croft and other video game characters. See: Paasonen, "The Affective and Affectless Bodies," 15–18.

16 *Simpsons: The XXX Parody.*

17 As Carolyn Dean remarks, "While it is true that eroticized violence was a predominant theme in underground pornography in England and North America during the nineteenth century, contemporaries generally viewed it as a manifestation of its authors' and readers' weakness of moral will; its violence was one among many examples of the human susceptibility to sin which was evident in all pornographic material. After the Great War, however, there is a new continuity between the thematics of war and pornography, in which sexualized violence becomes the primary example of human moral failure." Dean, "The Great War," 61.

18 See Simon Hardy on the *Iraq Babes* website, which "shows porn actors dressed up as American troops and 'raping' Iraqi women, thus allowing the average American citizen to vicariously share in the tradition of invading armies that rape the women of a defeated power." Hardy, "The New Pornographies?," 16. Matteo Pasquinelli also provides an interesting account of this "sub-genre of trash porn" in "WARPORN WARPUNK!," par. 7.

19 Johnny Maldoro, "Abu Gag!," *Village Voice*, 27 July 2004, http://www.villagevoice.com/2004-07-27/people/abu-gag/ (accessed 10 November 2009), par. 3.

20 I had intended to include a screen grab from *Gag Factor 15* at this point, but the copyright holder refused permission to use the image. I had also wanted to include images depicting the positioning of this opening scene and *Gag Factor* DVD box covers, but, again, permission to use the images was refused. As it is, I have done my best to describe these visuals accurately, but acknowledge that elements of my descriptions will inevitably be somewhat subjective.

21 Bataille, *Eroticism*, 38.

22 See: Ha, "Vivid Entertainment."

23 Martin, "Never Laugh at a Man," 196.

24 Johnston, "The 2010 End-of-Year," par. 1.

25 Kit, "Superhero Porn Parody," par. 3.

26 Indeed, one post on *Bleeding Cool* suggests that, in creating *Batman XXX*, director Axel Braun has "created one of the few porn movies where the non-sex

version may be watched more than the sex version." "Bleeding Cool's One Year Anniversary," par. 5.

27 O'Toole, *Pornocopia*, 298, 342.

28 Leonard, "Pornography and Obscenity," 200.

29 This is reflected in the slippage occurring around the word "sex," too. As Feona Attwood notes, "as sex appears to become more and more important to contemporary cultures, permeating every aspect of our existence and providing a language for talking about all kinds of things, its meaning becomes more elusive and more ambiguous; politicians and their dossiers can be 'sexed up,' and the term 'sexy' may simply indicate something that is noteworthy." Attwood, "Introduction: The Sexualization of Culture," xv.

30 Jacobs, *Netporn*, 118.

31 Pasquinelli, "WARPORN WARPUNK!," par. 7.

32 See: Jacobs, *Netporn*, 122–5.

33 Mooney and Hancock, "Poverty Porn," par. 4.

34 I attempt to begin this process of theorization in my book *Beyond Explicit: Pornography and the Displacement of Sex*. However, there is still much more work to be done.

BIBLIOGRAPHY

Arcand, Bernard. *The Jaguar and the Anteater: Pornography Degree Zero*. Translated by Wayne Grady. London: Verso, 1993.

Attwood, Feona. "Introduction: The Sexualization of Culture." In *Mainstreaming Sex: The Sexualization of Western Culture*, edited by Feona Attwood, xiii–xxiv. London: I.B. Tauris, 2009.

Bataille, Georges. *Eroticism*. Translated by Mary Dalwood. London: Marion Boyars, 1987.

– *The Tears of Eros*. Translated by Peter Connor. San Francisco: City Lights, 1989.

"Bleeding Cool's One Year Anniversary – LITG SPECIAL." *Bleeding Cool*. 1 June 2010. http://www.bleedingcool.com/2010/06/01/bleeding-cools-one-year-anniversary-litg-special/ (accessed 17 November 2011).

Braun, Alex, dir. *Batman XXX: A Porn Parody*. Vivid Video, 2010. DVD.

– *This Ain't Avatar: XXX*. Hustler Video, 2010. DVD.

Dean, Carolyn. "The Great War, Pornography, and the Transformation of Modern Male Subjectivity." *Modernism/Modernity* 3, no. 2 (1996): 59–72.

Gag Factor. JM Productions, n.d. http://www.gagfactor.com/gagfactordotcom.html, 22 March 2010.

Ha, Peter. "Vivid Entertainment Announces Vivid-Superhero String of Adult Films." *Time*. 10 May 2010. http://techland.time.com/2010/05/10/vivid-entertainment-announces-vivid-superhero-string-of-adult-films/ (accessed 17 November 2011).

Hardy, Simon. "The New Pornographies: Representation or Reality?" In *Mainstreaming Sex: The Sexualization of Western Culture*, edited by Feona Attwood, 3–18. London: I.B. Tauris, 2009.

Hester, Helen. *Beyond Explicit: Pornography and the Displacement of Sex*. Albany: SUNY Press, 2014.

Jackass: The Lost Tapes. MTV, 2009. DVD.

Jacobs, Katrien. *Netporn: DIY Web Culture and Sexual Politics*. Lanham, MD: Rowman and Littlefield, 2007.

Johnston, Rich. "The 2010 End-of-Year Lying in the Gutters Special." *Bleeding Cool*. 31 Dec. 2010. http://www.bleedingcool.com/2010/12/31/the-2010-end-of-year-lying-in-the-gutters-special/ (17 November 2011).

Kit, Borys. "Superhero Porn Parody Films Ready to Fly." *Reuters*. 12 May 2010. http://www.reuters.com/article/2010/05/12/us-porn-idUSTRE64B0N720100512 (accessed 17 November 2011).

Leonard, Sarah. "Pornography and Obscenity." In *Palgrave Advances in the Modern History of Sexuality*, edited by H.G. Cocks and Matt Houlbrook, 180–205. Basingstoke: Palgrave Macmillan, 2006.

Maddison, Stephen. "'Choke on It Bitch!': Porn Studies, Extreme Gonzo and the Mainstreaming of Hardcore." In *Mainstreaming Sex: The Sexualization of Western Culture*, edited by Feona Attwood, 37–53. London: I.B. Tauris, 2009.

Martin, Nina K. "Never Laugh at a Man with his Pants Down: The Affective Dynamics of Comedy and Porn." In *Pornography: Film and Culture*, edited by Peter Lehman, 189–205. New Brunswick: Rutgers University Press, 2006.

Mooney, Gerry, and Lynn Hancock. "Poverty Porn and the Broken Society." *Variant* 39/40 (2010). http://www.variant.org.uk/39_40texts/povertp39_40.html (accessed 16 June 2011).

O'Toole, Laurence. *Pornocopia: Porn, Sex, Technology and Desire*. London: Serpent's Tail, 1999.

Paasonen, Susanna. "The Affective and Affectless Bodies of Monster Toon Porn." In *Sex in the Digital Age*, edited by Paul G. Dixon and Isabel K. Düsterhöft, 10–24. London: Routledge, 2018.

Pasquinelli, Matteo. "WARPORN WARPUNK! Autonomous Videopoiesis in Wartime." *Generation Online*, n.d. http://www.generation-online.org/t/warporn.htm (accessed 18 May 2011).

Porn Jackass, n.d. http://tour.pornjackass.com/aa/index.php (accessed 22 March 2010).
"Porn Jackass." *Rabbit's Reviews*, 22 September 2004. http://www.rabbitsreviews.com/s507/Porn-Jackass.html (accessed 22 March 2010).
Rosen, Christopher. "*The Big Lebowski* Porn Parody Doesn't Include That Much Porn or Parody." *Movie Line*. 3 April 2010. http://www.movieline.com/2010/04/the-big-lebowski-porn-parody-doesnt-include-that-much-porn-or-parody.php (accessed 17 November 2011).
Shelton, Emily. "A Star Is Porn: Corpulence, Comedy, and the Homosocial Cult of Adult Film Star Ron Jeremy." *Camera Obscura* 17, no. 3 (2002): 115–46.
Sicko Games. Redslip LLC, 2005. http://www.sickogames.com/fff.html (accessed 20 May 2011).
Simpsons: The XXX Parody. Full Spread Entertainment, 2010. http://www.simpsonsporno.org/ (accessed 27 January 2011).
Tremaine, Jeff, dir. *Jackass: The Movie*. Paramount, 2007. DVD.
United States. Department of Justice. "News Release." 7 August 2003. http://www.usdoj.gov/criminal/ceos/Press%20Releases/WDPA%20Zicari%20indict%20PR_080703.pdf (accessed 9 January 2009).
Wicke, Jennifer. "Through a Gaze Darkly: Pornography's Academic Market." In *Dirty Looks: Women. Pornography, Power*, edited by Pamela Church Gibson and Roma Gibson, 62–80. London: British Film Institute, 1993.
Williams, Linda. *Hard Core: Power, Pleasure, and the "Frenzy of the Visible."* Berkeley: University of California Press, 1999.

CONTRIBUTORS

T. NIKKI CESARE SCHOTZKO is associate professor at the University of Toronto's Centre for Drama, Theatre, and Performance Studies. Her first monograph, *Learning How to Fall: Art and Culture after September 11* (Routledge, 2015), engages the changing relationship between world events and their subsequent documentation. Her current project considers the performance of radical acts of care. She has published in *TDR*, *Performance Research*, *Theatre Research in Canada*, *Canadian Theatre Review*, and *Theatre Journal*, and has dramaturged experimental-music theatre productions in the US, Canada, and internationally.

CHRISTOPHER VAN GINHOVEN REY is a lecturer in the Department of Romance Languages and Literatures at Pomona College. His most recent book is *Instruments of the Divinity: Providence and Praxis in the Foundation of the Society of Jesus* (Brill, 2013).

HELEN HESTER is associate professor of media and communication at the University of West London. Her research interests include technofeminism, sexuality studies, and theories of social reproduction, and she is a member of the international feminist collective Laboria Cuboniks. She is the author of *Beyond Explicit: Pornography and the Displacement of Sex* (SUNY Press, 2014) and *Xenofeminism* (Polity, 2018) and co-editor of the collections *Fat Sex: New Directions in Theory and Activism* (Ashgate, 2015) and *Dea ex Machina* (Merve, 2015). She is also the series editor for Ashgate's Sexualities in Society book series.

EMILY HOFFMAN is associate professor of English at Arkansas Tech University in Russellville, Arkansas. She has published articles on a variety of pop culture topics, including *Mad Men*, *The Mary Tyler Moore Show*, *The Closer*, *Diner*, and *A Place in the Sun*.

NATALIE B. PENDERGAST holds a PhD in comparative literature. She specializes in comics and *bande dessinée*. Her work has appeared in the *Journal of Graphic Novels and Comics*, *Broken Pencil*, *Vice Canada*, and *Graphic Details: Jewish Women's Confessional Comics in Essays and Interviews*, among other publications.

BETH SAUNDERS is curator and head of special collections and gallery at the Albin O. Kuhn Library and Gallery, University of Maryland, Baltimore County. Previously she was the assistant curator of photographs at the Metropolitan Museum of Art.

RACHEL F. STAPLETON is based at the Centre for Comparative Literature at the University of Toronto. Her research focuses on the rhetorical uses of life experiences in early modern women's letters from the British Isles and the Iberian Peninsula. Her work has been published in *Medieval Feminist Forum*, *Lives & Letters*, and two volumes of *L'histoire comparée de littératures de langues européennes* (Benjamins, 2011 and 2017). A chapter is forthcoming on early modern women's networks in *Women and Community in Early Modern Iberia* (University of Nebraska Press). With Jonathan A. Allan, she is co-editor of a special issue (38.4) of the *Canadian Review of Comparative Literature*.

ADAM SWANN is a librarian at the University of Glasgow. His research interests include early modern intellectual culture, politics, and theology, and in 2014 he completed a PhD, which explored the influence of seventeenth-century economic debates on Milton's soteriology.

MICHAEL TAUSSIG is Class of 1933 Professor of Anthropology at Columbia University. He studied medicine in Sydney, sociology in London, and real life in Colombia where he first went in 1969 and has returned every year since. He has written several books and essays, including a book on iconoclasm called *Defacement* and a short essay on the US flag in the aftermath of 9/11, in Bruno Latour's *Iconoclash*. Recent works include *Palma Africana* (2018), *The Corn Wolf* (2015), *Beauty and the Beast* (2012), *I Swear I Saw This: Drawings in Fieldwork Notebooks, Namely My Own* (2011), and *What Color Is the Sacred?* (2009).

ANGELA R. TOSCANO received her PhD in English literature from the University of Iowa in 2018. She was the recipient of the 2016 Humanities Without Walls Pre-Doctoral Fellowship. Her specialization is the eighteenth-century novel, with a particular emphasis on romance and amatory fiction. She has written extensively on genre romance, and her article "A Parody of Love: The Narrative Uses of Rape in Popular Romance" was published in the *Journal of Popular Romance Studies*. She has also written a brief history of the rakehell, titled "A Rake's Progress," for the Popular Romance Project, a collaborative project engaging public scholarship and the digital humanities. She has contributed a chapter on the Gothic romance to the forthcoming volume *The Ashgate Research Companion to Popular Romance*.

ANTONIO VISELLI is a lecturer and head of French studies at the University of Canterbury (New Zealand), following positions held at Trent University and Wilfrid Laurier University. His research focuses on the intermediality of musico-literary texts and on subjectivity in French symbolist and European modernist literature. He has published most recently on topics such as fugue, absence, alterity, and hospitality in the works of Rousseau, Tristan Corbière, Pound, Pavese, and Nanni Moretti.

BRENDON WOCKE is associate researcher at the University of Perpignan in France. He completed his doctoral thesis on the poetics of wordplay in the work of Jacques Derrida in cotutelle with the University of Perpignan and the University of Tübingen. His continuing research explores the deconstructive and psychoanalytic implications of the contemporary American novel. He has also published a series of articles on the relationship between the psychoanalytic notion of *jouissance* and contemporary gastronomic culture.

INDEX